SOCIOLOGY AS APPLIED
TO MEDICINE

SOCIOLOGY AS APPLIED TO MEDICINE

3rd Edition

edited by

Graham Scambler, BSC, PhD
*Senior Lecturer, University College and
Middlesex School of Medicine,
University College London, London, UK*

Baillière Tindall
London   Philadelphia
Toronto   Sydney   Tokyo

Baillière Tindall   24–28 Oval Road
London NW1 7DX

The Curtis Center,
Independence Square West,
Philadelphia, PA 19106–3399, USA

55 Horner Avenue
Toronto, Ontario M8Z 4X6, Canada

Harcourt Brace Jovanovich Group
(Australia) Pty Ltd.,
30–52 Smidmore St,
Marrickville, NSW 2204, Australia

Harcourt Brace Jovanovich (Japan) Inc.,
Ichibancho Central Building,
22–1 Ichibancho
Chiyoda-ku, Tokyo 102, Japan

© 1991 Baillière Tindall

Third edition 1991
Second printing 1992
Third printing 1993

This book is printed on acid-free paper

ISBN 0-7020-1559-8

A catalogue record for this book is available from The British Library

Typeset by Columns Design and Production Services Ltd,
Reading, England.
Printed and bound in Great Britain by
Mackays of Chatham PLC, Chatham, Kent

Contributors

David Blane, MB BS, MSc Lecturer in Medical Sociology, Department of Psychiatry, Charing Cross and Westminster Medical School, 22–24 St Dunstan's Road, London, W6 8RP, UK

Ray M. Fitzpatrick, BA, MSc, PhD Fellow, Nuffield College, Nuffield College, Oxford, OX1 1NF, UK. University Lecturer in Medical Sociology, University of Oxford

Sheila Hillier, BSc, MSc (Econ), PhD Senior Lecturer, Joint Department of Sociology Applied to Medicine, The London Hospital Medical College, Turner Street, London E1 2AD, UK. Senior Lecturer in Sociology, The Medical Colleges of St Bartholomew's Hospital and Queen Mary and Westfield (University of London)

David Locker, BDS, PhD Professor, Department of Community Dentistry, Faculty of Dentistry, University of Toronto, 124 Edward Street, Toronto, Ontario, M5G 1G6, Canada

Nicholas Mays, MA Lecturer in Medical Sociology, Department of Public Health Medicine, United Medical and Dental Schools of Guy's and St Thomas' Hospitals, St Thomas' Campus, London, SE1 7EH, UK

Myfanwy Morgan, BA, MA Senior Lecturer in Medical Sociology, United Medical and Dental Schools of Guy's and St Thomas' Hospitals, St Thomas' Campus, London, SE1 7EH, UK

Graham Scambler, BSc, PhD Senior Lecturer in Sociology, Department of Psychiatry, University College and Middlesex School of Medicine, University College London, Wolfson Building, Middlesex Hospital, Riding House Street, London W1N 8AA, UK

Contents

PART IV. THE SOCIAL PROCESS OF DEFINING DISEASE

PART V. ORGANIZATION OF HEALTH SERVICES

Foreword
(to the first edition)

Students of medicine and of other related disciplines may be forgiven for feeling that their schools and colleges insist that they learn more and more about an increasing number of aspects of the human condition in health and illness. There was a halcyon time, not so long ago, when the pre-clinical curriculum consisted of one course in human anatomy and another in physiology; the clinical phase involved merely learning the skills needed to recognize the signs and symptoms of a wide but ultimately limited range of diseases. Moreover, there was little institutional pressure on students to study since they were free to repeat examinations until they passed them.

The picture is very different today. Knowledge of the molecular structure of living beings and the factors which determine natural and pathological growth and decay has expanded exponentially in the last fifty years and continues to do so. Students are expected to know a good deal about the theories and research methods of the scientific disciplines, the 'ologies', which have led to this increased knowledge, as well as about the implications of their findings for medical practice. More and more disciplines claiming relevance to medical knowledge and practice jostle each other for a place in the pre-clinical curriculum; new clinical specialties want medical students to be exposed at some time during their clinical studies to what they have to offer. All make claims to the indispensable nature of their own contribution to the curriculum. Meanwhile, medical students are no longer free to work at their own pace. Examinations weed out those who cannot satisfy their teachers after a maximum of two failures. The pressures are those of the institution. Students of other health professions, such as nursing, dentistry, pharmacy and optometry, are exposed to broadly comparable pressures in the process of qualifying as practitioners.

Sociology is one of the disciplines which has recently claimed the attention of the medical and other related health professions and their students. Its formal introduction into the curriculum as a basic medical science, which by the 1980s had taken place in most of the medical schools of the United Kingdom, was a radical innovation. Compared with most of the other new subjects it involves a break away from the traditional preparation for medicine based exclusively on the detailed study of parts of the biological organism which we call the human body. Its focus is not on the human individual *per se*: it is on the two-way relationships between the individual and society. Sociology as applied to medicine is concerned specifically with those aspects of the relationship which influence the experiences of health and illness in individuals and the responce to them of others — relatives, doctors, nurses, administrators and governments.

Not surprisingly, not all those already involved in medical education welcomed the advent of sociological teaching. Some of the staff involved in teaching the traditional laboratory based or clinical subjects saw in it an intrusion of a largely unknown and untested quantity competing for the students' limited span of attention time. They were unfamiliar with its methods or potential and sceptical about its contribution to the making of a good practitioner. Some students, expecting the medical curriculum to resemble in essence the pre-medical natural science courses they had taken prior to entry, also needed to be persuaded that sociology was relevant to their preparation as future doctors, especially when they felt themselves to be under pressure to absorb all that the teachers of subjects which were more thoroughly examined put before them.

Such early doubts have not entirely disappeared, but they have substantially diminished. Indeed, the General Medical Council's recommendations for medical education in the 1980s are even more insistent than earlier recommendations on the necessity for broadening the students' basic understanding of the social context of health and illness and of the social determinants of medical practice and health service provision. This then is the major task and challenge for those responsible for the teaching of sociology as applied to medicine, and the contributors to this book are to be congratulated for providing a concise introduction to the subject.

In this book, which will form an admirable basic text upon which teachers and students can build, the contributors have shown how some of the theories, concepts and methods developed by sociologists can illuminate aspects of human experience in health and illness. They look at how such socially determined factors as marital status, social class and family composition influence the pattern of morbidity and mortality. They show that medical perceptions of what constitutes mental or physical illness are not necessarily shared by the populations served and that the absence of shared perceptions may frustrate much medical effort. They look at the variety of ways in which old age, death and ethnicity are regarded and treated and the dilemmas which such variety can pose for practitioners. They explore the social origins of contemporary systems of health care in order to obtain greater understanding of their present problems. They examine too the various interpretations which can be placed upon the collective and individual behaviour of members of the medical profession, and on the expansion of medical concern and metaphors into many aspects of social life. This list does not exhaust their concerns and there are many other developments in the sociology of health and illness which cannot be covered in a volume of this size.

It seems to me impossible to argue that acquaintance with such findings and with the methods and conceptual frames of the discipline on which they are based is not an essential ingredient in the preparation of the doctor for medical practice whether it be in general practiced, an age-band or body-system specialty, or community medicine. He or she needs it at the very least for protection against the very real hazard of frustration and unhappiness when it proves difficult to implement medical measures; but above all it is needed if the medical and other health-related professions are to make their greatest potential contribution to the welfare of the populations they are privileged to serve.

Margot Jefferys
August 1981

Preface

When the first edition of this textbook was published in 1982, sociology had only recently established itself on the curricula of medical, nursing and other schools and colleges preparing students for work in the health service. By the time the second edition was produced in 1986, not only had its contribution to education and training been consolidated, but it had also been associated with a rapidly expanding body of research in the health field, some of which was incorporated into the revised text. There has been no slackening of pace since then. Moreover, health issues, from the social and personal determinants of health to the evaluation of health-care interventions and systems, have gained a new prominence and salience for all health students and workers.

In this third edition of the text we have tried to take account of current research and policy developments. Accordingly, we have not merely rearranged and updated the previous material, but have undertaken a number of more substantial revisions. Some chapters have gone altogether, the more significant material now incorporated elsewhere; other chapters have been reworked or amended; and there are some new chapters — for example, on chronic disease, community care and the funding and organization of health care. A draft version of each chapter was commented on in detail by another author before reaching the editor, and we have all benefited once more from constructive feedback from both our colleagues and our students.

Sadly, two contributors to the previous editions, Donald Patrick and Ellie Scrivens, no longer teach health students and have withdrawn to take on new challenges. Our special thanks go to Donald Patrick who, as senior co-editor of the first and second editions, was instrumental in getting the venture off the ground a decade ago. We are fortunate to be joined by Nicholas Mays for this third edition.

Graham Scambler

PART I

Social aspects of disease

PART 1

Social aspects of disease

1

Society and changing patterns of disease

Ray M. Fitzpatrick

One of the most important recent developments in ideas about health care and illness has been the widespread recognition that social and economic conditions have a major effect upon patterns of disease and death rates. A wide range of sources—historical, medical and sociological—have provided the evidence for such influences. This chapter considers how we can trace lines of influence from society and the economy to patterns of disease.

The starting point of this analysis is the dramatic variation to be found in death rates both in the past and at present. For example, the death rate per annum has virtually halved in England and Wales over the last 150 years: in 1851 it was 22.7 per 1000 population and by 1990 it had fallen to 11.9. Another way to express the difference over this period is to talk in terms of the average number of years an individual could expect to live at birth, i.e. life expectancy. Whereas a man and woman in 1840 could, on average, expect to live to 40 and 43 years, respectively, by 1990 life expectancy had risen to 72 and 77 years. Such differences in overall mortality rates, however, disguise a more complex picture if we look at particular age groups. The higher death rates of the mid-nineteenth century were much more severe in particular age groups, especially in infancy and childhood. Thus, future life expectancy for those who have reached the age of 45 years has improved slightly over the last 100 years, but not nearly as dramatically as has the life expectancy of a child at birth.

The higher death rates and lower life expectancies are not of course simply an historical phenomenon. Many third world countries at present have crude death rates much higher than those of England;

for example, Ethiopia 23.6 per 1000 and Sierra Leone 23.4 per 1000. Third world countries with higher death rates resemble nineteenth-century England and Wales in that infant and child mortality are one of the main reasons for lower life expectancy.

VARIATION IN DISEASE PATTERNS IN HUMAN SOCIETY

The diseases that man has encountered have not remained the same over time. Man's history might be viewed as a progressive victory over disease, but this is an over-simplification. Whilst some diseases are less important than in the past, others have become more important. Complex social and biological processes have altered the balance between man and disease. A number of authorities (Powles 1973; McKeown 1979) now agree that man has passed through three characteristic disease patterns in historical sequence.

Pre-agricultural disease patterns

Before about 10 000 B.C., indeed for most of man's evolution as a distinct species, man lived as a hunter–gatherer, that is without any form of settled agriculture for subsistence. Although conclusions based on such early evidence are somewhat speculative, anthropologists and epidemiologists have argued that the infectious diseases which were later to become major causes of illness and death were relatively uncommon at this stage of social evolution. Furthermore, diseases which are sometimes described as diseases of civilization, such as heart disease and cancer, were less common than at the present time (Powles 1973). It is likely that mortality in adults arose from environmental and safety hazards, for example hunting accidents and exposure.

Diseases in agricultural society

Knowledge of the diseases which plagued agricultural societies is more certain. These were predominantly the infectious diseases, which for purposes of discussion can be divided into the following:

1. air-borne diseases such as tuberculosis;
2. water-borne diseases such as cholera;
3. food-borne diseases such as dysentry; and

4. vector-borne (i.e. carried by rats or mosquitoes) diseases such as plague and malaria.

In England and Wales, and in Europe generally, the plague was a particularly important cause of death and at its most virulent, in the Black Death of 1348, it killed one-quarter of the English population. It last occurred on any large scale in England and Wales in 1665 and disappeared from Europe shortly after. The plague was spread by the fleas carried by black rats. Its disappearance was due to the replacement of the black rat by the brown rat which was much less prone to infest human habitations.

Malaria was never as great a health problem in England and Wales as it has been in the tropics where conditions are ideal for the natural life cycle of both vector and parasite. By the mid-nineteenth century when reliable vital statistics were available in England and Wales and the country's economy was moving from agricultural to industrial, the major causes of death were tuberculosis, bronchitis, pneumonia, influenza and cholera.

The modern industrial era of disease

By the mid-twentieth century, infectious diseases had become relatively unimportant causes of death in England and Wales and in the western world in general, although some infectious diseases such as influenza remained common causes of death, particularly in the elderly. The infectious diseases have been replaced as major causes of death by the so-called degenerative diseases, cancer and cardiovascular disease.

Because of these changes in patterns of death the major medical problems of today are such chronic illnesses as atherosclerosis, diabetes and osteoarthritis. These are all problems involving multiple risk factors, rather than a single cause. Their onset is quite early in life; they tend to be progressive; and they appear in all modern societies. Fries (1983) argues that there appear to be quite definite limits to the extension of the human lifespan, so that life expectancy at age 100 years has barely changed in the last 80 years. However, if one looks at such indices as age at first heart attack or age-specific lung cancer rates in the USA there have been quite definite improvements in recent years. Fries concludes that health policy should make the compression of morbidity a major objective. Combining medical and social approaches to reducing the risk factors for chronic illnesses such as atherosclerosis would result in a life in which serious illness and decline in functioning were increasingly confined to later ages and the years of vigorous life extended.

This dramatic increase in importance of the chronic degenerative diseases is characteristic of almost all countries that have undergone industrialization, although the exceptions and the variations in rates from one country to another provide important and intriguing problems for the medical and social scientist. Japan, for example, has a much lower incidence of heart disease than comparable industrialized societies. On the other hand, the level of stomach cancer is considerably higher in Japan compared with, for example, the USA.

Explaining changes in disease prevalence

It would be all too easy to regard changes in disease patterns as the inevitable consequences of medical and technical progress without further explanation. Close examination of the major influences on disease patterns, however, uncovers a complex picture which is increasingly recognized as important for the understanding of disease in the contemporary world. The study of how disease patterns have changed indicates the pervasive influence of social and economic factors on disease prevalence.

Three main factors seem important in the changes in disease patterns that followed the transition from nomadic hunting and gathering to agricultural life. Firstly, the development of cereals such as wheat allowed agricultural societies to feed more mouths and hence support higher population densities. Evidence from epidemiological studies, however, shows that many infectious organisms thrive when human populations grow above certain densities. Secondly, agricultural work necessitated permanent settlement, whereas hunter–gatherers periodically moved settlement in search of fresh food sources. However, in the absence of sanitation and awareness of its importance, permanent settlement often led to the contamination of water supplies by waste products, which increased the risks of infection from a number of organisms. Thirdly, the development of cereals as the major source of food, whilst supporting greater numbers of people, paradoxically narrowed the range and quality of diet, a factor which crucially reduced resistance to infection.

More careful examination is needed to explain the remarkable changes in death rates and the decline in significance of mortality from infectious disease that occurred with the transition from agricultural to industrial economies. The nineteenth and twentieth centuries' victory over death and diseases still represents the most dramatic improvement in health in the history of man. Death rates for the various infectious diseases did not decline simultaneously. Tuberculosis, the most common cause of death in the nineteenth century, began to decline in the first half of that century, as indicated

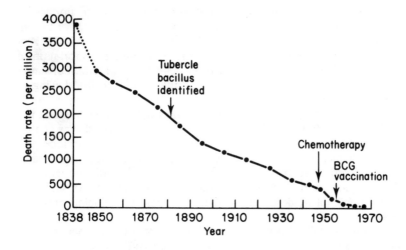

Figure 1. Pulmonary tuberculosis: annual death rates for England and Wales, 1838–1970. (Source: McKeown (1979).)

in Fig. 1. There are a limited number of possible explanations for such a marked decline in mortality from an infectious organism. It is possible that a change occurred in the virulence of the organism itself or that the genetic immunity of the population improved. Both these possibilities are generally discounted. There is no theoretical reason why the organisms responsible for tuberculosis and a number of other infectious diseases should fortuitously change in their virulence at approximately the same time; nor could genetic immunity improve in such a short time. The most convincing explanation for the decline in mortality from tuberculosis and, later in the century, from air-borne diseases such as pneumonia, is that an increased resistance to infection resulted from improvement in nutritional intake as agricultural techniques improved and transportation of produce became faster and more efficient.

In many third-world countries today, diseases such as measles or tuberculosis have a much higher fatality, especially amongst the very young in populations whose resistance is reduced by malnutrition. McKeown cites the conclusion of the World Health Organization report that one-half to three-quarters of all statistically recorded deaths of infants and young children are attributed to a combination of malnutrition and infection (McKeown 1979).

The incidence of illness and mortality from water-borne diseases such as cholera declined somewhat later in the nineteenth century, largely as the result of concerted efforts by the public health movement to prevent the contamination of drinking water supplies by sewage; gastroenteric infectious diseases came under control by the beginning of the twentieth century, resulting in a dramatic impact on infant mortality. The sterilization and more hygienic transportation of milk in particular, and improved food hygiene in general, constitute another form of environmental change that produced the decline in infectious disease mortality.

Thus, most of the decline in death rates achieved in this country and in the western world generally by the Second World War can be attributed to environmental factors such as improvements in food and hygiene which were the products of economic development. Other social changes, such as the decline in the birth rate, reduced the demand for food and housing resources. Improved housing and better personal hygiene also played their role in reducing mortality rates.

Historians still dispute the precise nature of the changes that brought about the decline in mortality rates just described. Some would argue that the main mechanism emphasized by McKeown, that is improvements in diet produced by steadily increasing levels of income, is over-emphasized. In particular this interpretation presents a view of economic improvements influencing health as if with an 'invisible hand' (Szreter 1988), thereby under-stating the often intense political struggles by protagonists in the public health movement, especially at the level of local government, to implement reforms in water supply, housing standards and the regulation of the quality of food sold to the public. Szreter thus underscores the role of conscious public health interventions such as the Public Health Act (1872), which obliged local authorities to ensure a pure water supply. He argues that, contrary to the 'invisible hand' thesis, at some stages in the course of the nineteenth century, increased levels of income coincided with periods of *deteriorating* mortality rates, particularly as working-class families migrated rapidly and in large numbers into the unplanned and unhygienic industrial cities of England and Wales.

THE HISTORICAL ROLE OF MEDICINE

To this point nothing has been said about the role that medical intervention has played in the relationship between man and disease. At first glance, this might seem an important omission, given that medical knowledge was accumulating throughout the period and that hospitals had grown in number since the latter part of the eighteenth century. The evidence that McKeown and others have gathered, however, suggests that very little of the decline in mortality rates can be attributed to improvements in medical care. For example, when Florence Nightingale began to reform the hygienic conditions in hospitals, it was widely thought that hospitals constituted a risk to health; in other words, one stood a high risk of cross-infection, contracting a disease from other patients, since wards were unsegregated as well as unhygienic. Similarly, in spite of the advances in surgery made possible by the development of anaes-thetics, there is little evidence that surgical procedures made any impact on life expectancy in the nineteenth century (McKeown & Brown 1969). As for drugs, prior to the twentieth century a large armoury of medicines appears to have been available to the Victorian doctor. However, only a few, such as digitalis, mercury and cinchona, used in the treatment of heart disease, syphilis and malaria, respectively, would be recognized by modern standards as having specific efficacy and, in any case, dosages were unlikely to have been appropriate. The first drugs which can be shown to have influenced mortality rates did not appear until the end of the 1930s. The antibiotics used in the treatment of a wide range of bacterial infections were developed in the 1930s and 1940s. Prophylactic immunization against such diseases as whooping cough and polio date from the 1950s. In the case of these medical breakthroughs, however, it is easy to overstate the contribution that they made to mortality rates. The decline in mortality for most infectious diseases took place before the introduction of antibiotics. For tuberculosis the period of decline can be seen in Fig. 1, while the mortality rates for bronchitis, pneumonia and influenza are shown in Fig. 2. Moreover, it is difficult to distinguish between the improvements in disease mortality that can be attributed to the introduction of treatment or immunization and those due to the continuing influence of improving social and economic conditions. Most likely, the immunization programmes for diphtheria and polio brought about the greatest improvement which can be attributed to specific medical intervention.

DISEASE RATES AND SOCIAL FACTORS IN MODERN SOCIETY

The association between diseases and social and economic cir-cumstances is not a purely historical phenomenon. In many parts of the third world life expectancy at birth is much lower than in Europe or North America. Many aspects of the environment in the third world provide much more favourable conditions for the spread of infectious diseases than those that prevailed in historical Europe. For example, tropical ecology is particularly favourable for such vectors of disease

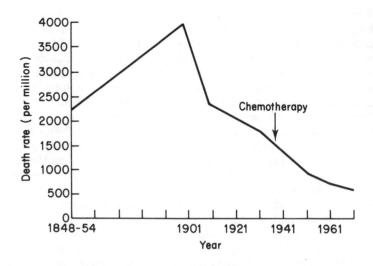

Figure 2. Bronchitis, pneumonia and influenza: death rates for England and Wales, 1848–1971. (Source: McKeown (1979).)

as the mosquito (malaria) and tsetse fly (sleeping sickness). Nevertheless it is the extremely low standard of living above all else that produces high mortality rates in countries such as Bangladesh and Ethiopia.

In countries like Britain, the social and environmental factors that are responsible for many kinds of commonly occurring disease are somewhat different and may require different explanation. The association between standard of living and the risk of disease, however, is still apparent in the social-class differences in illness and mortality rates discussed in Chapter 8. It is evident that environmental factors, whether in the home or at work, continue to play an important role in influencing the risks of illness and mortality.

The report of the Research Working Group on Inequalities in Health (DHSS 1981) makes clear in many of its recommendations which aspects of the social and economic environment it considers responsible for inequalities in health in Britain. Firstly, benefits such as the maternity grant and child benefits need to be increased, according to its authors, in order to reduce child poverty. Secondly, major programmes are needed in housing improvement, the prevention of accidents to children and the provision of school meals. Lastly, more action is needed to prevent accidents in the work place. Their recommendations are a clear reminder that, for large sections of society, health is harmed by material deprivation in terms of income, diet and housing, rather than because of the 'diseases of affluence'.

Whilst environmental conditions associated with poverty increase the risk of disease, many kinds of disease are now associated with behaviour which may have little or nothing to do with poverty. Increasingly, the mass media are focussing attention on the role that over-eating or inappropriate diet, smoking and excessive alcohol consumption have in a wide variety of disorders such as heart disease, diabetes, lung cancer and cirrhosis of the liver.

The association between smoking and lung cancer has been established beyond all reasonable doubt. It is important to recognize, however, that contemporary health risks associated with behaviour are just as certainly a function of current social conditions as were the infectious health risks associated with the social conditions of the nineteenth century. This is an essential point to grasp, since it is all too easy to view behaviour such as smoking simply as reflecting an individual's decisions and preferences. To focus on an individual smoker would not only lead to erroneous and over-simplified explanations of the causes of his behaviour, but more importantly it might lead to misguided or naive attempts to change his behaviour.

At present, while 17% of men and 15% of women in social-class I are smokers, 49% of men and 36% of women in social-class V still smoke (see Chapter 8 for definition of the five social classes). It is widely assumed that advertising and marketing strategies, governmental health warnings and taxation on tobacco all have a direct influence on attitudes and behaviour. If effective health policies are to be devised, however, evidence on the social factors which influence smoking is required. There may be little point, for example, in increasing expenditure on mass health-education programmes to alter behaviour associated with health risks in those particularly vulnerable groups who do not respond to such influences.

A realistic analysis of smoking in modern society would have to include a number of complex political and economic, as well as health, issues. For example, an increase in taxation on cigarettes might make their cost prohibitive to many. However, one consequence for the Treasury would be a decline in an important source of revenue. Similarly, whilst the National Health Service (NHS) might cost less if smoking were reduced, much more money would be needed for the pensions of the increased numbers surviving into old age. Again, reduction in the tobacco industry, although reducing the number of days of sickness absence in industry in general, could result in heavy unemployment in cities that depend heavily on the tobacco industry itself.

The example of smoking illustrates that disease is as much a reflection of the economy today as it has been in the past. Diet is another example. It has been estimated by Lock and Smith (1976) that 56% of women and 52% of men in Britain over the age of 40 years are at least 15% overweight. The mortality risks of men who are 10% overweight are one-fifth higher than average, especially in mortality associated with diabetes and vascular disease. Clearly, overeating may be a major health risk. Burkitt (1973) and others have argued that inappropriate diet is also a problem. He argues that diverticular disease, cancer of the bowel, diabetes and indeed various venous diseases such as varicose veins and deep vein thrombosis may all be linked to lack of fibre. Populations which have diets with high fibre content seem relatively free of many such diseases. In Britain the daily fibre intake from bread has been reduced to about one-tenth of its level in 1850, whereas we have almost doubled our consumption of sugar and other refined carbohydrates. Again the statistics of change do not reveal the causal links. Changes in diet have reflected changes in the food-producing industries which are now concentrated in a small number of multinational companies more concerned with producing standardized and well-accepted, easily transported commodities: nutritional values have taken second place to the expansion of profits.

Another essentially modern form of health hazard may be identified in the 6000 deaths and 80 000 serious injuries that occur annually as a result of road traffic accidents. Doll (1983) makes the point that the rate per million of deaths on the roads is actually lower now than it was in the 1930s and is in this sense a testament to the beneficial effects of legislation with regard to prevention. Nevertheless, some 2000 hospital beds are occupied each day by the victims of road traffic accidents (Butler & Vaile 1984) which represents a considerable demand upon health-care resources. Risks of accidents are 18 times higher to motorcyclists than to car drivers, and much more still could be achieved to prevent accidents to this group by, for example, legislation on training and testing riding ability.

It may seem that an analysis of the relationship of social and economic factors to health is unhelpful and depressing because it points to features of our economic system that are central, firmly established and difficult to change. If this is the case, then another parallel is suggested with the nineteenth-century problems of environmental disease. The changes in sanitation, urban planning and building that were required to transform the pattern of infectious diseases in Victorian times were similarly regarded as unrealistic and resisted for long periods by politicians and business interests, but the reforms were slowly adopted and growing awareness of the relationship between commercially promoted behaviours such as smoking and unhealthy eating in our own time should help to speed the process of securing reforms.

A multi-disciplinary committee has produced a major report to assess the effectiveness of existing public health policies and to stimulate new national strategies (Smith & Jacobson 1988). They identify six areas of current life-styles that influence health, for which research evidence of harmful effects is strong and support for the feasibility of action is clear cut:

1. tobacco,
2. diet,
3. physical activity,
4. alcohol,
5. sexuality, and
6. road safety.

Similarly, they identify five areas of preventive services where evidence is very strong that public health interventions could now produce dramatic improvements:

1. maternity services,
2. dental health,
3. immunization,
4. early cancer detection (breast and cervix), and
5. high-blood-pressure detection.

Their approach in each of these 11 priority areas is to identify precise quantitative targets and make specific recommendations to public bodies and institutions. Thus one of a number of specific nutritional targets is to increase the total dietary fibre intake from 20 g per person per day to 30 g. The list of agencies to whom nutritional targets and specific actions are recommended includes the food industry, local authorities, health authorities and government. Their view is that agencies need specific targets to stimulate action and to provide a ready means of monitoring results.

THE ECONOMY AND HEALTH POLICY IN MODERN SOCIETY

Some of the most recent research on the relationship between the economy and health suggests that, even in modern societies, economic factors play the predominant role in determining patterns of illness, and that the role of health services is negligible by comparison. Brenner (1977) has argued that most of the variation in annual overall mortality rates for the USA can be statistically explained in terms of changes in the annual level of employment, provided that a time lag of 5 years is allowed for unemployment to have its effect on health. This impact is produced in two ways: firstly, unemployment reduces family income and, therefore, material standard of living; and secondly, the individual loses a sense of meaning and purpose found at work and experiences increased fears about the future and tension at home and is thereby more vulnerable to ill health. From USA data, Brenner concluded that a 1% increase in unemployment, if sustained for 5 years, was statistically responsible for nearly 37 000 extra deaths. Similar results have been found from analyses of data collected in England and Wales and Sweden (Brenner 1979).

This work has been challenged by Eyer (1977), who argues that the influence on health of experience such as unemployment generally occurs within a much shorter time than the 5-year lag that Brenner allows. If this is the case, the association between unemployment and mortality is considerably reduced. Instead, Eyer argues that death rates increase at the time of business booms when employment rates are high. The association between employment and mortality he explains in terms of four connected social factors that attend business cycles.

1. Economic booms increase workers' migration, which weakens social networks that normally protect individuals against disease.
2. 'Stress' through overwork in times of business peaks increases ill health.
3. The unhealthy consumption of alcohol and tobacco increases.
4. Conversely, during low periods of the economy, social networks are strong and act to protect individuals.

Support for the position taken by Brenner in this dispute may be found in a number of other studies. Bunn (1979) examined national statistics for ischaemic heart disease in Australia. He found that economic recessions and their associated problems of high unemployment were associated not only with subsequently higher levels of heart disease mortality, but also with increased rates of drug prescribing. The latter he interpreted as a potential indicator of the stress of the recession, which resulted in increased general practice prescribing. One of the most convincing pieces of statistical evidence is the Office of Population Censuses and Surveys (OPCS) Longitudinal Study (OPCS 1984), which found that men who were unemployed in 1971, and their wives, experienced a 20% higher mortality rate than those men employed in the following 10 years (Moser et al. 1987).

Other studies, instead of looking at correlations in national statistics, have examined at close hand the experiences of unemployed families. Fagin (1981) examined in detail a small sample of families in which the male bread-winner had been without work for at least 16 weeks. In many families the bread-winners developed clinical depression, loss of self-esteem, insomnia and suicidal thoughts, much of which necessitated psychotropic drug treatment by their general practitioners. Physical symptoms included asthmatic attack, back ache and skin lesions. The health of younger children in some families also seemed to be affected.

The issues raised by these two contrasting approaches of Brenner and Eyer are complex and far from resolution, but both at least agree in placing the main responsibility for health and illness on economic policy rather than on the health services. This controversial position is partly shared by more radical writers who are more concerned with analysing directly the contribution of modern medicine to health. Perhaps the best known is Illich (1977), who argues that medicine has played a very small role in improving health and that its contribution has actually been negative, insofar as it has:

1. raised public expectations of 'wonder cures' which in reality are ineffective;
2. extended too far the kinds of problem that are thought to be medical;
3. been responsible for large amounts of iatrogenic (medically produced) illness; and
4. decreased the ability of individuals to cope with their own illness by fostering a debilitating dependency on the expert (see Chapter 14).

Illich's own solution is firstly to break down medicine's monopoly in health care, so that there is a 'free market' in which anyone can practise healing, and secondly to reverse the social trend towards dependency by restoring the value of personal responsibility.

This approach, which is attractive to many advocates of 'alternative medicine' and self-help groups, is rejected as mistaken and utopian by writers such as Navarro (1975) because it wrongly blames the medical profession and a 'gullible' public for aspects of ill health which are best understood as products of a capitalist economy. It is this which directly creates much illness, maintains an unequal distribution of illness and encourages a very inappropriate health-care system for treating illness once it has occurred. Hence Navarro advocates radical political changes in society as the only solution to the kinds of problems that have been identified in this chapter.

Other writers such as McKeown and Powles place more emphasis on the need to reform health care rather than concerning themselves with wider issues of social change. Firstly, they argue that, since much disease is environmentally caused and preventable medicine should give more attention in teaching, research and practice to the prevention of disease rather than dealing with it after it has occurred. Not only has prevention had a significant impact in the past, it would appear a simple, more humane and sound means of reducing disease in the present.

Secondly, these analysts also maintain that health-care resources and energy have become too concentrated on high technology and hospital-based acute medicine at the expense of preventive and community resources. In the light of the evidence reviewed above, it seems that there is an unwarranted faith in technological medicine. With the possible exception of antibiotics and immunization, few improvements in health can be attributed to breakthroughs in laboratory medicine. Cochrane (1972) argues that all too few medical procedures have been submitted to rigorous evaluation of their effectiveness (see Chapter 18).

Thirdly, it is argued that another shift in the emphasis of medicine is needed, that from cure to care. Since medicine can claim few cures to be effective, it must confront the task of caring for the sick with greater zeal and effectiveness. Caring necessitates concern with the quality of life of the ill and reduction in any handicap or disadvantage consequent to disease. However, financial and other resources, reflecting medical values, are at present spent more in efforts in acute medicine than in the psychiatric or geriatric units. Medical education perpetuates such values because it is conducted predominantly in acute hospitals where consultants maintain traditional values in their teaching.

Clearly these arguments are controversial and have not gone unchallenged. Lever (1977) has argued that inferences about current health planning based on historical patterns are hazardous. To prove that environmental factors were the most important determinants of mortality in the past does not necessarily prove that environmental measures will produce such beneficial effects in the present. Given limited funds for health services, a major shift towards environmental and preventive health care would be a major gamble. Whatever the merits of such points, it has to be acknowledged that at present insufficient resources have been committed to such preventive services as health education and occupational medicine, compared with expenditure on hospital technology, to allow any serious examination of their potential role.

It might also be argued that analysts like McKeown are too pessimistic in their interpretation of the impact of medical treatments which have been shown to have led to markedly improved survival rates for many forms of childhood cancers and Hodgkin's disease and cancer of the testis amongst adult cancers (Doll 1990). Moreover, the debate has tended to focus upon death rates, thereby ignoring substantial benefits that may have been derived from medical treatments in improving individuals' quality of life, for example by mitigating symptoms of pain, discomfort or disability.

At present there remains much work to be done regarding the influence that social and economic factors exert on health. At the same time controversial debates continue unresolved about the priorities in efforts and expenditure that are most appropriate to modern patterns of illness.

REFERENCES

Brenner, M. (1977) Health costs and benefits of economic policy. *Int. J. Hlth Serv.*, **7**, 581–623.

Brenner, M. (1979) Mortality and the national economy. *Lancet*, **ii**, 568–73.

Bunn, A. (1979) Ischaemic heart disease mortality and the business cycle in Australia. *Am. J. pub. Hlth*, **69**, 772–81.

Burkitt, D. (1973) Some diseases characteristic of modern Western civilization. *Br. med. J.*, **1**, 274–8.

Butler, J. & Vaile, M. (1984) *Health and Health Services.* London: Routledge & Kegan Paul.

Cochrane, A. (1972) *Effectiveness and Efficiency: Random Reflections on the Health Service.* London: Nuffield Provincial Hospitals Trust.

Department of Health and Social Security (1981) *Inequalities in Health.* London: HMSO.

Doll, R. (1983) Prospects for prevention. *Br. med. J.*, **286**, 81–8.

Doll, R. (1990) Are we winning the fight against cancer? An epidemiological assessment. *Eur. J. Cancer*, **26**, 500–8.

Eyer, J. (1977) Does unemployment cause the death rate peak in each business cycle? *Int. J. Hlth Serv.*, **7**, 625–62.

Fagin, L. (1981) *Unemployment and Health in Families.* London: DHSS.

Fries, J. (1983) The compression of morbidity. *Milbank mem. Fund Q.*, **61**, 397–419.

Illich, I. (1977) *Limits to Medicine. Medical Nemesis: The Expropriation of Health.* Harmondsworth: Penguin.

Lever, A. (1977) Medicine under challenge. *Lancet*, **i**, 353–5.

Lock, S. & Smith, T. (1976) *The Medical Risks of Life.* Harmondsworth: Penguin.

McKeown, T. (1979) *The Role of Medicine: Dream, Mirage or Nemesis*, 2nd edition. Oxford: Blackwell Scientific.

McKeown, T. & Brown, R. (1969) Medical evidence related to English population changes in the eighteenth century. In: *Population in Industrialisation*, ed. M. Drake. London: Methuen.

Moser, K., Goldblatt, P., Fox, A. & Jones, D. (1987) Unemployment and mortality: comparison of the 1971 and 1981 longitudinal study census samples. *Br. med. J.*, **294**, 86–90.

Navarro, V. (1975) The industrialization of fetishism or the fetishism of industrialization: a critique of Ivan Illich. *Int. J. Hlth. Ser.*, **5**, 351–71.

Office of Population Censuses and Surveys (1984) *Mortality Statistics.* London: HMSO.

Powles, J. (1973) On the limitations of modern medicine. *Sci. Med. Man*, **1**, 1–30.

Smith, A. & Jacobson, B. (eds) (1988) *The Nation's Health: A Strategy for The 1990s.* London: King's Fund.

Szreter, S. (1988) The importance of social intervention in Britain's mortality decline c. 1850–1914: a reinterpretation of the role of public health. *Soc. History Med.*, **1**, 1–38.

2

Social causes of disease

David Locker

In the last chapter evidence was presented to indicate that the improvements in health observed during the eighteenth and nineteenth centuries were the product of rising standards of living and sanitary reform. This illustrates the general principle that the health of a population is closely tied to the physical, social and economic environment. The focus of this chapter is on the more specific social factors involved in causing disease. Over the past 40 years research in this field has grown significantly, with relatively new disciplines such as social epidemiology and psycho-physiology devoted to the investigation of the links between the social environment, psychological and emotional states, physiological change and disease. The broad implication of this work, and the view of health it embodies, is that health and illness are social, as well as medical, issues.

THEORIES OF DISEASE CAUSATION

Prior to the rise of modern medicine, disease was attributed to a variety of spiritual or mechanical forces. It was interpreted as a punishment by God for sinful behaviour or the result of an imbalance in body elements or 'humours'. Cholera, which was epidemic during the early nineteenth century, was ascribed to a life of vice or a weak moral character or believed to be due to 'miasma', that is, bad air arising out of dirt and decaying organic matter.

Ideas about disease emerging during the nineteenth century were influenced by two developments which provided a philosophical and empirical basis for the biomechanical approach characteristic of modern medical practice. These developments were the 'Cartesian revolution', which gave rise to the idea that the mind and body were independent, and the doctrine of specific aetiology, which flowed from the discovery of the microbiological origins of infectious disease. These effectively denied the influence of social and psychological factors in disease onset. Rather, the body was viewed as a machine to be corrected when things go wrong by procedures designed to neutralize specific agents or modify the physical processes causing disease. These ideas have been progressively challenged as the monocausal view of disease has been modified by multicausal models of disease onset.

The germ theory of disease

During the latter half of the nineteenth century, the work of Ehrlich, Koch and Pasteur revealed that the prevailing health problems of the time were the product of living organisms which entered the body through food, water, air or the bites of insects or animals. In 1882, Koch identified and isolated the bacillus causing tuberculosis, and between 1897 and 1900 the organisms responsible for 22 infectious diseases were identified. This work gave rise to the doctrine of specific aetiology, the idea that each disease has a single and specific cause. This is embodied in Koch's postulates, a set of rules for establishing causal relationships between a micro-organism and a disease. These state that, to be ascribed a causal role, the agent must always be found with the disease in question and not with any other disease. This doctrine with its monocausal approach came to dominate, and to some extent still dominates, medical research and practice. As a result, research effort moved from the community to the laboratory and concentrated on the identification of the noxious agents responsible for a given disease, while medical practice became devoted to the destruction or eradication of that agent from individuals already affected (Najman 1980).

Multicausal models of disease

Although the germ theory of disease made a significant contribution to explaining and solving the major health problems of its time, it has serious limitations in terms of our understanding of disease processes. The most important of these is that there is no direct relationship between the presence of micro-organisms and the existence of disease; not all those exposed to pathogens become ill. Clearly, an organism or other noxious agent is a necessary, but not a sufficient, cause of disease. The *epidemiological triangle* approach sees disease as the product of an interaction between an agent, a host and the environment. Host and environmental factors determine exposure and/or susceptibility to the noxious agent in question. In this respect, all diseases, including infections, are multifactorial and have multiple causes. One of the benefits of this broader view is that the health of a population may be promoted by procedures which modify suscep- tibility and exposure as well as by procedures which attack the agent involved in the disease. That is, disease can be prevented as well as cured.

The epidemiologic triangle is useful in understanding infectious disorders, but is less useful with respect to chronic, degenerative disorders such as heart disease, stroke and arthritis, for here no specific agent can be identified against which individuals and populations may be protected. Many contemporary medical problems are better understood in terms of a *web of causation* (MacMahon & Pugh 1970). According to this concept, disorders such as heart disease develop through complex interactions of many factors which form interlocking chains. These factors may be biophysical, social or psychological and may promote or inhibit the disease at more than one point in the causal process. For example, some of the factors implicated in heart disease are high blood pressure, blood cholesterol levels, diet, smoking, physical inactivity, Type A personality and stress. Since many of these factors can be modified, prevention offers better prospects for health than cure. It is also important to note that many of the factors implicated in heart disease have been identified as increasing the risk of other disorders, such as stroke and cancer.

It should be apparent that both these models accord some significance to the physical and social environment and/or the patterns of behaviour they may engender.

The theory of general susceptibility

The theory of general susceptibility has emerged over the past 20 years and departs in important ways from monocausal and multicausal models of disease. It is not concerned with identifying single or multiple risk factors associated with specific disorders, but seeks to understand why some social groups seem to be more susceptible to disease and death in general. For example, numerous studies have shown that social class, measured by occupation, education, income or area of residence, is closely related to health, even in countries with nationalized and egalitarian health-care systems such as the National Health Service (NHS) in the UK (see Chapter 8). Other examples, such as social integration, social support and marital status, are discussed below. While the processes involved

are multicausal, involving some complex combination of environment, life experiences and behaviours, they also involve a general
susceptibility of certain groups to death from a wide variety of
conditions. As a consequence, social and political change may be
necessary to modify the health experience of these groups.

These four theories of the causes of disease have been presented
in a more or less historical sequence. From the brief descriptions
offered it is clear that the role ascribed to the physical, social and
psychological environment increases as we have progressed from the
germ theory to the theory of general susceptibility. The latter
completely overturns the doctrine of specific aetiology central to the
former, for broad non-specific social and psychological factors are
seen to be associated with a variety of disease outcomes.

It would, however, be a mistake to assume that the role of social
and psychological factors as causes of disease has been realized only
in modern times. Many of the so-called 'pre-scientific' explanations of
disease gave recognition to the part played by such factors. In many
cultures, disease is still seen in social terms, as the outcome of a lack
of harmony in social relationships. In the context of modern medical
history the idea that disease can be brought about by psychological
influences was integral to the work of Freud, who explained disorders
such as asthma and gastric ulcers as the product of unresolved
psychological conflict. Freud's work gave rise to the notion that some
diseases were 'psychosomatic' while others were not. The contemporary view is that social and psychological factors are implicated in
all diseases, although the mechanisms by means of which they
influence health are complex and variable.

SOCIAL AND PSYCHOLOGICAL FACTORS
AND HEALTH

The research effort invested in studies of social and psychological
factors and health is enormous and the body of work that has been
produced is difficult to summarize. One reason for this is that a wide
variety of factors having a potential influence on health have been
studied. These factors fall into three broad types: socio-environmental, behavioural and psychological. Socio-environmental factors
include poverty, social support and relationships with others, work
and unemployment; behavioural factors include smoking, exercise
and dietary practices; and psychological factors include personality
type, coping capacities and health beliefs. Physical

Clearly, there are close links between many of these factors and
contemporary models of illness attempt to specify how and when

they are involved in the mechanisms leading to disease. Even though behaviours such as smoking are individual acts, a number of social and cultural factors influence whether someone will become a smoker and continue to smoke. These factors include cultural themes associated with smoking such as relaxation, adulthood, sexual attractiveness and emancipation; the socioeconomic structure of tobacco production, processing, distribution and legislation; explicit and continual advertising by the tobacco companies and the influence of peers, siblings and significant others' (Syme 1986).

Some of the socio-environmental factors having an influence of health and contemporary explanations of their role as causes of disease are reviewed below.

Social and cultural change

Most of the early studies of social factors and disease onset were concerned with the effects of social and cultural change. They included studies of industrialization and urbanization, migration and social, occupational and geographical mobility. The major disease outcome studied was coronary heart disease since this is predominantly a disease of industrialized, urbanized nations. Some populations isolated from western culture have low blood pressure which does not rise with age. However, blood-pressure levels and coronary heart disease rates increase when these populations move to urban settings (Prior 1974). Recent studies of this type have focussed on the downward occupational and social mobility associated with short- and long-term unemployment.

A number of studies conducted during the 1960s and early 1970s found higher rates of disease among people who changed jobs, place of residence or life circumstances. For example, one study found that men reared on farms who moved to urban centres to take middle-class jobs had higher rates of coronary heart disease than men who continued to work on the farm or who took up labouring jobs in cities (Syme et al. 1964). Similar observations have been made with respect to cancer. Men raised on farms who moved to cities had higher rates of lung cancer than those who did not, even at comparable levels of smoking (Haenszel et al. 1962). However, a study of the impact of oil development in the north of Scotland showed that rapid social change did not have negative consequences on the health of the population if the community was well integrated prior to the change, if the change was anticipated and planned, and if it had more advantages than disadvantages for the community.

A number of mechanisms might be responsible for the negative effects of social and cultural change on health. The adverse effects may be the direct result of change itself, a product of the circumstances to which individuals move or the product of personal characteristics which predispose individuals to both mobility and poor health. One study which attempted to evaluate these explanations compared rates of heart disease among Japanese immigrants to California and Hawaii with those of Japanese men still living in Japan (Marmot et al. 1975). Coronary heart disease and mortality rates were highest among those living in California and lowest in Japan. This difference was not explained by differences in risk factors such as cholesterol levels, diet, blood pressure or smoking. However, among those living in California, some had become 'acculturated' and had adopted western lifestyles, while others retained traditional Japanese ways. The former had disease rates up to five times as high as the latter. This suggests that being mobile is not, in itself, the important factor.

In recent years, more emphasis has been placed on the health effects of unemployment. There are two main reasons why unemployment could conceivably affect health (Marmot & Madge 1987). First, it is related to standard of living and the material conditions of life, and second it is a stressful event which may become chronic and deprive an individual of a social role, meaningful daily existence and contact with others.

Two approaches are evident in studies of unemployment and health and both are subject to problems in interpretation, largely because it is difficult to separate the effects of unemployment from the effects of other social and economic conditions (Marmot & Madge 1987). The first of these approaches attempts to demonstrate an association between unemployment rates and mortality rates and the way these co-vary with the ups and downs of the economic cycle. The most recent of this work was conducted by Brenner (1979) and is reviewed in Chapter 1. The second approach attempts to assess the health of people who are, or have recently become, unemployed. Since ill health can lead to unemployment as well as vice versa, such studies need to be conducted carefully before it can be concluded that unemployment is a cause of poor health. Nevertheless, evidence from well-designed research does suggest that the unemployed experience more illness, have higher blood pressure and increased mortality (Arber 1987; Moser et al. 1987).

Social support

One of the earliest studies of the relationship between social environment and health was undertaken by the French sociologist Durkheim and published in 1897. In this work Durkheim pioneered the use of statistical methods for exploring and explaining differences in suicide rates across different social groups. Although suicide is an

——————— **Table 1** ———————
Mortality, all causes: ratio of
mortality rate of the unmarried to the
mortality rate of the married; whites
aged 25–64 years, USA, 1960.

Marital status	Sex	Ratio
Single	Male	1.96
	Female	1.68
Widowed	Male	2.64
	Female	1.77
Divorced	Male	3.39
	Female	1.95

Source: Gove (1979).

individual act, these differences in rates have persisted over time and
across cultures. Durkheim explained suicide in terms of the social
organization of these groups, particularly the extent to which individuals
were integrated into the group, and the way in which this encouraged or
deterred individuals from suicide. High rates of suicide were associated
with groups which had very high and very low levels of integration.

More recent studies of social ties and health have focussed on the
relationship between social support and individual well-being. Some
of this early work looked at differences in health according to marital
status. The single, widowed and divorced have higher mortality rates
than the married, the differences being much larger for men than for
women (Table 1). These differences, which were first observed and
reported in the mid-nineteenth century, have been remarkably
consistent over time, and are consistent across cultures and health-
care systems. Only a small part of the differences in mortality rates
can be explained by the selective effects of marriage (Morgan 1980).

One possible explanation of these differences is that marital status
has an influence on psychological states and life-styles (Gove 1973).
Studies have shown that the married tend to be happier and more
satisfied with life than the unmarried, they are less likely to be socially
isolated and have more social ties. In a society in which marriage and
family life are a central value, being married gives meaning and
significance to daily life, promotes a sense of well-being and is a
source of social and emotional support. This explanation tends to be
supported by data on marital status and specific causes of death.
Variations in mortality rates are large where psychological states or
aspects of life-style play a direct role in death, as in suicide or death
from accidents, or are associated with acts such as smoking or alcohol
consumption. Large differences are also observed with respect to

———— **Table 2** ————

Mortality, specific causes: Ratio of mortality rate
of the unmarried to the mortality rate of the married;
whites aged 25–64, years, USA, 1960.

Marital status	Cause				
	Suicide	Lung cancer	Cirrhosis	Tuberculosis	Diabetes
Single					
Male	2.00	1.45	3.29	5.37	2.69
Female	1.51	1.11	1.19	3.31	2.03
Widowed					
Male	5.01	2.24	4.61	7.70	2.46
Female	2.21	1.20	3.45	3.31	1.71
Divorced					
Male	4.75	3.07	8.84	9.27	4.32
Female	3.43	1.11	4.43	3.10	1.67

Source: Gove (1979).

diseases such as tuberculosis, where family factors may influence entry into medical care, willingness to undergo treatment or the availability of help and support (Table 2).

The high death rates of widowed men have also been confirmed in studies which have documented the mortality experience of recently bereaved men. Parkes et al. (1969) found that mortality rates of widowers aged 55 years and over were 40% higher than those of men the same age in the 6 months following the loss of a spouse.

An influential study which clearly demonstrated that integration into the community has a direct effect on health was undertaken by Berkman and Syme (1979). They followed a random sample of adults over a 9-year period. At the start of the study a social network score was calculated for each subject based on marital status, contacts with friends and relatives and membership of religious and other social groups. Over the 9-year period of the study those with low network scores were more likely to die than those with high network scores. After controlling for other factors such as weight, cigarette smoking, alcohol consumption, physical activity, health practices and health status at baseline, mortality rates for the socially isolated were two to three times higher than those with extensive social networks.

Other evidence suggests that social integration and social support have a broad influence on health. They have been linked to heart disease (Reed et al. 1983), complications of pregnancy (Nuckolls et al. 1972) and emotional illness (Henderson et al. 1978). A 2-year follow-up study of people with disabilities living in an urban community found that people with few social contacts were more likely to deteriorate in physical and psycho-social functioning than people with high levels of contact with others (Patrick et al. 1986). However, the greatest and most significant difference between those with and without social support occurred among those reporting an adverse life event during the period of the study.

Social support refers to a fairly broad category of events and includes practical assistance, financial help, the provision of information and advice and psychological support. The mechanisms by means of which it enhances or protects health are not known. One hypothesis concerning this mechanism has emerged in the context of studies of the negative health impact of stressful life circumstances. This research suggests that social support has no direct influence on health but acts as a buffer against adverse events that would otherwise have health-damaging effects. In their research on the social origins of depression, Brown and Harris (1978) found that social support was protective only in the context of a severe life event. While this and other studies strongly suggest that social support enhances coping and the ability to tolerate stressful life circumstances, further research is needed to specify what types of support buffer which kinds of life problems and precisely how they promote health and well-being.

Life events

A more comprehensive attempt to assess the influence of life experiences such as bereavement and unemployment is to be found in studies of life events and health. This approach emerged at the end of the 1960s with the development of instruments such as the Social Readjustment Rating Scale (SRRS) (Holmes & Rahe 1967). This scale consists of a list of 42 events, each of which involves personal loss or some degree of change in roles or personal relationships. Each event is given a score depending upon how much life change it involves. These scores were based on the judgments of a large sample of healthy adults. The top of the scale is the death of a wife or husband and is given a score of 100. Divorce has a score of 73 and losing a job a score of 45. Scores for an individual are totalled to give a numerical estimate of the amount of life change experienced in a defined period, usually the past year. A number of studies have shown that there is some relationship between scores on this scale and future changes in health.

There have been a number of criticisms of this method of measuring the frequency and severity of life events. Perhaps the most important is that scales such as the SRRS fail to take account of variations in the meaning and significance of life events. The birth of a child, for example, may be a positive event for some women but a negative event for others, depending upon the social context in which it occurs. More sophisticated measures of life events have been developed which take account of variations in the meaning of life events based on contextual factors (Brown & Harris 1978).

A second criticism of the SRRS is that it focusses on major life events and ignores less severe but more common life difficulties. A measure which attempts to tap such difficulties is the Hassles Scale (Kanner et al. 1981). Its proponents claim that measures of life stress based on daily 'hassles' are better predictors of changes in physical and psychological health than measures based on major life events.

Clearly, the measurement of life stress is a complex issue and establishing a relationship between such stress and negative health outcomes is methodologically challenging. Many studies which have shown such a relationship have design weaknesses which makes interpretation of their results difficult.

One particularly noteworthy study is that conducted by Brown and Harris (1978). This was an investigation of the social and economic circumstances causally implicated in the onset of depression in women. Using measures which were context sensitive, they were able to show a clear relationship between life events with long-term threatening implications and the onset of depression in women. Events with short-term implications, no matter how stressful, were not associated with depression. However, whether or not a woman became depressed after an event involving long-term threat was dependent upon the presence of four 'vulnerability factors'. These were: the absence of a close, confiding relationship with a spouse or other person, loss of mother before age 11 years, lack of employment outside the home, and having three or more children under the age of 15 living at home. The greater the number of these factors present, the greater was the likelihood of depression following an event with long-term threatening implications. Brown and Harris (1978) believe that these vulnerability factors produce ongoing low self-esteem and an inability to cope with the world. These interact with life events to produce generalized feelings of hopelessness and, subsequently, depression.

This model also explains why working-class women have higher rates of depression than middle-class women. They are more likely to experience severe life events and, because their lives are more likely to be characterized by one of these vulnerability factors, they are more prone to become depressed as a result.

Life events have also been implicated in the mechanisms leading to physical disorders (Creed 1985). They have been linked to disturbances in the control of diabetes (Bradley 1979), to diseases such as duodenal ulcer (Murphy & Brown 1980) and to abdominal pain leading to appendicectomy (Creed 1981). The study by Murphy and Brown suggested that the development of physical conditions was dependent on the prior development of a psychiatric disorder, while the study by Creed suggested that life stress was an important component of functional disorders.

THE SOCIAL CAUSES OF DISEASE: EXPLANATORY MODELS

Two explanations have been developed to account for the relationship between broad social factors and the experience of disease. The first has been referred to as the *stress–illness model*. Although there are a number of formulations of this model, most assume that *stressors* (threatening environmental circumstances) give rise to *strains* (psychological and physiological changes) which increase an individual's susceptibility to disease. There is evidence to suggest that stress, or its outcome in the form of depression, leads to a number of changes in the human body. It interferes with the normal functioning of hormonal and immune systems, leads to increased heart rate and respiration, dilatation of blood vessels to the muscles and alterations in gastrointestinal function. These changes are believed to cause disease directly or render an individual more prone to disease.

This essentially simple model is more complex than it seems. Firstly, the link between stressors and illness is mediated by a number of factors which may increase or decrease an individual's vulnerability when faced with a stressor. Psychological variables such as personality characteristics, perceptual processes and coping styles, along with social factors such as social support, socio-economic and family status, interact in complex ways to affect health outcomes.

The second explanatory model gives greater weight to environmental and behavioural factors (Najman 1980). These include exposure to hazardous community, occupational and domestic environments, smoking, alcohol consumption, diet, exercise and use of self-care practices. The assumption here is that groups characterized by these broad social variables related to health are also characterized by health-damaging environments and behaviours.

While there is evidence to support both the stress model and the environment–behaviour theory, neither is complete and both are contradicted by the results of some studies (Najman 1980). One approach which attempts to link the stress–illness model and the environment–behaviour theory suggests that health-damaging behaviours are themselves the product of stress. Some support for this point of view is to be found in the fact that rates of smoking and alcohol consumption are highest among those in occupations which have the highest levels of stress.

The main conclusion to be drawn from this research is that patterns of health and disease are largely the product of social and environmental influences. While health and illness may involve biological agents and processes, they are inseparable from the social settings in which people live. Ultimately, it is these which influence the challenges people encounter in daily life and their capacity to manage them.

REFERENCES

Arber, S. (1987) Social class, non-employment and chronic illness: continuing the inequalities in health debate. *Br. med. J.*, **294**, 1069–73.

Berkman, L. & Syme, S. (1979) Social networks, host resistance and mortality: a nine-year follow-up of Alameda County residents. *Am. J. Epidem.*, **109**, 186–204.

Bradley, C. (1979) Life events and the control of diabetes mellitus. *J. psychosom. Res.*, **23**, 159–62.

Brenner, M. (1979) Mortality and the national economy. *Lancet*, **ii**, 568–73.

Brown, G. & Harris, T. (1978) *The Social Origins of Depression.* London: Tavistock.

Creed, F. (1981) Life events and appendicitis. *Lancet*, **i**, 1381–5.

Creed, F. (1985) Life events and physical illness: a review. *J. psychosom. Res.*, **29**, 113–24.

Gove, W. (1979) Sex, marital status and mortality. *American J. Sociol.*, **79**, 45–67.

Haenszel, W., Loveland, D. & Sirken, M. (1962) Lung cancer mortality as related to residence and smoking histories: I. White males. *J. natn. Cancer Inst.*, **28**, 947–1001.

Henderson, S., Byrne, D., Duncan-Jones, P., Adcock, S., Scott, R. & Steale, G. (1978) Social bonds in the epidemiology of neurosis. *Br. J. Psychiat.*, **132**, 463–6.

Holmes, T. & Rahe, R. (1967) The social readjustment rating scale. *J. psychosom. Res.*, **11**, 231–218.

Kanner, A., Coyne, J., Schaefer, C. & Lazarus, R. (1981) Comparison of two modes of stress measurement: daily hassles and uplifts versus major life events. *J. behavior. Med.*, **4**, 1–39.

MacMahon, B. & Pugh, T. (1970) *Epidemiological Principles and Methods.* Boston, MA: Little, Brown and Co.

Marmot, M. & Madge, N. (1987) An epidemiological perspective on stress and health. In. *Stress and Health: Issues in Research Methodology*, ed. S. Kasl & C. Cooper. Winchester: Wiley.

Marmot, M., Syme, L. & Kagan, A. (1975) Epidemiological studies of heart disease and stroke in Japanese men living in Japan, Hawaii and California. Prevalence of coronary and hypertensive disease and associated risk factors. *Am. J. Epidem.*, **102**, 514–25.

Morgan, M. (1980) Marital status, health, illness and service use. *Soc. Sci. Med.*, **14A**, 633–43.

Moser, K., Goldblatt, P. & Fox, A. (1987) Unemployment and mortality: a comparison of the 1971 and the 1981 longitudinal study census samples. *Lancet*, **ii**, 1324–8.

Murphy, E. & Brown, G. (1980) Life events, psychiatric disturbance and physical illness. *Br. J. Psychiat.*, **136**, 326–38.

Najman, J. (1980) Theories of disease causation and the concept of general susceptibility: a review. *Soc. Sci. Med.*, **14A,** 231–7.

Nuckolls, K., Cassel, J. & Kaplan, B. (1972) Psychosocial assets, life crises and the prognosis of pregnancy. *Am. J. Epidem.*, **95,** 431–41.

Parkes, C., Benjamin, B. & Fitzgerald, R. (1969) Broken heart: a statistical survey of increased mortality among widowers. *Br. med. J.*, **1,** 740–4.

Patrick, D., Morgan, M. & Charlton, J. (1986) Psychosocial support and change in the health status of physically disabled people. *Soc. Sci. Med.*, **22,** 1347–54.

Prior, I. (1974) Cardiovascular epidemiology in New Zealand and the Pacific. *N.Z. med. J.*, **80,** 245–52.

Reed, D., McGee, D., Yano, K. & Feinleib, M. (1983) Social networks and coronary heart disease among Japanese men in Hawaii. *Am. J. Epidem.*, **117,** 384–96.

Syme, S. (1986) Social determinants of health and disease. In: *Public Health and Preventative Medicine* (ed. J. Last) Norwalk, Conn.: Appleton–Century–Crofts.

Syme, S., Hyman, M. & Enterline, P. (1964) Some social and cultural factors associated with the occurrence of coronary heart disease. *J. chron. Dis.*, **17,** 277–89.

PART II

Social factors in medical practice

3

Health and illness behaviour

Graham Scambler

Definitions of 'health' and 'illness' vary within cultures, subcultures and communities, and even within households, between generations for example. There may be gaps too between lay and medical concepts. The primary focus of this chapter is on lay beliefs about, and attitudes toward, health and illness, and on the various ways in which these, together with a host of other social factors, can influence people's behaviour when faced with what they perceive to be threats to their well-being.

Consideration is given first to differences in people's perspectives on health and illness. A brief review is then given of studies of the prevalence of illness and disease in the community. Special attention is paid to those factors known to influence help-seeking behaviour, and especially to those known to affect whether or not people who define themselves as ill consult a physician, usually a general practitioner. Finally, self-help and sources of help other than allopathic medicine are considered, ranging from informal lay networks to alternative therapies.

PERCEPTIONS OF HEALTH AND ILLNESS

The modern study of how lay people define health and illness was pioneered by Herzlich (1973) with her research with 80, largely middle-class, adults in France. Analysing their accounts of health and illness, she found that illness was generally perceived as *external* and as a product of a way of life, notably urban life. This covered not merely pathological agents such as germs, but also accidents and diseases like cancer and various mental disorders. Health, on the other hand, was perceived as *internal* to the individual, with three different and discernible dimensions: an absence of illness ('health in a vacuum'); a 'reserve of health', determined by constitution and temperament; and a positive state of well-being or 'equilibrium'.

Several studies in Britain have since led to similar distinctions. Pill and Scott (1982) interviewed mothers of families with young children from working-class backgrounds. They encountered definitions of health in terms of the absence of illness. A functional definition of health was also common, that is, in terms of the capacity to perform or cope with normal roles. As in Herzlich's study, a positive definition of health was apparent as well, although among Pill and Scott's sample it was associated with being cheerful and enthusiastic rather than with a state of equilibrium.

Such a positive dimension was missing, however, from the accounts of mothers and daughters in socially disadvantaged families questioned by Blaxter and Paterson (1982). References were made to health as the absence of illness, but the majority seemed to have a functional definition of health. They also had a functional definition of illness, many of them distinguishing between *normal* illness, which they accommodated, and *serious* illness, like cancer, heart disease and tuberculosis, which called for radical adjustment and change. These conceptions of health and illness, especially the lack of a positive definition of health, clearly reflected the high prevalence of health problems amongst the sample.

Reviewing these and other studies, Blaxter (1990) writes: 'Health can be defined negatively, as the absence of illness, functionally, as the ability to cope with everyday activities, or positively, as fitness and well-being'. She adds that health also has moral connotations, as salient in modern urban communities as among pre-modern or primitive societies. There is a sense in which people feel a duty to be healthy and experience illness as failure. Health can be seen in terms of will-power, self-discipline and self-control.

The national *Health and Lifestyle* survey found that 71% of participants defined their health as at least 'good' (Blaxter 1990). This did not mean that none of these people had symptoms of illness or, indeed, medically defined disease. For example, many disabled and/or elderly people defined their health as 'excellent', clearly meaning 'my health is excellent despite my disability/considering my advanced years'. Comparisons were made between participants' own assessments of their health and a series of objective measures. Although there was a general correspondence between the two, most obviously at the extremes, 10% of men and 7% of women in the top category of health, objectively measured, described their health as only 'fair' or 'poor'; and as many as 40% of those with undoubted

——— **Table 1** ———
Levels (%) of self-defined acute and chronic illness
in Britain, 1972 and 1987

	Acute illness		Chronic illness		Limiting chronic illness	
	1972	1987	1972	1987	1972	1987
Men	7%	12%	20%	32%	13%	19%
Women	8%	14%	21%	35%	15%	22%
All	8%	14%	21%	33%	14%	21%

Source: OPCS (1989).

health problems, objectively measured, described their health as
'good' or 'excellent'.

ILLNESS AND DISEASE IN THE COMMUNITY

In the *General Household Survey* for 1987 (OPCS 1989), 14% of
those questioned, 12% of men and 14% of women, reported
episodes of acute sickness leading to restricted activity in a 14-day
reference period. Regarding chronic illness, in 1987 as a whole,
33% (32% of men and 35% of women) reported experiencing some
long-standing sickness, and 14% (12% of men and 14% of women)
had their activity 'limited' in some way as a consequence. As Table 1
shows, there has been a slight increase in the tendency to report both
acute and chronic illness over the period 1972–87 (OPCS 1989).

The same survey shows that people do not always seek medical
help when they define themselves as ill. Only 41% of those reporting
restricted activity due to acute sickness over the 2-week period in
1987 had consulted their general practitioners. Only 22% of those
reporting chronic or long-standing illness had taken this same option.
At the same time, 8% of those with no reported illness had consulted
their doctors over the same 2-week period (OPCS 1989).

Overall, 15% of participants in the *General Household Survey*
(13% of men and 18% of women) consulted their general
practitioners in the 2-week period before interview in 1987; and the
average number of general practitioner consultations throughout
1987 was five: four for men and six for women (OPCS 1989). People
consult slightly more often than was the case 15 years ago. The
average number of prescriptions per person has also risen, reaching
7.5 in 1988, when a total of 427.7 million were dispensed (Central
Statistical Office 1990).

The rate of reporting of individual *symptoms* of illness is, of course,

———— **Table 2** ————

Two-week incidence of symptoms and
subsequent behaviour in a random sample
of 1000 adults living in London.

Individuals with no symptoms	49
Individuals with symptoms taking no action	188
Individuals with symptoms taking non-medical action	562
General practitioner patients	168
Hospital out-patients	28
Hospital in-patients	5
Total	1000

Source: Wadsworth et al. (1971).

considerably higher. The findings of Wadsworth et al. (1971) remain typical of retrospective studies in this area. As Table 2 reveals, 95% of their sample of 1000 adults had experienced symptoms in the 14 days prior to interview; and only one in five had consulted a doctor. In a prospective study conducted by Scambler et al. (1981) a sample of women aged 16–44 years kept 6-week health diaries in which they recorded any disturbances in their health. Symptoms were recorded on an average of one day in three. The 10 most frequently recorded symptoms are given in Table 3, which also shows how often these precipitated medical consultations and the ratio of medical consultations to symptom episodes. Overall, there was one medical consultation for every 18 symptom episodes.

It might be thought that most symptoms not precipitating consultations are mild and not indicative of diseases requiring medical intervention. Ingham and Miller (1979) found that symptom severity for seven selected symptoms was indeed greater in consulters than in non-consulters. There is convincing evidence, however, that general practitioners are often not consulted for diseases which would undoubtedly respond to treatment. Epsom (1978) carried out a classic investigation of the health status of a sample of adults using a mobile health clinic. Of the 3160 people investigated, 57% were referred to their general practitioners for further tests and possible treatment. Major diseases detected included seven instances of pre-invasive cervical cancer, one confirmed case of carcinoma of the breast and one active case of pulmonary tuberculosis. A follow-up study of those referred to their general practitioners indicated that 38% of the findings had not previously been known to the general practitioners, and that 22% of the findings made known to the general practitioners for the first time were judged serious enough to warrant hospital referrals. This study and others confirm that a significant clinical iceberg exists: the professional health services treat only the tip of the sum total of ill health.

——— **Table 3** ———
Symptom episodes and medical consultations
recorded in health diaries.

Main types of symptoms recorded	No. of symptom episodes	Percentage of total number of symptom episodes	Mean length of symptom episodes (days)	No. of occasions on which symptom episode precipitated medical consultation	Ratio of medical consultations to symptom episodes
Headache	180	20.9	1.3	3	1:60
Changes in energy, tiredness	109	12.6	1.4	0	—
Nerves, depression, or irritability	74	8.6	1.7	1	1:74
Aches or pains in joints, muscles, legs or arms	71	8.2	1.6	4	1:18
Women's complaints like period pain*	69	8.0	1.7	7	1:10
Stomach aches or pains	45	5.2	1.5	4	1:11
Backache	38	4.4	1.6	1	1:38
Cold, flu, or running nose	37	4.3	4.1	3	1:12
Sore throat	36	4.2	2.4	4	1:9
Sleeplessness	31	3.6	1.5	1	1:31
Others	173	20.0	1.9	21	1:8
Total	863	100.0	1.7	49	1:18

Source: Scambler et al. (1981).
*Stomach aches and pains and backache were classified as period pains if so defined by the women themselves.

The existence of a clinical iceberg has important implications. Most obviously there is the problem of unmet need: many people of all ages are enduring avoidable pain, discomfort and handicap. There is a gap in other words between the need for and the demand for health care. It must be remembered, however, that any substantial increase in the existing level of demand would swamp the primary care services. Many general practitioners also argue that there is currently a widespread tendency for people to consult for trivial, unnecessary or inappropriate reasons: in one national study, one-quarter of the general practitioners questioned felt that half or more of their surgery consultations fell into this category (Cartwright &

Anderson 1981). Basic to these issues, of course, is the question of how to define 'need'.

UNDERSTANDING ILLNESS BEHAVIOUR

A number of studies have documented the socio-demographic characteristics of users and non-users of medical services. It is known, for example, that women consult more than men, children and the elderly more than young adults and the middle-aged; social class, ethnic origin, marital status and family size are other factors which have been shown to be related to utilization. These studies tell us who does and does not make use of the services, rather than why. To begin to answer the more complex question of why people seek or decline to seek professional help is to begin to theorize about illness behaviour.

It is crucial to recognize that whether or not people consult their doctors does not depend only upon the presence of disease, but also upon how they, or others, respond to its symptoms. Mechanic (1978) has listed 10 variables known to influence consulting behaviour:

1. visibility, recognizability, or perceptual salience of signs and symptoms;
2. the extent to which the symptoms are perceived as serious (that is, the person's estimate of the present and future probabilities of danger);
3. the extent to which symptoms disrupt family, work and other social activities;
4. the frequency of the appearance of the signs or symptoms, their persistence, or their frequency or recurrence;
5. the tolerance threshold of those who are exposed to and evaluate the signs and symptoms;
6. available information, knowledge and cultural assumptions and understandings of the evaluator;
7. basic needs that lead to denial;
8. needs competing with illness responses;
9. competing possible interpretations that can be assigned to the symptoms once they are recognized; and
10. availability of treatment resources, physical proximity, and psychological and monetary costs of taking action (not only physical distance and costs of time, money and effort, but also such costs as stigma, social distance and feelings of humiliation).

Mechanic acknowledges that this list is far from exhaustive and that in reality different variables tend to interact together. He also introduces a basic underlying distinction between 'self-defined' and 'other-defined' illness: the major difference is that, in the latter, individuals tend to resist the definitions that others attempt to impose upon them, and it may be necessary to bring them into treatment under great pressure, even involuntarily.

Since it is not possible to explore all the multifarious and interrelated influences on illness and consulting behaviour here, six broad categories have been selected for emphasis.

/. Cultural variation

The significance of cultural factors in determining how symptoms are interpreted has been well documented, perhaps most convincingly in studies of ethnicity and the experience and reporting of pain. In a pioneering study conducted in New York, Zborowski (1952) found that patients of Old-American or Irish origin displayed a stoical, matter-of-fact attitude towards pain and, if it was intense, a tendency to withdraw from the company of others. In contrast, patients of Italian or Jewish background were more demanding and dependent and tended to seek, rather than shun, public sympathy. Subsequent research has both corroborated Zborowski's findings and afforded support for the more general view that there is a marked cultural difference in the interpretation of and response to symptoms between so-called Anglo-Saxon and Mediterranean groups. It is tempting to assume that such cultural variation is explicable in terms of socialization alone, namely that differences in illness behaviour merely reflect different culturally learned styles of coping with the world at large. The authors of a study of Anglo-Saxon, Anglo-Greek and Greek groups in Australia, however, have suggested that other factors may also be important. They found, for example, that immigrant status and, relatedly, the stress of adapting to a majority culture, played a significant part in accounting for the different patterns of illness behaviour among the Anglo-Saxon and Mediterranean groups (Pilowski & Spence 1977). In short, cultural patterns may vary depending on the social context.

2. Phenomenology of symptoms and knowledge of disease

Studies have indicated that symptoms which present in a 'striking' way — for example, a sharp abdominal pain or a high fever — are more likely to be interpreted as illness and to receive prompt medical attention than those which present less dramatically. Consultation in such circumstances may simply be a function of the pain or discomfort; alternatively, it may be a function of the degree of incapacitation or disruption engendered by the pain or discomfort (see 'Triggers' below). Many distressing symptoms are not indicative of serious diseases; but, equally, some serious diseases — for example, some cancers — rarely appear in a striking fashion: their onset may be slow and insidious. The actions of potential patients are thus also dependent on their knowledge of disease, and on their capacity to differentiate between diseases which are threatening/non-threatening and which can/cannot be effectively treated.

3 . 'Triggers'

While many of the symptoms people experience are recognized as indicating disease processes, it is not necessarily the case that treatment is sought. What, when and if action to resolve any problems is undertaken often depends upon a number of other factors. Zola (1973) has looked at the *timing* of decisions to seek medical care. He found that most people tolerated their symptoms for quite a time before they went to a doctor, and that the symptoms themselves were often not sufficient to precipitate a consultation: something else had to happen to bring this about. He identified five types of 'trigger':

1. the occurrence of an interpersonal crisis (e.g. a death in the family);
2. perceived interference with social or personal relations;
3. 'sanctioning' (pressure from others to consult);
4. perceived interference with vocational or physical activity; and
5. a kind of 'temporalizing of symptomatology' (the setting of a deadline, e.g. 'If I feel the same way on Monday . . .', or 'If I have another turn . . .').

The decision to seek professional help is, then, very much bound up with an individual's personal and social circumstances. Zola also found that, when doctors paid insufficient attention to the specific trigger which prompted an individual or which an individual used as an excuse to seek help, there was a greater chance that the patient would eventually break off treatment.

4 Perceptions of costs and benefits

Doctors and other health-care personnel tend to assume that a rational individual will report any symptoms which are causing him or her distress or anxiety; in other words, they take it for granted that the restoration of 'good health' is a natural first priority. Good health, however, is one goal among others: it is not always supreme. At any given time a person may deem obtaining treatment, which may perhaps involve hospitalization, to be less important or urgent than, for example, looking after young children or a dependent mother at home, preparing for an examination, being at work or going on holiday. Thus the value an individual attaches to good health varies in accordance with his or her perception of the benefits versus the costs of its accomplishment. The 'health belief model' represents one sustained attempt to bring together all these factors — from the demographic to the psychological — which influence an individual's assessment of the costs and benefits involved in seeking help.

5. Lay referral and intervention

It is comparatively rare for someone to decide in favour of a visit to the surgery without first discussing his or her symptoms with others. Scambler et al. (1981) found that three-quarters of those participating in their study discussed their symptoms with some other person, usually a relative, before seeking professional aid. Freidson (1970) has claimed that, just as doctors have a professional referral system, so potential patients have 'lay referral systems': 'the whole process of seeking help involves a network of potential consultants from the intimate confines of the nuclear family through successively more select, distant and authoritative laymen until the "professional" is reached'. Friedson has himself produced a model in terms of: (a) the degree of congruence between the subculture of the potential patient and that of doctors; and (b) the relative number of lay consultants interposed between the initial perception of symptoms and the decision whether or not to go to the doctor. Thus, for example, a situation in which the potential patient participates in a subculture which *differs* from that of doctors and in which there is an *extended* lay referral system would lead to the 'lowest' rate of utilization of medical services. In line with this example, one Scottish study reported that a high degree of interaction with interlocking kinship and friendship networks might well have 'inhibited' women in social class V from using antenatal care services (McKinlay 1973).

Occasionally lay persons may take it upon themselves to intervene and to initiate medical consultations (see Mechanic's other-defined illness above). This is most common when symptoms are perceived to be serious or life-threatening or when the sufferer is temporarily incapable of self-help: parents may take action on behalf of a child, a wife on behalf of a husband who is psychotic or who has experienced a tonic–clonic seizure. Scambler (1989) found that four out of five first consultations for epilepsy were other-initiated, many of them involving the calling of an ambulance. It has been suggested, however, that lay persons who are *not* members of the sufferer's family may be less likely than those who are to tolerate delays in help-seeking resulting from the normalization or denial of symptoms. Finlayson and McEwen (1977), for example, have described how the wives of some men tried in vain to persuade their husbands to see a doctor in the hour preceding myocardial infarction.

6. Access to health-care facilities

Ease of access to health-care facilities has obvious implications for usage. Tudor-Hart (1971) has argued that, what he terms an *inverse care law*, applies in Britain; that is, the provision of health care is inversely related to the need for it (i.e. poor facilities in depressed areas characterized by high morbidity and good, or better, facilities in affluent areas characterized by low morbidity). He relates this to the market economy: the more prosperous areas attract the most resources, including skilled health workers, in both primary and secondary care. Empirical support for this 'law' has accumulated steadily, notwithstanding the reduction in *inter-regional* inequality in health-service provision secured since 1976 under the auspices of the Resource Allocation Working Party. More specifically, it has often been shown that, as the distance between home and general practice increases, the likelihood of consultation diminishes; this is particularly true for elderly or disabled people, who are relatively immobile (Whitehead 1987).

SELF-CARE, SELF-HELP AND ALTERNATIVE THERAPY

Clinical Iceberg

Evidence cited earlier showed that only a small minority of all symptoms are presented to a doctor. This suggests that self-care, and especially *self-medication*, may be of considerable importance. Wadsworth et al. (1971) found that self-treatment with non-prescribed medicines and home remedies is indeed extremely common. Dunnell and Cartwright (1972) found lower consultation rates among people who reported self-medication. They also found that in a 2-week period the ratio of non-prescribed to prescribed medicines taken by adults was approximately two to one; 67% of their sample had taken one or more non-prescribed medicines during this period. Moreover, only one in ten of the non-prescribed medicines consumed had been first suggested by a doctor; most were recommended by members of lay referral systems. The data suggested that adults tended to use self-medication as an alternative to medical consultation. Anderson et al. (1977) provide support for this interpretation, but add that, while self-medication seems to be more popular among non-users than among users of the primary-care services, non-users are also less inclined than users to obtain medical help for potentially serious symptoms. Dunnell and Cartwright found that, for children, self- or parent-medication seemed to be used more as a supplement to medical consultation.

Of particular interest too is the rapid growth of *self-help groups*. Some, like Alcoholics Anonymous, have been established for a long time and are well known, but there are many newer and less well-known groups — for people with schizophrenia, skin diseases, depression, hypertension, cancer, the parents of handicapped children, victims of disasters, and so on. Some of these were the brainchildren of health workers who are still active within them, but many operate quite independently of the formal health services: in fact, the impetus for the formation of a number of groups has been the lack of adequate understanding, care, treatment or support from the various health professions. Some commentators regard self-help groups as a poor substitute for people who are starved of 'real' services. Others, like Robinson (1980), argue that 'it is the professional health services which should be seen as specific technical, organizational or expert assistance'; they contend that self-help should be regarded as one of the basic components of primary health care.

Apart from simply ignoring symptoms, another alternative to consulting a doctor or pursuing some form of self-care or self-help is to rely on *alternative* or *non-orthodox therapies*. Thomas et al. (1991) have estimated that in 1987 there were 1909 registered, non-medical practitioners of non-orthodox health care — that is, of acupuncture, chiropractic, homoeopathy, medical herbalism, naturopathy and osteopathy — working in Britain (see Table 4). The same authors report that of the 70 600 patients seen by this group of practitioners in an average week, 78% were attending for musculoskeletal problems. Two-thirds of the patients were women. Thirty-six per cent of the patients had not received previous medical care for their main problem; 18% were receiving concurrent non-orthodox and medical care. It has been estimated that alternative or non-orthodox medicine is growing five times as rapidly as orthodox allopathic medicine.

It has been shown that, very often, the decision whether or not to consult a doctor is not simply a function of the degree of pain or

——— **Table 4** ———
Main treatment offered and use of multiple treatments
by the membership of the professional association for estimated
numbers (%) of registered non-orthodox practitioners.

Main treatment	Registered practitioners		Practitioners in each group offering multiple trreatments and having membership of only one association	
	No.	%	No.	%
Acupuncture	507	27	100	20
Chiropractic	290	15	6	2
Homoeopathy	93	5	12	13
Medical herbalism	115	6	45	39
Naturopathy with osteopathy	128	7	41	32*
Osteopathy	680	36	34	5
Member of more than one association	96	5	—	
Total	1909	100	238	12

Source: Thomas et al. (1991).
*Practitioners offering at least one treatment in addition to naturopathy and osteopathy.

disability associated with symptoms or of their perceived seriousness. What Hannay (1980) has termed 'incongruous referral behaviour' is commonplace. The heterogeneous assembly of factors which are known to influence decisions about medical consultaton has been indicated. It should perhaps be stressed, however, that the study of illness behaviour is not concerned exclusively with whether or not people visit doctors. On the basis of anthropological work, Kleinman (1985) has suggested that there are typically three major arenas of care in what he calls 'local health care systems': popular, folk and professional (Fig. 1).

Most health care takes place in the popular sector, which embraces self-care, including self-medication, and those self-help groups which function independently of professional health workers. The folk sector comprises non-professional 'specialists' who offer some form of alternative or non-orthodox therapy. Professionalization, Kleinman contends, has a tendency to distance practitioners from patients and to lead to a focus on (medically defined) disease as opposed to (patient defined) illness. Of the professional sector in western societies he writes: 'Western-oriented biomedicine seems to be the more extreme example of this trend, perhaps because biomedical ideology and norms are more remote from (one almost wants to say estranged

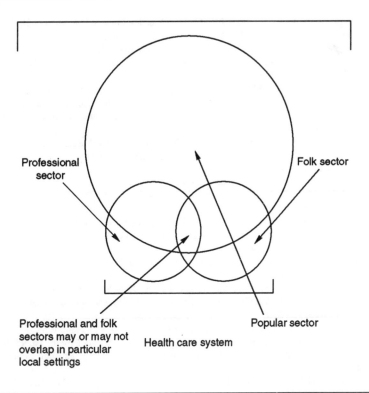

Figure 1. Local health-care system: internal structure. (From Kleinman 1985.)

from) the life world of most patients'. He considers that the major challenge is to 're-work medicine's paradigm of clinical practice to make it more responsive to indigenous patient values, beliefs and expectations'. Agree or disagree, there is no question that the study of illness behaviour must address itself to the popular and folk as well as to the professional sectors of local health-care systems.

REFERENCES

Anderson, J., Buck, C., Danaher, K. & Fry, J. (1977) Users and non-users of doctors — implications for care. *J. R. Coll. gen. Practnr,* **27,** 155–9.

Blaxter, M. (1990) *Health and Lifestyles.* London: Tavistock/Routledge.

Blaxter, M. & Paterson, E. (1982) *Mothers and Daughters.* London: Heinemann Educational.

Cartwright, A. & Anderson, R. (1981) *General Practice Revisited: A Second Study of Patients and their Doctors.* London: Tavistock.

Central Statistical Office (1990) *Social Trends 20.* London: HMSO.

Dunnell, K. & Cartwright, A. (1972) *Medicine-Takers, Prescribers and Hoarders.* London: Routledge & Kegan Paul.

Epsom, J. (1978) The mobile health clinic: a report on the first year's work. In: *Basic Readings in Medical Sociology,* ed. D. Tuckett & J. Kauffert. London: Tavistock.

Finlayson, A. & McEwen, J. (1977) *Coronary Heart Disease and Patterns of Living.* London: Croom Helm.

Freidson, E. (1970) *Profession of Medicine.* New York: Dodds, Mead.

Hannay, D. (1980) The iceberg of illness and trivial consultations. *J. R. Coll. gen. Practnr,* **30,** 551–4.

Herzlich, C. (1973) *Health and Illness.* London: Academic Press.

Ingham, J. & Miller, P. (1979) Symptom prevalence and severity in a general practice. *Epidem. commun. Hlth,* **33,** 191–8.

Kleinman, A. (1985) Indigenous systems of healing: questions for professional, popular and folk care. In: *Alternative Medicines: Popular and Policy Perspectives,* ed. J. Salmon. London: Tavistock.

McKinlay, J. (1973) Social networks, lay consultation and help-seeking behaviour. *Soc. Forces,* **53,** 255–92.

Mechanic, D. (1978) *Medical Sociology,* 2nd edition. New York: Free Press.

OPCS (Office of Population Censuses and Surveys) (1989) *General Household Survey, 1987.* London: HMSO.

Pill, R. & Scott, N. (1982) Concepts of illness causation and responsibility: some preliminary data from a sample of working-class mothers. *Soc. Sci. Med.,* **16,** 43–52.

Pilowski, I. & Spence, N. (1977) Ethnicity and illness behaviour. *Psychol. Med.,* **7,** 447–52.

Robinson, D. (1980) The self-help component of primary care. *Soc. Sci. Med.,* **14A,** 415–21.

Scambler, A., Scambler, G. & Craig, D. (1981) Kinship and friendship networks and women's demand for primary care. *J. R. Coll. gen. Practnr,* **26,** 746–50.

Scambler, G. (1989) *Epilepsy.* London: Routledge.

Thomas, K., Carr, J., Westlake, L. & Williams, B. (1991) Use of non-orthodox and conventional health care in Great Britain. *Br. med. J.,* **302,** 207–10.

Tudor Hart, J. (1971) The inverse care law. *Lancet,* **i,** 405–12.

Wadsworth, M., Butterfield, W. & Blaney, R. (1971) *Health and Sickness: The Choice of Treatment.* London: Tavistock.

Whitehead, M. (1987) *The Health Divide: Inequalities in Health Care in the 1980s.* London: Health Education Council.

Zborowski, M. (1952) Cultural components in response to pain. *J. soc. Issues,* **8,** 16–30.

Zola, I. (1973) Pathways to the doctor: from person to patient. *Soc. Sci. Med.,* **7,** 677–89.

4

The doctor–patient relationship

Myfanwy Morgan

$\mathbf{M}$eetings between doctors and patients are frequent and regular occurrences. In the UK over half a million such meetings occur between general practitioners and their patients every working day, while a large number of consultations also take place at hospital level. The success or otherwise of these medical encounters is often influenced by the nature of the relationship between doctor and patient. For example, central to medical diagnosis and treatment is the exchange of information between doctor and patient. However, unless patients feel at ease and are encouraged to talk freely they may not disclose the 'real' problems that are troubling them or express their worries and concerns which thus remain 'hidden'. For example, in a study of general-practice patients it was found that two-thirds of those patients who reported symptoms in answer to a brief health questionnaire had not mentioned some of these in the consultation (Tuckett et al. 1985).

Creating an atmosphere which allows a sensitive discussion not only assists the doctor in diagnosing a patients' problem but also influences the patients' response. It is estimated that up to 40% of patients do not comply with drug therapy and that large numbers of prescriptions are not taken to the chemist, important reasons being that patients feel dissatisfied with the diagnosis or continue to have questions or worries which they did not feel able to raise in the consultation or which were not responded to satisfactorily by the doctor (Pendleton & Hasler 1983). The advice, reassurance and support provided by the doctor can also help play an important role in helping people tackle or come to terms with their health problems and may even have a positive effect on the pain and other symptoms experienced. This was demonstrated in a longitudinal study of patients attending neurological clinics for the diagnosis and treatment of severe headache, which showed that for half the patients seen the main factor related to a reduction in symptom severity appeared to be patients' satisfaction with the initial consultation and, in particular, being given information and advice which they felt to be relevant to their worries and concerns and enabled them to make sense of their symptoms and achieve a sense of control over the illness (Fitzpatrick et al. 1983). This benefit derived from social aspects of the doctor–patient relationship has been termed the 'placebo' effect (which literally means 'I will please') and has been calculated to account for as much as one-third of the success of any drug (Beecher 1955).

Recognition that the nature of the relationship between doctor and patient plays a vital role in diagnosis and treatment decisions, as well as contributing more generally to patients' feelings of well-being and satisfaction with the consultation, has focussed attention on the forms and determinants of this relationship. Some sociologists have depicted the general social expectations which surround the behaviour of doctors and patients and emphasized their shared values. Others have examined the ways in which doctors and patients may differ in their beliefs and expectations and have shown how each may seek to influence the process and outcome of the consultation.

PARSONS' MODEL OF THE DOCTOR–PATIENT RELATIONSHIP

Parsons (1951) was one of the earliest sociologists to examine the relationship between doctors and patients. His interest in this area arose from a concern with the question of how society is able to function smoothly. Parsons regarded this as being partly achieved because people act out social roles which are associated with socially prescribed patterns of behaviour. As a result we are all aware of how people are likely to behave when they occupy the role of father, teacher, shop assistant, etc., and similarly we are aware of their expectations of us when we occupy the complementary role of child, pupil or customer. In a similar way, Parsons regarded doctors and patients as occupying social roles with socially prescribed patterns of behaviour.

Parsons' description of the doctor–patient relationship is presented as an 'ideal type'. An ideal type is a model that abstracts and presents what are regarded as the fundamental features of a particular social organization or social role and constitutes an important method of analysing and describing very complex social phenomena. He depicted the role of sick people as involving four general expectations. Firstly, sick people are allowed, and may even be required, to give up some of their normal activities and responsibilities, such as going to work or playing football for the local team, and secondly they are regarded as being in need of care. These two expectations and privileges are, however, contingent on the sick person fulfilling the obligations of wanting to get well as quickly as possible, seeking professional medical advice and, most importantly for the doctor–patient relationship, cooperating with the doctor (Table 1). As Parsons points out, the specific expectations of the sick person, such as the number and type of activities the ill person is expected to give up, will be influenced by the nature and severity of the condition. It is also recognized that not all illness requires people to relinquish their normal social roles and occupy the status 'sick'. For example, much minor illness can be and is coped with without recourse to the doctor and does not require any changes to a person's everyday life (see Chapter 3). Similarly, people with chronic illness, although often needing to consult the doctor regularly, are not generally expected to occupy a permanent sick role, and only occupy the status 'sick' if they experience a change in their usual health. Parsons thus viewed the sick role as a temporary social role which has been instituted by society with the aim of returning sick people to a state of health and restoring them to fully functioning members of society as quickly as possible. The sick role is also regarded as a universal role, in that its obligations and expectations apply to all sick people whatever their status in other spheres.

Parsons viewed the role of the doctor as complementary to that of the patient; whereas the patient is expected to cooperate fully with the doctor, doctors are expected to apply their specialist knowledge and skills for the benefit of the patient. In order to carry out the tasks of diagnosis and treatment, doctors often need to know intimate details about the patient that are not usually known between strangers. It may, for example, be necessary to carry out intimate physical examinations and to ask for information about the patient's personal affairs. The potential tensions arising from the personal nature of medical practice are, however, reduced by the obligation on the doctor to remain objective and emotionally detached, and to use this privileged position for the benefit of the patient and not for personal advantage.

Parsons analysis is important in identifying the general social expectations which guide the behaviour of doctors and patients. However, his model overlooks the conflict and tensions that may be experienced by doctors and patients, as well as the differing forms this relationship may take.

One source of conflict and tension for doctors arises from their

——— **Table 1** ———

Parsons' analysis of the roles of patients and doctors.

Patient: sick role	Doctor: professional role
Obligations and privileges	*Expected to*
1. Must want to get well as quickly as possible	1. Apply a high degree of skill and knowledge to the problems of illness
2. Should seek professional medical advice and cooperate with the doctor	2. Act for welfare of patient and community rather than for own self-interest, desire for money, advancement, etc.
3. Allowed (and may be expected) to shed some normal activities and responsibilities (e.g. employment and household tasks)	3. Be objective and emotionally detached (i.e. should not judge patients' behaviour in terms of personal value system or become emotionally involved with them)
4. Regarded as being in need of care and unable to get better by his or her own decisions and will	4. Be guided by rules of professional practice
	Rights
	1. Granted right to examine patients physically and to enquire into intimate areas of physical and personal life
	2. Granted considerable autonomy in professional practice
	3. Occupies position of authority in relation to the patient

Source: Parsons (1951).

obligation to act in the best interests of individual patients and his or her duty to serve the interests of the state. As Parsons recognized, doctors are the official gatekeepers to the sick role and decide who is 'healthy' and who is 'sick', while people who are officially designated as 'sick' are generally entitled to various privileges, including time off work or financial benefits. However, although patients may request, or even demand, a sick note, problems can arise for the doctor in determining whether disease exists and whether the designation of 'sick' can be justified. For example, back pain forms a major reason for time off work but it is often difficult to determine its causes or assess its severity. This means that the doctor generally has to rely on patients' reports and may experience problems in determining the legitimacy of patients' claims to the sick role. In such situations should doctors give priority to the interests of the patient? Similarly, should doctors inform the licensing authority if they are aware that a patient diagnosed as epileptic is driving a car and thus contravening the state's regulations, and should they inform patients thinking of being tested for human immunodeficiency virus (HIV) of the potential problems of being diagnosed as a carrier for insurance premiums when this might discourage testing?

Other conflicts for doctors arise from the competing interests of individual patients and the larger patient population. For example, doctors are often involved in rationing scarce resources of staff time, beds and medical equipment and may have to decide which patients should be given a transplant or undergo other medical procedures, as well as the priority to be assigned to treating different cases. In the absence of clear and explicit criteria, such choices rest on the judgement of individual clinicians. Doctors may also experience conflicts between maintaining the confidentiality of the doctor–patient relationship and disclosing information to a patient's parent or spouse. This raises the question of whether medical confidentiality is absolute or whether there are any situations when interests are best served by passing on information about a patient. For example, are there any circumstances in which a clinic doctor should disclose that a patient has acquired immunodeficiency syndrome (AIDS), or is positive for HIV, when this is against the patient's wishes? Similarly, should a doctor agree to prescribe contraceptive pills to a girl aged under 16 years if the girl makes it clear that she does not want her parents to be told or consulted, and the doctor is both aware that the girl is aged under 16 years and knows the girl's parents? Such situations frequently pose dilemmas for doctors and raise questions concerning their primary duties and responsibilities, as well as possibly presenting conflicts in relation to their own beliefs and values. However, there are powerful arguments to support the view that priority should be given to maintaining the confidentiality of the doctor–patient relationship and thus preserving patients' trust in doctors and their willingness to consult and discuss their problems freely in the future, for destroying this trust would undermine the foundation of the relationship between doctor and patient (Lockwood 1985).

TYPES OF DOCTOR–PATIENT RELATIONSHIP

Parsons' analysis remains important in identifying fundamental principles of the doctor–patient relationship. However, his broad model has since been extended to depict four types of doctor–patient relationship based on the degree of control exercised by both doctors and patients (Table 2).

——— **Table 2** ———
Types of doctor–patient relationship.

Patient control	Physician control	
	Low	High
Low	Default	Paternalism
High	Consumerist	Mutuality

Source: Stewart and Roter (1989: 21).

A *paternalistic* relationship involving high physician control and low patient control corresponds to Parsons' sick role. In this situation the doctor is dominant and acts as a 'parent' figure who is trusted by the patient and decides what he or she believes to be in the patient's best interest. At some stages of illness patients derive considerable comfort from being able to rely on the doctor in this way and being relieved of burdens of worry and decision-making.

Traditionally, a paternalistic relationship has been most common. However, medical consultations are now increasingly characterized by greater patient control and hence in relationships based on *mutuality*. In this situation both doctors and patients bring knowledge; the doctor brings clinical skills and knowledge and patients bring their own theories, experiences, expectations and feelings. Both parties thus participate as a joint venture on a relatively equal footing and engage in an exchange of ideas and a sharing of belief systems.

However, in some instances another form of power imbalance occurs and produces a *consumerist* relationship. This describes a situation in which power relationships are reversed and the patient takes the active role, whereas the doctor adopts a fairly passive role and accedes to the patients' requests for a second opinion, referral to hospital, a sick note, etc. Such a relationship mainly occurs in a competitive market situation where doctors are dependent on patients' goodwill for their business and financial security.

A fourth type of relationship termed *default* may occur if patients continue to adopt a passive role, even though doctors reduce some of their control of the consultation. This may occur because patients are not aware of the alternatives and are timid in negotiating a more participative relationship.

Different types of relationship, and particularly those characterized by paternalism and mutuality, can be viewed as appropriate to different conditions and stages of illness. For example, at an acute stage of illness it may be necessary or desirable for the doctor to be dominant, whereas at later stages it may be beneficial for patients to be more actively involved and to engage in an adult–adult relationship rather than the adult–child relationship which underlies a paternalistic approach. For example, patients with diabetes mellitus rely episodically on the doctors expertise, but are required to assume considerable responsibility for their condition and to monitor their own blood sugar level and alter the dose of insulin or tablets accordingly. However, the nature of the doctor–patient relationship and the interaction that occurs in the consultation often cannot be explained solely in terms of the patients' medical condition. Other important influences are the beliefs and expectations of patients, the doctor's clinical-practice style, and the setting within which the consultation takes place.

Patients' beliefs and experience of illness

Patients coming to a medical consultation have generally been through a process of evaluating and assessing the seriousness of their symptoms, and may have developed their own explanations of the possible causes of their problems and the actions required of the doctor. These lay views derive from previous contact with medical professionals, as well as from popular literature and the media, and the advice and experience of family and friends. In some cases patients' beliefs and assessments differ from clinical scientific views but can nevertheless be seen as rational when viewed in terms of the patient's context and experiences. For example, a man may be very anxious about a slight chest pain if his father died at a young age from a heart attack and perhaps expect to be referred to hospital for a specialist opinion. Similarly, a woman may appear overly anxious about whether her pregnancy is progressing normally if she has already experienced several miscarriages, while a mother may not be knowledgeable about norms of growth and development but is nevertheless aware of what is normal in her own two-year old. Patients' concerns and assessments of the seriousness of a condition may also be influenced by cultural values. For example, the prevalence of hypertension among people of West Indian origin encourages a tendency to normalize the condition and reduces its significance, while the emphasis often given by patients to stress as a cause of hypertension may reduce the importance they attach to drug therapy (Morgan & Watkins 1988). Other differences may arise from the importance attached to the social significance of medical problems in terms of their impact on patients' everyday life. For example, although acne is clinically trivial and fairly common among adolescents, it has important implications for the individual's self-concept and social relationships, and can thus be viewed as serious when judged in social terms. Similarly, for more serious medical conditions, such as epilepsy, the negative social meanings and feelings of stigma may have a greater impact on the patient's life than do the medical problems directly associated with the disease or disorder (see Chapter 13).

Patients' social contexts and experiences not only influence the meanings attributed to symptoms but may also increase risks of illness. For example, family problems, job problems and other adverse life events have been shown to increase the risk of depression, abdominal pain, heart disease and other medical problems (see Chapter 2). Patients who are grieving or worried may also sometimes feel ill and benefit from the affective quality of the doctor–patient relationship, although they have no detectable disease.

Patients' experiences of illness thus often have important social dimensions and individual meanings. These feelings and concerns in turn influence their expectations of the medical consultation and their needs for information and reassurance. However, whether patients' beliefs and feelings are made known and responded to depends both on the doctor's clinical-practice style and the patient's ability to influence the consultation.

Doctors' orientations and practice styles

Whereas doctors' behaviour in the medical consultation is guided by the general social and professional expectations outlined by Parsons, there are important differences between doctors in terms of whether they define their task in fairly narrow clinical terms or are concerned more broadly with the patient's experience of illness. This difference in doctors' orientations and practice style has important implications for the nature of the relationship they seek to create with patients and hence for the opportunities available for patients to participate in the consultation rather than merely cooperate with the doctor.

The different ways in which doctors perceive their role and the nature of the medical task were identified by Byrne and Long (1976) based on tape-recorded interviews of nearly 2500 general-practitioner consultations. From these interviews they identified two polar types of consultation which they termed 'doctor-centred' and 'patient-centred'. They found that for three-quarters of the doctors their clinical-practice style tended toward the doctor-centred end of the spectrum. This was characterized by the traditional paternalistic approach, based on the assumption that the doctor is the expert and the patient is required to cooperate. Doctors in this category employed tightly controlled interviewing methods aimed at reaching an organic diagnosis as quickly as possible. Questions were thus mainly of a 'closed' nature, such as 'how long have you had the pain?', 'it is sharp or dull?', and there was little opportunity for patients to express their own beliefs and concerns. At the other end of the spectrum were doctors characterized by a patient-centred approach. These doctors adopted a much less authoritarian style and encouraged patients to participate in the consultation and to express their own feelings and concerns. They therefore made considerable use of 'open' questions, such as 'tell me about the pain', 'how do you feel?', 'what do you think is the cause of the problem?' They also spent more time listening to patients' problems, picking up cues, encouraging patients' expressions of their ideas or feelings and clarifying and interpreting their statements.

Byrne and Long found that individual general practitioners could be fairly consistently classified as holding *either* doctor-centred *or* patient-centred consultations. This suggests that doctors develop a particular consulting style which they then employ fairly consistently, and often do not vary their behaviour significantly in relation to the patient's presenting problem, although doctors classified as patient-centred showed the greatest flexibility. These different consulting styles can be linked to differences in doctors' orientation and perception of the nature of the medical task. A doctor-centred approach is concerned with identifying and treating disease through the traditional diagnostic framework and knowledge of disease processes. Doctors adopting this approach thus ascertain the patient's complaint and seek information that will enable them to interpret the patient's illness within their own biomedical framework (Fig. 1). Doctors adopting a more patient-centred approach also use these clinical skills and knowledge, but at the same time they acknowledge that patients may have specific ideas about the causes of their illness and expectations of the consultation, and that people may respond in different ways to similar disease states. They therefore attach greater importance to eliciting patients' ideas, feelings and expectations and integrating this with their own disease-centred concerns (Fig. 1). Doctors adopting a patient-oriented approach also frequently pay greater attention to the psycho-social aspects of illness in terms of its possible social origins and to patients' experience of anxiety, depression and other emotional problems.

These differences in practice style and the differing opportunities they afford for patient participation not only characterize the clinical interview but also influence the broader relationship between doctors and patients. For example, treatment decisions may be controlled by the doctor based on the belief that the doctor as the medical expert is in the best position to act in the patient's interests, thus giving rise to a paternalistic relationship (Table 2). Alternatively, doctors may adopt a more participative style, recognizing that the benefits of different forms of treatment may depend on the patient's own evaluations and life circumstances, or may require that patients assume considerable responsibility for their own treatment.

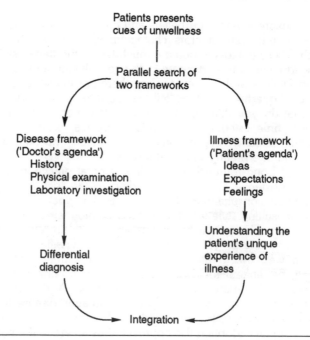

Figure 1. The patient-centred clinical interview. (Source: Levenstein et al. (1989: 109).)

Structural influences on the consultation

General practitioners frequently identify a shortage of time as the major constraint on adopting a patient-oriented approach, with consultations averaging about 6 min (although this obscures wide variations in the actual length of consultations, which range from about 2 min to over 20 min). Pressures of time encourage a more tightly controlled doctor-centred (or 'paternalistic') consultation, with the aim of reaching a diagnosis as quickly as possible. As a result, shorter consultations have been shown to be associated with more prescriptions being issued and fewer psychological problems identified (Howie et al. 1989). However, doctors' practice styles probably exert a more important influence on the content of consultations than the time available. Thus general practitioners with a disease-oriented approach often do not change their practice style as a result of increased consultation time, but merely do more of the same. Similarly, general practitioners with a more patient-oriented approach often prefer to run over time, and possibly keep other patients waiting, if they feel that it is necessary to spend more time with a particular patient. They may also deliberately restrict their list size, so that they are able to provide what they regard as good-quality care. As a result, the length of time available for consultations is itself partly a function of practice style, as well as serving to constrain patterns of interaction in the consultation. Committing sufficient time to listen and respond to patients' worries and concerns may also reduce the number of return visits, and hence the total length of consultation time for an episode of illness.

The length of consultations tends to be greater and the practice style of doctors more patient-oriented where medical care is financed on a fee-for-service basis. This is because a fee-for-service payment is often associated with a greater availability of resources and greater priority being given to pleasing the patient, and hence the development of a more consumerist approach (Fig. 1). These differences are illustrated by Silverman's (1987) comparison of doctor–patient interaction in a private oncology clinic with doctor–patient interaction in two oncology clinics at a London teaching hospital in the National Health Service (NHS). This showed that doctors and patients interacted on more equal terms in the private sector, with the patient exercising greater control of the consultation. However, as Silverman notes, a continuum of different forms of relationship does occur within NHS hospitals. SILVER MAN

Patients' influence on the consultation

Whereas two major determinants of the nature of the doctor–patient relationship and the interaction that occurs in the consultation are the doctors' clinical-practice style and the structural constraints on the consultation, a third influence is the patient's ability to exercise control and participate in the consultation. This active involvement in the consultation is most likely to occur when patients possess considerable knowledge and familiarity with their condition. West (1976), in a study of doctor–patient encounters where the child was diagnosed as having epilepsy, showed that during the initial consultation patients were passive, uncritical and appeared satisfied. However, by the third consultation parents had moved from a situation of low to high control and had begun to initiate questions themselves and to force information out of the doctor. They were also more critical and less satisfied with the doctor, and in some cases this led to a threatened rejection of the doctor's authority and expertise.

Personal characteristics of patients associated with greater participation in the consultation include being of a high social and educational level, being male, and not belonging to an ethnic minority group. The influence of social class was demonstrated in a study of 1470 general-practice consultations, which showed that only 27% of working-class patients sought clarification from the doctor about what he/she had said compared with 45% of middle-class patients (Tuckett et al. 1985). This request for information by patients in turn led to fuller explanations being given by doctors and a rather longer consultation. Subsequent interviews with 98 patients revealed that 60% had questions that they had not expressed. Major reasons given for this included feeling that it was not appropriate to ask (36%), feeling hurried (27%), being frightened that the doctor would think less well of them (14%) and being frightened of a bad reaction from the doctor (14%). In another study of women having their first baby in a public hospital, 57% of working-class women were identified as wanting more information from the doctor about labour compared with 26% of middle-class women (Shapiro et al. 1982). The authors suggest that this partly reflects the doctor's lack of awareness of the information required by patients. Patients also experienced difficulties in eliciting this information as they tended to be 'processed' through the hospital system and had few opportunities to establish a relationship with medical staff. In contrast, women attending private hospitals received more personal attention and were less likely to feel that they would have liked further information.

Doctor–patient relationships, although surrounded by general social expectations, are thus characterized by differing degrees of control by both doctors and patients. The type of relationship which best promotes positive outcomes depends on the nature of the patient's medical condition, and their general expectations of the consultations, and thus requires that doctors are sensitive to the patient's needs and concerns.

CONFLICT AND CONTROL

Medical consultations are rarely characterized by overt conflict between doctor and patient. Nevertheless, differences in the interests, expectations and knowledge of the lay person and the professional may give rise to tensions (Friedson 1970). As we have seen, doctors are trained to diagnose and treat disease, whereas patients are concerned with their personal experience of illness and may bring to the consultation ideas and expectations that differ from professional medical views. A failure to reconcile these perspectives may thus give rise to tension and dissatisfaction. For example, a patient's condition may be dismissed by the doctor as 'trivial', reflecting a failure to identify the underlying reason for the consultation or the significance of the condition for the patient. Patients may also have expectations for the outcome of the consultation, such as a prescription or referral to a specialist, which may not be judged necessary by the general practitioner. However, the doctor's reasons for his or her chosen cause of action may not be fully explained or accepted by patients.

Except in situations characterized by a strong consumerist relationship, doctors retain ultimate control of the consultation as a result of their professional status and specialist knowledge, and their greater experience in managing the encounter. Nevertheless, patients may be successful in influencing the outcome of the consultation and achieving their desired end through persuasion and negotiating with the doctor. This may involve patients in trying to persuade the doctor that a particular type of treatment is appropriate by presenting information in a form which they believe is likely to lead the doctor to their desired course of action. For example, a study of parents and specialists in ear, nose and throat (ENT) clinics showed that parents commonly mentioned the general practitioner's diagnosis, and the general practitioner's feelings that tonsillectomy might be necessary, rather than directly stating their opinion that their childs' tonsils should be removed (Bloor 1977); the assumption was that the consultant was more likely to be impressed by the general practitioner's opinion than by that of the patient. Doctors, rather than accepting patients' requested or suggested course of action, may in turn try to convince patients that their approach is best. This may involve overwhelming patients with evidence in the form of laboratory tests, or their own previous experience in treating patients with similar types of conditions, in support of their chosen course of action, perhaps accompanied by a warning of the likely consequences of neglecting their advice.

In some situations either the doctor or patient manages to achieve their desired outcome, but often a compromise or temporary agreement is reached. For example, a patient may agree to try a course of tablets on the understanding that if they do not achieve a beneficial effect within a specified time they will then be referred for a specialist opinion. Waissman (1990) similarly describes the process of negotiation to reconcile doctors' and parents' choices regarding the use of home or hospital dialysis for children with renal disease. She also shows how the doctor's decision and choice of home dialysis may later be renegotiated by parents and other arrangements made if they continue to experience difficulty in managing the dialysis at home.

Control of the consultation may be exercised not only through verbal techniques but also through non-verbal behaviours. It is estimated that in a normal two-person conversation the verbal component carries less than 35% of the social meaning of the situation, and 65% or more is carried by the non-verbal component

(Pietroni 1976). Non-verbal cues in the consultation, as in other forms of interaction, contribute to the rapport between doctor and patient and influence the amount of information exchanged. For example, by looking interested, nodding encouragingly and other gestures doctors can provide positive feedback to patients, whereas by continued rifling through notes, twiddling with pens, or failing to look directly at patients, they may convey disinterest and result in patients failing to describe their problems.

Interaction is also influenced by the seating and relative positions of doctor and patient in the consulting room. In one simple experiment a cardiologist removed the desk from his clinic on alternate days. He found that when he removed his desk 50% of the patients sat back in their chair in an at-ease position, whereas only 10% did so when he was sitting behind his desk (Pietroni 1976). The influence of the physical organization of the consultation on interaction is also illustrated by Bloor's (1977) study of ENT clinics. In one consultation the doctor examined a child who was accompanied by his mother and in carrying out the examination the doctor placed himself between the child and the mother and kept his back to the mother throughout, thus making it difficult for her to speak to him. Carrying out certain diagnostic tests which require the doctor's attention and concentration is also in itself an effective way of silencing a patient. Non-verbal techniques may also be used to serve as a signal that the consultation has ended, as for example when doctors write out a prescription, rise to their feet or hold open the door.

COMMUNICATION AND SATISFACTION WITH THE CONSULTATION

A major criticism of medical care by both general-practice and hospital patients concerns the lack of information and explanations they receive about their illness and treatment. For example, in a national survey of general practices, 23% of patients felt that their doctor was not so good at explaining things to them (Cartwright & Anderson 1983). Similarly, among women who had experienced a miscarriage, 35% were fairly or very dissatisfied with the information they received from their general practitioner and 36% were dissatisfied with the post-operative information they received on discharge from hospital (Friedman 1989). Other surveys demonstrate that patients frequently fail to remember and recall what they are told. This was shown by Ley et al. (1973) who found that general-practice patients were often unable to remember more than 50% of the information they were given even 5 min after the end of the consultation. A more recent study of 328 general-practice patients found that, following the consultation, 36% of patients either did not remember, make sense correctly or were not committed to key points of diagnostic significance communicated by the doctor (Tuckett et al. 1985).

These findings of problems of communication have resulted in greater priority being given to teaching doctors communication skills, with the aim of making their communication clearer and better organized so that patients will comprehend it, remember it and feel satisfied that they have been informed. Successful communication, however, also depends on the perceived relevance and importance of what is being communicated and whether it makes sense in terms of patients' own beliefs and concerns. This requires that an exchange of views takes place, so that doctors are aware of and can respond more directly to patients expectations, ideas and concerns. For example, Tuckett et al. (1985) found a statistically significant relationship between patients' ideas being evaded or inhibited by doctors and their lack of commitment to the doctor's treatment advice. Studies of patients' adherence to treatment advice and control of diabetes and hypertension have similarly identified the importance not only of clear instructions to patients but also of qualitative aspects of communication in promoting patient satisfaction and positive treatment outcomes, including the doctor's sensitivity to and understanding of patients' feelings (Bartlett et al. 1984; Kaplan et al. 1989). These interpersonal qualities are also of particular importance for patients experiencing considerable anxiety and emotional distress (Friedman 1989).

Doctors are often not aware of whether or not patients are satisfied with the consultation since, whatever their views, patients may retain a deferential attitude reflecting the traditional expectations of the patient role. Thus they rarely express their dissatisfaction or tell the doctor when they disagree with his or her advice or have no intention of following it. Indeed, some patients regularly attend for repeat prescriptions even if they do not take the medication or take it only irregularly, in order to keep up the appearance of being a good patient.

CHANGES IN THE DOCTOR–PATIENT RELATIONSHIP

A number of changes are encouraging greater patient control and participation in medical care. One change is that people are becoming more knowledgeable about health matters. This partly reflects the greater emphasis on individual responsibility for health and the increasing attention to health issues given by the media. A number of general practices and hospital clinics also now make case notes available to patients, which promotes patients' knowledge and confidence in asking questions and contributes to a more equal relationship with the doctor. More generally, medicine like other areas of life is increasingly characterized by a questioning of professional authority. Maternity care forms one area in which a consumerist approach has been particularly strong and has resulted in more account being given to individual women's needs and choices in decisions regarding pain control and other aspects of their care.

Another source of change arises from doctors' changing perception of their role. This is seen in the greater readiness of doctors to disclose a terminal illness and the trend, especially in the USA, for patients to be increasingly involved in decisions regarding treatment, especially in situations where the benefits and risks of different therapies and procedures are uncertain. This change reflects a greater acceptance of a participative approach to medical care, as well as increased fears of malpractice claims which emphasize the importance of joint responsibility and of promoting patients' feelings of confidence and trust in the doctor. Many general practitioners are also extending their role beyond the traditional disease model to engage in counselling, health education and other activities requiring more active involvement by patients, while homeopathy, acupuncture and other forms of alternative medicine are gaining acceptance. A recent survey of general practitioners indicated that 31% had a working knowledge of at least one form of alternative medicine (Anderson & Anderson 1987).

Structural changes which have implications for the doctor–patient relationship include the growth of private medicine, which forms a small but expanding component of medical care in Britain; in 1987, 9% of the population was covered by private medical insurance, although coverage was mainly confined to hospital care. The views of the consumer are likely to be given greater priority as a result of the introduction by the 1990 National Health Service and Community Care Act of major reforms to the financing of hospital and general-practitioner services (see Chapter 14). In the reformed NHS, the size of a hospital's budget will depend on its ability to attract contracts for services. This is expected to lead to competition between hospitals in terms of both price and quality, with one indicator of quality being patients' evaluations and satisfaction with the organization and process of care. Other changes in the reformed NHS at a general-practitioner level include the greater proportion of general practitioners' income which derives from capitation fees, changes in regulations which make it easier for patients to shift their custom to another practice if they are not satisfied, and the wider availability of information about practices which will enable patients to be more selective in their choice of doctor.

These trends suggest that patients will continue to become increasingly better informed about health and medical matters and that doctors working at both general-practice and hospital level will attach greater importance to the patient's perspective and to the broader social context of disease. This is likely to produce a greater participation of patients in the consultation and in medical decision-making and thus in relationships characterized as mutual, as well as a greater concern in the health service with patients' evaluations and satisfaction with health care.

REFERENCES

Anderson, E. & Anderson, P. (1987) General practitioners and alternative medicine. *J. R. Coll. gen. Practnr.*, **37**, 52–5.

Bartlett, E., Grayson, M., Barker, R., Levine, D.M., Golden, A. & Zibber, S. (1984) The effects of physician communication skills on patient satisfaction, recall and adherence. *J. chron. Dis.*, **37**, 755–64.

Beecher, R. (1955) The powerful placebo. *J. Am. Med. Ass.*, **159**, 602–6.

Bloor, M. (1977) Professional autonomy and client exclusion: a study in ENT clinics. In: *Studies in Everyday Medical Life*, ed. M. Wadsworth & D. Robinson. London: Martin Robertson.

Byrne, P.S. & Long, B.L. (1976) *Doctors Talking to Patients*. London: HMSO.

Cartwright, A. & Anderson, R. (1983) *General Practice Revisited: A Second Study of Patients and their Doctors*. London: Tavistock.

Davis F. (1960) Uncertainty in medical diagnosis — clinical and functional. *Am. J. Sociol.*, **66**, 41–7.

Fitzpatrick, R.M., Hopkins, A.P. & Howard-Watts, O. (1983) Social dimensions of healing. *Soc. Sci. Med.*, **17**, 501–10.

Friedman, T. (1989) Women's experiences of general practitioner management of miscarriage. *J. R. Coll. gen. Practnr*, **39**, 456–8.

Friedson, E. (1970) Dilemmas in the doctor–patient relationship. In: *A Sociology of Medical Practice*, ed. C. Cox & A. Mead. London: Collier MacMillan.

Howie, J.G., Porter, A.M. & Forbes, J. F. (1989) Quality and the use of time in general practice: widening the discussion. *Br. Med. J.*, **298**, 1008–10.

Kaplan, S., Greenfield, S. & Ware, J.E. (1989) Assessing the effects of physician–patient interactions on the outcomes of chronic disease. *Med. Care*, **2**, 8110–27.

Levenstein, J.H., Brown, J.B., Weston, W.W. et al (1989) Patient centred clinical interviewing. In: *Communication with Medical Patients*, ed. M. Stewart & D. Roter. New York: Sage Publications.

Ley, P., Bradshaw, P.W., Eaves, D. & Walker, C.M. (1973) A method for increasing patients' recall of information presented by doctors. *Psychol. Med.*, **3**, 217–20.

Lockwood, M. (ed.) (1985) *Moral Dilemmas in Modern Medicine*. Oxford: Oxford University Press.

Morgan, M. & Watkins, C.J. (1988) Managing hypertension: beliefs and responses to medication among cultural groups. *Soc. Hlth Illness,* **10,** 561–78.

Parsons, T. (1951) *The Social System.* Glencoe, IL: Free Press.

Pendleton, D. & Hasler, J. (eds) (1983) *Doctor–Patient Communication.* London: Academic Press.

Pietroni, P. (1976) Language and communication in general practice. In: *Communication in the General Practice Surgery,* ed. B. Tanner. London: Hodder & Stoughton.

Shapiro, M.C., Najman, J.M., Chang, A., Keeping, J.D., Morrison, J. & Western, J.S. (1983) Information control and the exercise of power in the obstetrical encounter. *Soc. Sci. Med.,* **17,** 139–46.

Silverman, D. (1987) *Communication and Medical Practice: Social Relations in the Clinic.* London: Sage Publications.

Stewart, M. & Roter, D. (1989) *Communicating with Medical Patients.* New York: Sage Publications.

Tuckett, D., Boulton, M., Olson, C. & Williams, A. (1985) *Meetings Between Experts: An Approach to Sharing Ideas in Medical Consultations.* London: Tavistock Publications.

Waissman, R. (1990) An analysis of doctor–patient interactions in the case of paediatric renal failure: the choice of home dialysis. *Soc. Hlth Illness,* **4,** 432–51.

West, P. (1976) The physician and the management of childhood epilepsy. In: *Studies in Everyday Medical Life,* ed. M. Wadsworth & D. Robinson. London: Martin Robertson.

5

Hospitals and patients

Myfanwy Morgan

During this century hospitals have developed from their role of providing a refuge for the sick and homeless, or for the dying poor, to occupy a central place in medical practice. In 1989–90 there were 1730 hospitals in England, providing approximately 283 000 beds, and employing more than half of the National Health Service (NHS) doctors, 350 000 nursing and midwifery staff and 80 000 other professional and technical staff. In financial terms, hospitals account for over 60% of revenue expenditure in the NHS.

Hospitals typically form large institutions with a diversity of activities. Many hospitals not only engage in patient care but also serve as centres of education and training for doctors, nurses and other health workers, and provide a setting for research. The patient admitted to hospital thus enters a complex organization with a variety of goals, and with a well-developed system of rules and procedures for coordinating the different activities and the large numbers and categories of staff. This chapter examines both the hospital as a social organization and patients' experience of hospital care.

HOSPITALS AS FORMAL AND INFORMAL ORGANIZATIONS

Hospitals are large institutions which share many characteristics of any formal organization. These include the existence of a hierarchical system of authority based on a rational and explicit set of rules. Thus staff members occupy positions with clearly defined responsibilities, recruitment of individuals is based on their qualifications, and there are possibilities of promotion based on seniority or merit, and so on. However, an important difference between hospitals and most other organizations is that many hospital personnel are members of a profession which enjoys considerable autonomy (see Chapter 15). Hospitals are therefore characterized both by a bureaucratic managerial authority structure and a separate professional authority structure.

Difficulties often arise in the relationship between these two structures. For example, doctors enjoy the clinical freedom to decide which and how many patients to refer to hospitals for treatment, which and how many shall be admitted and what treatments to give for how long. However, it is the manager's task to negotiate with doctors about space and ward facilities, to oversee contracts for the hospital services negotiated with district health authorities and general practitioners, and generally to ensure the successful running of the hospital. Conflicts may thus occur, if the doctor's clinical freedom interferes with the achievement of managerial goals. For example, a consultant who keeps patients in hospital longer than the norm, or prefers to perform selected procedures on an in-patient basis rather than as day surgery, reduces the opportunities for treating a greater number of patients and thus of maximizing a hospital's revenue and contributing to the fulfilment of its contracts.

As a result of such conflicts between professional and managerial authority and objectives, a number of reforms have been introduced since the early 1980s with the aim of strengthening the management structure and giving clinicians greater responsibility for budgets. Most recently, the 1989 White Paper, 'Working for Patients', and the 1990 National Health Service and Community Care Act, contained requirements which reduce professional autonomy and increase clinical involvement in management. These include the requirement for fuller job descriptions for consultants, the provision for district management to take a formal part in appointing consultants, and the requirement that doctors should be involved in reviewing the quality of medical care, including their use of resources.

The analysis of institutions in terms of their authority structures has been complemented by approaches which focus on the formal goals of the institution. The primary goal of the hospital can be regarded as the provision of good patient care, although views may differ as to the most appropriate forms of care for individual patients. However, in reality patient care forms only one of several goals of the hospital. For example, psychiatric hospitals were also traditionally expected to fulfill social goals by protecting the public from frightening patients, as well as protecting patients from actions that might be a danger to themselves and from an incapacity to meet social demands. These goals of treatment and custody or care are also often complemented by other goals of providing training, conducting research and achieving financial security. The existence of a diversity of goals means that they may sometimes conflict. For example, the goals of providing good quality care for an individual patient and training medical students may conflict if several students are required to examine a patient and this results in some stress or inconvenience to the patient, although such procedures may be justified in terms of their long-term contribution to patient care. Similarly, the procedures undertaken in the name of patient care may sometimes be a response to scientific or medico-legal concerns rather than for the immediate benefit of the individual patient.

Recognizing the diversity of interests and goals within hospitals and other large institutions, some writers have suggested that their workings can only be fully understood by focussing on their informal organization. A key characteristic is thus seen as the fluidity and negotiation that occurs. This is made possible because job descriptions and procedures are rarely specified in such detail as to dictate everyday activities, and instead allow tasks and relationships to be negotiated and renegotiated. For example, junior doctors and nursing staff frequently negotiate their respective roles and responsibilities on the ward.

The scope for negotiation and influencing priorities is generally greatest in large and expanding organizations and where authority is delegated rather than centralized. In hospitals the opportunities for negotiation regarding treatment is usually greater on medical than surgical wards, as medical treatments are generally less routine and may benefit from the opinions and observations of different categories of staff. This is formalized in the team approach to medical care which has received particular emphasis in the provision of geriatric services, and is aimed at achieving a greater coordination of activities and communication between different health-care workers. However, in practice, problems often arise because different professional groups tend to emphasize different patient needs and give priority to different goals. For example, a clinician caring for a stroke patient may be primarily concerned about the patient's need for treatment in terms of antihypertensive drugs and the suitability of alternative forms of accommodation. In contrast, the physiotherapist is primarily concerned to achieve anatomically specific goals such as an improvement in hand muscle, while the occupational therapist is primarily concerned with functional applications to everyday life in terms, for example, of the ability to make a cup of tea. Thus each professional employs different assessment scales and criteria of successful outcome. Achieving a coordinated approach therefore requires negotiation and acceptance by professional groups of their respective roles within the team.

Staff who have little formal authority within an organization may nevertheless exert considerable influence in certain situations. For example, Hall (1977) showed how attempts to introduce play leaders for children in hospitals were modified by nurses who felt that the very notion of play and the arrangements required for its occurrence threatened the conventional routines of ward life. As a result, nursing staff successfully renegotiated the opportunities children had for play, and confined play leaders to a more marginal position within the ward than official policy decreed. Indeed, staff who have a fairly low position within an organization are often the most resistant to change. This is because they possess task-specific rather than more general and adaptable skills and are, therefore, likely to be less successful in negotiating new roles.

HOSPITAL ACTIVITY

Hospital activity can be considered both in terms of rates of hospital use and the content or type of hospital work undertaken.

Rates of hospital use

The routine statistics show that people are now more frequently admitted to non-psychiatric hospital care but tend to have shorter lengths of stay. For example, over the period 1975–85, the admission rate to non-psychiatric hospitals in England (excluding maternity admissions) increased from 81 per 1000 population to 107 per 1000 population, reflecting a 26% increase in the total number of admissions (Department of Health and Social Security 1979; Department of Health 1989). The higher admission rate partly reflects the increased proportion of elderly people in the population (Chapter 11). However, of greater importance is the increasing number of procedures and forms of treatment available at a hospital level which creates new needs and demands for care. For example, hip-replacement surgery, coronary artery bypass surgery, liver and kidney transplants, cancer chemotherapy and computerized axial tomography (CAT) scans have all become commonly performed procedures since the early 1960s, thus creating new needs and demands for hospital care. One response to the increased pressures on NHS hospitals has been the growth of the private sector which caters particularly for varicose-veins surgery, hip replacement, inguinal hernia repair and other elective procedures with long waiting lists for treatment in the NHS. In England and Wales, 1986, independent hospitals accounted for 7% of all non-psychiatric and non-maternity stays and treated 16.7% of all residents undergoing elective surgery (excluding abortions) as in-patients.

Although people are now more often admitted to hospital, lengths of stay have declined, with this being made possible by new procedures and forms of treatment as well as by changing ideas regarding the value of early ambulation (Morgan & Beech 1990). The mean length of stay for general medical patients declined from 13.5 days in 1975 to 9.8 days in 1985, and for general surgery from 9.5 to 7.0 days over the same period. This reduction in length of stay has been associated with a 19% decrease in the number of non-psychiatric hospital beds during 1975–85. As a result, the numbers of patients treated per available bed has increased, thus placing greater demands on medical and nursing staff. In addition, greater numbers of patients are now treated on a day basis for inguinal hernia repair, cataract extraction, laparoscopy and other intermediate procedures that previously required several nights in hospital. Such patients occupy a designated day bed for a period of time but are generally discharged home several hours after the operation rather than spending the night in hospital.

Table 1 shows the percentage of in-patient beds occupied in non-psychiatric NHS hospitals in England, 1985 (excluding maternity admissions). Nearly two-thirds (62%) of all beds are occupied by people aged 65 years and over, whereas this age group comprises 15% of the population (see Chapter 11). The relatively large number of elderly people occupying hospital beds reflects both their higher admission rates and longer lengths of hospital stay. Major causes of hospital use in terms of the total bed-days occupied are malignant neoplasms (12% bed-days), heart and circulatory diseases (12%), stroke (11%), fractures (8%) and arthritis (7%). For these conditions hospital admission generally forms one episode in a long process of treating and managing the disorder and the multiple problems it presents.

Since the 1960s, psychiatric hospitals have also been characterized by a trend of declining lengths of stay and a reduction in the number of hospital beds, reflecting the adoption of a policy of community care. This involves the move from hospital-based care for mentally ill and chronically sick people to care in the community in small residential homes, sheltered accommodation and other facilities, as well as substantial numbers of people living in private households and receiving care mainly from relatives with some support from community nursing, social work and other formal services (see Chapter 16). Psychiatric hospitals (or wards) are therefore increasingly being used for diagnosis and treatment rather than for long-term care.

Comparisons of lengths of stay at discharge show that 59% of patients discharged in 1986 had been in a psychiatric hospital for less

——— **Table 1** ———
Percentage of beds occupied in NHS non-psychiatric hospitals
by different age groups in England, 1985.

Age (years)	All beds (excludes maternity)	General-medicine beds (%)	General-surgery beds (%)
0–4	3.9	0.3	1.4
5–14	2.8	2.3	2.7
15–24	4.3	3.0	5.6
25–44	9.0	8.3	13.1
45–64	17.3	30.2	27.4
65–74	19.5 ⎫ 62.5	28.1 ⎫ 58.9	23.5 ⎫ 49.7
≥75	43.0 ⎭	29.8 ⎭	26.2 ⎭

Source: Department of Health (1989).

than 1 month, whereas in 1967 only 45% of discharges had stayed less than 1 month. Despite this move towards short lengths of stay, there are still substantial numbers of people who have been a patient in a psychiatric hospital for 5 years or more, including some with stays of over 20 years. Such patients pose particular problems in relation to the current move from institutional to community care, while there are also questions of whether in the future there will be a new group of patients requiring long-term care. By 1988–89, some large psychiatric hospitals had already closed and others had reduced the numbers of patients admitted, resulting in a 41% reduction in the numbers of psychiatric hospital beds available daily since 1978. However, in 1988–89 there were still 488 psychiatric hospitals in England, including 50 hospitals with over 500 beds (Department of Health 1990).

Types of hospital work

Strauss et al. (1985) classified the various kinds of work involved in medical and nursing care into five categories based on their studies of seven hospitals in California. These types of work are:

1. *Machine work* involves the selection and purchase of machines, their use for diagnosis, therapy or the maintenance of life (requiring the monitoring of patients, interpretation of films or print out, instructing patients, and so on), as well as work to ensure the safety and efficiency of machines.
2. *Safety work* is concerned with saving patients or reducing risks to their life or functioning through various forms of diagnosis and treatment. This often involves the balancing of

costs and benefits of whether, how, and how much to
intervene. It also involves efforts to prevent, monitor and
rectify errors, such as machines not being corrected properly,
results being misinterpreted, or the wrong treatment dosage
ordered or given.

3. *Comfort work* consists of all activities designed to promote the
physical comfort of patients. This includes treatment to reduce
pain, high temperatures or dizziness, physiotherapy to increase
functioning, the efficient scheduling of procedures to reduce
waiting times, and the provision of pleasant waiting areas and
good facilities on the ward.

4. *Sentimental work* aims to reduce patients' anxiety, fear, panic
and threats to their self-esteem by explaining, providing
reassurance, seeking consent and building up trust. By contributing to patients' psychological well-being these activities
may also assist staff in carrying out diagnostic and other clinical
procedures. Sentimental work is also involved in eliciting
biographical details regarding the patients' life-style and social
circumstances to assist in the management of chronic conditions, and in helping patients come to terms with terminal illness
or to cope with other stresses.

5. *Articulation work* is concerned with the development of a
coherent plan of clinical care, its reassessment as necessary in
relation to developments in the course of illness, and the
coordination of the various activities required to fulfill this plan.
This involves the organization, setting up, supervision and
monitoring of the doctors requested jobs, as well as coordinating the cluster and sequence of tasks necessary to accomplish
specific jobs, such as getting an X-ray taken.

The emphasis given to these different types of hospital work varies
for different categories of medical and nursing staff. It is also
influenced by the nature of patients' medical problems, and by the
general philosophy of care in terms of the importance attached to
technical and patient-oriented work. Patients for their part not only
react to these types of work but also frequently participate. For
example, they may try to ensure their own comfort and to identify
any errors with drugs or intravenous drips, as well as monitoring
dialysis and other machines. Patients also try to maintain their
composure during procedures, and respond to staff requests for
information or requirements to swallow barium, to cough, and so on.
Although patients generally conform with staff expectations and
requests, they may sometimes challenge or disobey instructions.
Some patient participation, such as monitoring the dialysis machine
or checking their drugs, may also not be explicit and thus not be
recognized by staff.

PATIENTS' EXPERIENCE OF HOSPITAL CARE

Patients' expectations and experience of hospital care is influenced by the nature of their medical problem, their age, previous contact with hospital services, and other factors. However, for most patients admission to hospital forms a major event and is often accompanied by considerable anxiety and stress.

Stress and hospitalization

The fact that 'something is wrong', requiring diagnosis, treatment or both, often forms a source of anxiety in itself. For some patients there are further uncertainties about whether they may be cured, left with a physical disability or faced with an early death. As well as these worries about the outcome of treatment, patients are frequently apprehensive about the discomfort and pain they may experience in undergoing diagnostic or operative procedures, and may worry about having an anaesthetic. The actual experience of being a patient in hospital is also often found to be stressful. Particular sources of stress identified by patients include the lack of privacy, their lack of familiarity with the different categories of staff and with the general routines on the ward, and not being given sufficient information about their medical condition or treatment. Patients are also often disturbed by the noise on the ward and perhaps seeing a very ill patient. In addition, patients frequently worry about things beyond the hospital, including their work, how their family will manage without them, how their spouse will cope, or, if their home is empty, about possible break-ins, burglaries and vandalism (Davies & Peters 1983). Not surprisingly, patients' major concerns change during the course of their hospital stay. For example, a source of anxiety experienced particularly by maternity and surgical patients shortly before discharge is about how they will manage at home.

Recognition of the high level of stress often experienced by hospital patients has led to a greater emphasis on sentimental work to reduce patients' anxiety and fears of the unknown. Patients are therefore now frequently given booklets and other written information explaining their treatment and hospital stay. Hospital staff also now generally attach considerable importance to listening and responding directly to patients' concerns. In particular, the large number of scientific evaluations demonstrating the positive effects of pre-operative discussion and explanations for patients' experience of pain and coping in the post-operative period has encouraged greater attention to this aspect of patient care (Newman 1984).

Providing comfortable, homely surroundings and reducing the clinical atmosphere of maternity wards, day surgical units and other settings also helps to reduce patients' anxiety and promotes satisfaction with their hospital care.

One group of patients who often exhibit considerable emotional stress are children. Many young children admitted to hospital show an immediate reaction of acute stress and crying; this is followed by a period of misery and apathy, and later a period of detachment, while disturbed behaviour may persist for several months after the child returns home. Children who are shown to be most distressed by hospitalization are those who are generally uncommunicative, isolated, shy, very young or without brothers or sisters (Wilson-Barnett 1979). To reduce the adverse effects of hospitalization on child patients, emphasis is now given to encouraging a greater amount of contact with parents through open visiting times, the involvement of parents on the ward, and provision in some hospitals for a parent to stay overnight, while wards are made attractive to children with toys and pictures. Also, where possible, the hospitalization of children is avoided altogether and procedures undertaken as an out-patient or day case.

Depersonalization

The experience of hospital in-patient care not only gives rise to feelings of fear and anxiety but often also produces a sense of depersonalization, or loss of self-identity. Unlike the psychiatric symptom of the same name, this type of depersonalization stems from the loss of the patient's normal social roles and separation from their familiar environment. It is accentuated by the impersonality of hospital care, with patients often feeling that they have been treated as 'just another case' rather than as individuals with their own feelings, concerns and experiences. These feelings are promoted both by styles of communication and management practices that are designed to achieve technical efficiency but give little attention to patients' psychological needs. For example, on admission to hospital each individual is immediately transformed into 'a patient', who is expected to change from his or her everyday clothes into night clothes, get into bed, and wait for 'things to be done' in terms of ward rounds, investigation and treatment procedures, meals and so on. Patients are also often treated as 'non-persons' by staff, who may talk in their presence as if their social selves have gone home and only damaged physical containers are left for repair.

The depersonalization of patients can be viewed as an unintended and unwelcome effect of organizational efficiency. However, depersonalization is also believed by some to have positive functions for both patients and staff. For example, it can be argued that the treatment of patients on an impersonal basis helps to protect nursing staff from the strain that arises from close involvement with chronically sick and dying patients and so enables them to cope with situations of inherently great psychological stress. In some circumstances, depersonalization may also facilitate the carrying out of medical procedures of a potentially embarrassing nature, as for example when the medical consultation relates to a gynaecological or obstetric problem. However, although the use of technical and impersonal language and the matter-of-fact stance adopted by the staff serve to emphasize the medical content of such consultations and protect both doctor and patient from a potentially embarrassing encounter, the depersonalization of patients can constitute an indignity in itself, arousing anxiety and hostility, especially if doctors do little to reassure patients or to recognize feelings of pain. Thus, whereas the efficiency of management is increased and medical procedures are sometimes facilitated by adopting an impersonal approach, neglecting an individual's personal feelings and concerns and thus failing to do adequate comfort and sentimental work, can also be a source of anxiety and stress.

Although feelings of stress and depersonalization are often experienced by patients admitted to acute wards, they rarely have major long-term effects. This is partly because lengths of stay are generally quite short. The individual nature of patients' medical treatment also serves to limit the extent to which acute hospital patients can be subjected to general routines and treated on an impersonal basis.

Institutionalization

This refers to the process by which patients who spend long periods in a custodial environment become dependent on the institution. This dependency is shown at a psycho-social level among long-stay hospital patients in terms of a lack of any interest in leaving the institution, a general apathy, and a lack of concern about what is going on around them. Institutionalized patients also generally demonstrate an inability to make choices and decisions, to plan activities or to undertake simple everyday tasks. Frequently speech is mumbled and patients often exhibit a characteristic shuffling gait with their head bent forward.

The view put forward by Goffman (1961), based on his study of a 7000-bed psychiatric hospital in Washington, DC, and by Townsend (1963), as a result of his study of large institutions for the elderly in the UK, is that this form of dependency is the product of a particular type of institutional environment. These writers identify a key feature of such institutions as being the need to cater for all the requirements of large numbers of people over a long period of time, which in turn encourages depersonalization and 'batch management'. This means that all residents are treated in a similar manner, irrespective of any personal preferences, while activities (waking times, bathing, meals, etc.) are carried out with a large number of others according to a schedule which is imposed on inmates and gives little scope for individual choice. Ease and efficiency of management is also facilitated if patients merely cooperate with staff, rather than being encouraged to be independent and undertake everyday tasks for themselves. Similarly, a number of other practices tend to develop which, although contributing to the efficiency of management, have adverse psychological effects on residents. These include the restriction of personal possessions, a lack of privacy, restrictions on mobility within the institution, little emphasis given to maintaining contacts outside the institution, and a lack of information about what is going on both within the institution and in relation to patients' own care. Patients may react initially by rejecting both a passive patient role and conformity to the staff's expectations. However, in the long term, they generally succumb to institutional pressures and adopt a dependent patient role. If this is associated with their acceptance of a new self-image, rather than merely 'playing along' with staff, the process of institutionalization is regarded as occurring and this will have long-term effects on the patients' self-concept and behaviour.

This notion that dependency is a product of a particular type of institutional environment has been challenged by some, who have suggested that the characteristics associated with institutionalization formed the inevitable outcome of disease processes. This question of the effects of hospital environment on patients' attitudes and behaviour was examined by Wing and Brown (1970), based on studies of women patients with schizophrenia. These patients had spent between 2 and 6 years in one of three psychiatric hospitals that differed markedly in their social conditions. Poverty of the hospital environment (measured in term of ward restrictiveness, lack of occupation, lack of personal possessions, lack of contact with the outside world and unfavourable nurse attitudes) was found to be highly correlated with patients' clinical poverty (measured in terms of lack of expressed emotion, poverty of speech and social withdrawal). The hospital with the richest social environment contained patients with the fewest negative symptoms, even though patients do not appear to have differed in the severity of their illness at the time of admission. They also found that attitudes to discharge became progressively more unfavourable with increasing length of stay, regardless of the patients' clinical condition. A follow-up study of the same group of patients 8 years later showed that the improvement in the social environment of the three hospitals over the intervening period was associated with a reduction in the clinical poverty of patients — an improvement that could not be explained by changes in drug treatment. Such findings strongly supported the notion that social environment is a key factor in producing the attitudes and behaviours associated with institutionalization. However, patients' susceptibility to institutional pressures depends on their clinical condition, length of hospital stay, and the extent of their contacts with the outside world.

Evidence of the adverse effects on patients of long periods of time spent in psychiatric hospitals and other institutions organized to care for large numbers of people played an important part in contributing to the shift in policy from institutional to community care and the attempt to provide a more rehabilitative environment within institutional settings. This humanitarian critique of institutional care was reinforced in the UK by a series of scandals in the late 1960s and early 1970s initiated by staff who exposed the cruelty and neglect of patients by staff at a number of long-stay hospitals. Another factor contributing to the policy of community care for mentally ill people was the development of the phenothiazine drugs, which reduced problems of control and facilitated care outside custodial settings. These changes were associated with a more general change in attitudes to mentally ill and handicapped people, who were increasingly viewed as requiring treatment and rehabilitation rather than as dangerous and violent and requiring control. The considerable economic costs of renovating and maintaining institutions built mainly in the Victorian era also encouraged the adoption of a policy of 'community care' which was viewed by its proponents as not only better but also often cheaper than long-term institutional care. As Chapter 16 shows, the term 'community care' encompasses many different levels of provision which vary in their costs and the degree of support they provide. However, despite the current policy of caring for elderly and chronically ill people outside institutions, it is likely that there will continue to be some severely dependent people whose needs can best be met in an institutional setting.

Key requirements for creating a rehabilitative environment within a hospital, a home for elderly people, a children's home or other residential setting, include the availability of staff in sufficient numbers to provide more individualized care and to attend to patients' physical comfort and needs for sentimental work. It is also essential that staff accept the importance of providing personal care and of encouraging independence. This means that talking with patients, providing choices, encouraging patients' participation in everyday activities, encouraging visitors and keeping routines flexible need to be viewed as important by staff at all levels within the institution. These tasks may sometimes conflict with and require greater priority than the achievement of 'efficient' management, which involves the completion of tasks on schedule, having tidy living areas and so on.

A third requirement for achieving a more rehabilitative environment relates to the physical organization of the institution. Of particular importance is whether individuals have a room or area that they can call their own, and whether they are able to retain and display some of their personal possessions, photos and other reminders of their self-identity, life experiences and social relationships. A more personal environment and greater interaction is also encouraged by arranging leisure areas so that people sit in groups around small tables rather than all chairs being placed against the wall or in a circle. Clark and Bowling (1989), in their comparison of the quality of life of elderly people in two different types of long-stay care (two NHS nursing homes and a hospital geriatric ward), also identified the importance of the Patients' Club in the hospital setting for facilitating a relaxed informal atmosphere, and providing a choice of activities and a high level of interaction between staff and patients. They also noted that the involvement of nursing and care staff in organizing a daily programme of activity ensures that this is accorded a central role rather than being viewed as a peripheral activity and the concern only of therapists.

Improvements in the quality of life of people in residential homes or on geriatric wards thus requires a philosophy of care and physical organization of the home or institution that promotes a rehabilitative environment, as well as the acceptance of this goal by staff. The greater importance attached to promoting the quality of life of people in residential settings has led to a broadening of the criteria of 'success' employed in evaluative studies. Traditional measures of residents' functional ability, level of activity, mental state and longevity are now often supplemented by data relating to patients' feelings about the environment, meals, degree of choice, and their relationships with other patients and staff.

Staff evaluations and patient care

Medical and nursing staff commonly evaluate patients in social and moral as well as medical terms. One form of evaluation relates to the staff's perception of the appropriateness of the demands placed by patients on hospital services. A study involving interviews with doctors and observation at three hospital casualty departments in an English city over a 7-month period indicated that four groups of patients were regarded as 'trouble' or 'rubbish': drunks, overdoses, tramps and those attending with medical trivia (Jeffrey 1979). Drunks, overdoses and tramps were regarded as unpleasant to deal with and as not conforming to the legitimate category of 'sick' (see Chapter 4).

This is because they were viewed as responsible either directly or indirectly for their illness. For example, drunks will continue to fall over or be involved in fights because they are drunk, and tramps were seen as seeking a warm bed for the night and as bringing on bronchitis through their way of life. Normal overdosers were also regarded as knowing what they were doing and as taking an overdose to seek attention or as moral blackmail. Doctors' social evaluations were thus based on notions of patients' responsibility for their medical problems, but did not necessarily raise questions of the causes of homelessness or of the personal and social situations which resulted in behaviour such as taking an overdose. These negative evaluations generally led to patients being kept waiting longer and receiving less sympathetic treatment from staff.

Patients presenting at Accident and Emergency (AE) departments with medical trivia are frequently regarded by casualty officers as misusing a service which is designed to provide skilled hospital care for medical emergencies at any time of day or night. A study of the AE department of a London teaching hospital found that of the 587 new patients attending during 1 week, 226 (39%) were not accidents or emergencies; of these, 67% were self-referrals who had not previously seen their general practitioner, 21% were self-referrals who had previously seen their general practitioner, and 12% were referred by their general practitioner (Davison et al. 1983). A major reason for self-referral was that the patient thought the condition needed immediate attention. Other reasons included the greater convenience of the hospital, having a condition they preferred not to take to their general practitioner, wanting a second opinion, not being registered with a general practitioner, or being a visitor to the area. The use of AE departments for medical 'trivia' may thus be rational from the patient's perspective and raises questions of the differing definitions of an 'emergency' and the appropriate functions of AE departments.

Social evaluations of patients' behaviour continues in the hospital in-patient setting, with some patients being labelled as 'problem' patients by staff who have to bear the brunt of the trouble. 'Problem' patients are of two kinds. One group are those who are seriously ill and who complain a great deal, are very emotional, anxious and need a lot of reassurance, encouragement and attention from the staff. These patients are viewed as problematic but 'forgivable' because the situation is not of their own making. Such patients are often given the time and attention they demand, particularly if they are grateful for it, but are 'problem' patients in that they take up a large amount of time and attention. A second group of 'problem' patients are those who are *not* seriously ill in the staff's eyes but are regarded as being over-emotional, uncooperative and over-demanding. This group are the most condemned by staff and tend to be ignored, discharged early and sometimes given tranquillizers to control their behaviour (Lorber 1975).

Social evaluations may also influence treatment decisions. For example, one widely held belief in western industrial society is that the young are more valuable than the old, which has been shown to be associated with differences in efforts to resuscitate young and old patients (Sudnow 1967). Similarly, doctors may take into account a patient's age and family responsibilities in determining priorities for transplants and other procedures for which medical needs exceed the opportunities for treatment.

Thus, while the hospital can be viewed as a formal organization the members of which have clearly defined duties and responsibilities, as this chapter has shown, the activities and relationships between staff are influenced by individual interests and philosophies of care and are subject to a continuous process of negotiation. Similarly, patients' experiences of hospital care are influenced by the social meaning ascribed to their condition, as well as by the organization of care and the general characteristics of the hospital environment.

REFERENCES

Clark, P. & Bowling, A. (1989) Observational study of quality of life in NHS nursing homes and a long-stay ward for the elderly. *Ageing and Soc.,* **9,** 123–48.

Davies, A.D. & Peters, M. (1983) Stress of hospitalization in the elderly: nurses and patients perceptions. *J. advd Nurs.,* **8,** 99–105.

Davison, A.G., Hildrey, A.C. & Floyer, M.A. (1983) Use and misuse of an accident and emergency department in the East End of London. *J. R. Soc. Med.,* **76,** 37–40.

Department of Health (1989) *Hospital In-patient Enquiry: In-patient and Day Case Trends 1985–89.* London: HMSO.

Department of Health (1990) *Health and Personal Social Services Statistics for England.* London: HMSO.

Department of Health and Social Security (1979) *Hospital In-patient Enquiry: Main Tables.* London: HMSO.

Goffman, E. (1961) *Asylums.* New York: Doubleday.

Hall, D. (1977) *Social Relations and Innovation.* London: Routledge & Kegan Paul.

Jeffrey, R. (1979) Normal rubbish: deviant patients in the casualty department. *Soc. Hlth Illness,* **1,** 90–107.

Lorber, J. (1975) Good patients and problem patients. *J. Hlth soc. behav.,* **16,** 213–25.

Morgan, M. & Beech, R. (1990) Variations in lengths of stay and rates of day case surgery: implications for the efficiency of surgical management. *J. Epidemiol. commun. Health,* **44,** 90–105.

Newman, S. (1984) Anxiety, hospitalization and surgery. In: *The Experience of Illness,* ed. R. Fitzpatrick, J. Hinton, S. Newman, G. Scambler & J. Thompson. London: Tavistock.

Strauss, A., Fagerhaugh, S., Suczek, B. & Wiener, C. (1985) *Social Organization of Medical Work*. Chicago, IL: University of Chicago Press.

Sudnow, D. (1967) *Passing On: the Social Organisation of Dying*. New York: Prentice Hall.

Townsend, P. (1962) *The Last Refuge: a Survey of Residential Institutions and Homes for the Aged in England and Wales*. London: Routledge & Kegan Paul.

Wilson-Barnett, J. (1979) *Stress in Hospital: Patients' Psychological Reactions to Illness and Health Care*. London: Churchill-Livingstone.

Wing, J.K. & Brown, G.W. (1970) *Institutionalism and Schizophrenia: a Comparative Study of Three Mental Hospitals, 1960-68*. Cambridge: Cambridge University Press.

6

Living with chronic illness

David Locker

Since the early 1970s sociologists have increasingly turned their attention to the issues and challenges involved in chronic illness and disability. Studies of people with disabilities were common before this time, but were predominantly concerned with psychological factors and their role in the rehabilitation process.

During the 1970s considerable effort was invested in developing appropriate measures of chronic illness and disability, estimating the prevalence and severity of disability, assessing the needs of people with disabilities and identifying gaps in service provision for these individuals and the families who cared for them. In the 1980s more attention was paid to the experience of living with chronic illness and disability (Conrad 1987; Anderson & Bury 1988). A growing number of studies have begun to describe in some detail what it is like for individuals and families to live with a long-term, disabling disorder. The rationale underlying this work is that 'a sound, effective and ethical approach to chronic illness must lie in awareness of and attention to the experiences, values, priorities and expectations of (these people) and their families' (Anderson & Bury 1988: 1). This means that a detailed understanding of the impact of chronic illness and disability on daily life is necessary for the providers of medical and social services to offer appropriate care and support.

This recent emphasis on chronic illness reflects the fact that chronic disabling disorders, rather than acute infectious diseases, are the major cause of mortality in industrial societies and present a significant challenge to the medical-care system (see Chapter 1). Even where chronic conditions are not fatal, they are major sources of suffering for individuals and families. Given that the populations of western societies are ageing (see Chapter 11), it is predicted that the proportion of consultations in medical practice devoted to the psycho-social and other problems of daily living associated with chronic illness will increase. As a result, there will be a fundamental shift in medical practice from 'cure' to 'care' (Williams 1989).

The emergence of an interest in chronic illness also coincided with an increase in government provision for people with disabling disorders. In the UK, 1970 saw the passing of the Chronically Sick and Disabled Persons Act, which made it mandatory for local authorities to identify people with disabilities, to determine their needs and to provide services to meet those needs (Topliss 1979). In 1974, a Minister for the Disabled was appointed with specific responsibilities for the group. These developments led to an increase in services and financial benefits for people with disabilities and those who cared for them, although these were somewhat eroded during the late 1980s.

A further development which stimulated a greater awareness of the needs and priorities of people living with chronic illness was the emergence of the 'disability movement' (Conrad 1987). This consisted of groups dedicated to self-help and political action. The former offered help and support through the sharing of individual experience, while the latter used the political process to secure fundamental rights and to promote independent living. The aim here was to ensure that people with chronic disabling disorders would themselves define their needs and the most appropriate way of providing for them, rather than having these imposed by putative 'experts' and professionals.

CHARACTERISTICS OF CHRONIC ILLNESS

The term 'chronic illness' encompasses a wide range of conditions affecting almost all body systems. Cancer, stroke, end-stage renal disease, poliomyelitis, multiple sclerosis, rheumatoid arthritis, psoriasis, epilepsy and chronic obstructive airways disease are common examples. The most fundamental characteristic of chronic illnesses is that they are long-term and have a profound influence on the lives of sufferers. Some are fatal and some are not; some are stable with a certain prognosis, others may show great variation in terms of their day-to-day manifestation and their long-term course and outcome. In the majority of cases medical intervention is palliative; it seeks to control symptoms but cannot offer a cure. Consequently, maximizing the welfare of these individuals means maintaining or improving the quality of daily life rather than attempting to eradicate the disease process itself.

Some of the problems encountered by people with a chronic disabling disorder stem directly from the symptomatic character of their illness. In this respect, every chronic condition is somewhat distinct. For example, the person with rheumatoid arthritis must cope with chronic pain, the person with respiratory disease must live with breathlessness and an inadequate oxygen supply, while the person with end-stage renal failure must cope with the demands of a dialysis machine. In other respects the problems faced by people with chronic illness may be common to all, irrespective of the nature of their condition. Unemployment or reduced career prospects, social isolation and estrangement from family and friends, loss of important roles, changed physical appearance and problems with self-esteem and identity are experienced by many such individuals. Another fundamental characteristic of chronic conditions is that these assaults on the *body*, *daily activities* (encompassing home, work and leisure) and *social relationships* (including relationships with self and others) must be managed in the course of everyday life. When chronic illness becomes severe, daily life may be entirely consumed in coping with its symptoms, the medical regimens intended to control it and its social consequences (Locker 1983).

Prevalence of chronic illness and disability

A number of surveys of national and local populations have been undertaken in order to estimate the prevalence of disability. These have produced somewhat different results, largely because different definitions and measures of disability have been employed. The most recent study, the Survey of Disability in Great Britain undertaken in 1985 by the Office of Population Censuses and Surveys (OPCS), found that 14.2% of the adult population were disabled (OPCS 1988). Rates increased substantially with age and were higher among women than men. Other studies have reported that the most common causes of significant disability are neurological, musculo-skeletal and respiratory diseases such as stroke, multiple sclerosis, Parkinson's disease and rheumatoid arthritis.

Studies of disability probably underestimate the prevalence of chronic illness. Conditions such as diabetes, psoriasis and epilepsy may not be identified by conventional measures of disability. Consequently, the percentage of the population living with a chronic condition is likely to be higher than the 14.2% identified by the OPCS survey. One estimate derived from work by the Royal College of Physicians suggested that just over one-fifth of the population was subject to some type of chronic illness.

Impairment, disability and handicap

A systematic approach to thinking about disease and its consequences is to be found in a taxonomy developed by Wood (1980) for
the World Health Organization. He defined three concepts which
refer to distinct and important dimensions of human experience in the
context of disease. *Impairment* is defined as 'any loss or abnormality
of psychological, physiological or anatomical structure or function'.
Disability is 'any restriction or lack of ability to perform an activity in a
manner or within the range considered normal for a human being';
and *handicap* is defined as 'the disadvantage for a given individual,
arising out of impairment and disability, that limits or prevents the
fulfillment of a role that is normal (depending on age, sex and social
and cultural factors) for that individual'. Consequently, 'impairment'
refers to changes in the individual's body, disability to changes in
what the individual can and cannot do and handicap to changes in
his/her relationship with the physical and social environment.
According to Wood, handicap is the area that can best be understood
by sociological enquiry.

These concepts are linked dynamically in the following way:

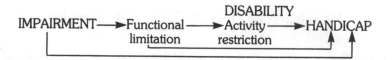

The relationships between impairment, disability and handicap are
not necessarily direct. Disability and/or handicap *may* result from
impairment, and handicap *may* be the outcome of disability, but this
is not necessarily the case. Nor is there any necessary relationship
between the severity of impairment and disability and the extent of
handicap experienced. For example, a recent study of people with
multiple sclerosis found that the psycho-social handicaps they
suffered were not related to the severity of the underlying disease
(Harper et al. 1986). Similarly, a study of individuals with chronic
respiratory disease found that clinical measures of lung function were
not good predictors of disability, and there was considerable
variability in the extent of handicap associated with a given level of
disability (Williams & Bury 1989a, b). This highlights the fact that
these relationships are mediated by a number of social, cultural and
other factors. In fact, for any given person, handicap is the result of
an interaction between impairment and disability and the personal
characteristics of the individual, the physical environment and the
particular social setting in which the individual lives.

THE MEANING OF CHRONIC ILLNESS

Early sociological approaches to chronic illness and disability drew on the theory of the sick role (Parsons 1951) (see Chapter 4), labelling theory (Lemert 1967) and Goffman's analysis of stigma (Goffman 1963) (see Chapter 13). More contemporary approaches have used detailed case studies to understand what it means to live with a chronic disabling disorder. This 'experience of illness' perspective is to be found in numerous books and scholarly papers published over the last 10 years and all have quality of life as their central concern.

The meaning of chronic illness is to be found in its practical and symbolic consequences (Blaxter 1976; Bury 1988). These consequences take the form of problems which chronically sick people and their families must solve if they are to attain a quality of life of minimal tolerability.

One study of people with rheumatoid arthritis found that all faced the following: problems managing the symptoms of the disease and the medical treatments designed to control them; problems with the practical matters of everyday living, such as self-care, household management and mobility around the home and community; problems with respect to finding work or maintaining a meaningful role in the work-force; economic problems following unemployment; and problems in social relationships and family life (Locker 1983). The subjects in this study also encountered what might be termed cognitive problems. That is, they were faced with the task of making sense of the onset of chronic illness and sought answers to the unanswerable question 'Why me?'. In addition, they were constantly engaged in efforts to make sense of the day-to-day variation in levels of pain and stiffness in an attempt to establish order in their world and render their unpredictable existence predictable. As many studies have revealed, a significant aspect of being or caring for a person with a disability is the 'daily grind' of the never-ending and unrewarded hard work involved in coping with these problems on a daily basis.

One crucial factor which has an influence on how, and the extent to which, these problems are managed is the resources to which individuals have access. These resources may take many forms: time, energy, money, social support, appropriate physical environment, formal services which foster independence rather than exacerbate dependence and knowledge and information are perhaps the most important. The magnitude and range of resources available to individuals and families, and the coping strategies of which they form a part, influence how well the consequences of chronic conditions are managed.

In a sense, the fact that personal and social resources must be allocated to solving mundane practical matters is part of the handicap that flows from chronic illness. Money may have to be used to pay someone to clean the house and do the shopping rather than being used to make life more enjoyable. As chronic illness progresses, it is sometimes the case that available resources shrink. Physical resources may decline as a result of the worsening of the disease, money may decline when the individual becomes unemployed and his/her spouse gives up work to adopt a full-time caring role and social support may be eroded as friendship networks or families collapse under the strain of chronic illness. In these instances, life becomes nothing more than the work and effort of solving illness-related problems and getting through the day.

The concept of resources is a crucial one. On the one hand, it provides one of the mechanisms which link disability and handicap; while on the other, it draws attention to the unequal distribution of resources in society and the ability/inability of individuals from different socio-economic groups to maintain a satisfactory existence in the face of chronic illness. In this way, it links personal concerns with wider social and political issues. People from working-class backgrounds, women, ethnic minorities and those who live in deprived urban communities are the most vulnerable in the face of chronic illness.

It is also the case that the illness experience can vary with historical period and culture. As Bury (1988) has indicated, chronic illness has two levels of meaning. One is to be found in the kinds of problems described above. The other is to be found in the significance or connotations that particular conditions carry, and the extent to which a given condition renders an individual culturally incompetent, that is, unable to perform ordinary activities in socially appropriate ways. The extent to which an individual is devalued by chronic illness will also be influenced by what the illness means in its particular cultural environment. For example, chronic obstructive airways disease is 'linked in the public mind to smoking (so) that the image of a wheezing, coughing, breathless old man is often greeted with little sympathy' (Williams & Bury 1989b: 609). This lack of sympathy may reflect a lack of attention to and resources invested in those suffering from the disease. In this way, the handicapping nature of chronic illness flows directly from its social and cultural context.

MAJOR THEMES IN RESEARCH ON THE EXPERIENCE OF ILLNESS

It is not possible to convey the realities of living with chronic illness within the confines of a short chapter such as this. However, some impression can be gained of its pervasive effects by a brief discussion of some of the major themes evident in research on the experience of illness. Conrad (1987) has identified a number of such themes. Five are mentioned here; another, stigma, is the subject of Chapter 13.

Uncertainty

Many chronic conditions are surrounded by uncertainty. This may begin at the time when the individual first notices that something is wrong and may continue throughout the entire course of the illness. Many chronic illnesses have a slow and insidious onset and emerge in the form of vague symptoms which persist for years prior to diagnosis (pre-diagnostic uncertainty). With multiple sclerosis the delay between appearance of symptoms and diagnosis may be as long as 15 years (Robinson 1988). During this time sufferers are convinced that something is wrong, but often find their complaints dismissed by medical practitioners as trivial or as evidence of malingering or hypochondria. This can be a very trying time for the individual and his/her family. When a diagnosis is finally obtained, it often comes as a relief; it legitimates the person's complaints and experiences and brings to an end conflicts with others over the reality of the symptoms (Robinson 1988).

However, uncertainty may follow the diagnosis itself. This is often so with respect to predicting the course and outcome of the disease (trajectory uncertainty). Coupled with the uncertainty which can surround day-to-day fluctuations in symptoms (symptomatic uncertainty), this can severely disrupt family life. It makes both short- and long-term planning impossible and often means that living arrangements have to be constantly revised. Managing this uncertainty by whatever means available can become a major component of daily life.

A good example of uncertainty is provided by rheumatoid arthritis (RA). The symptoms of this disease, joint pain and stiffness, are highly unpredictable. The location and severity of the pain varies from day to day, and may even change during the course of a day. What seems to be a 'good day' in the morning may become a 'bad day' by the afternoon. This variability and unpredictability means that people with RA find it difficult to make sense of their symptoms and to contain them within acceptable boundaries. Many attempt to impose a degree of certainty on their existence by trying to identify events which precede acute phases or particularly painful days. Cold or damp weather and physical and emotional stress are frequently seen as the cause of pain and avoided as far as possible. However, a 'bad day' for which no apparent reason can be found leaves sufferers confused and adds to their distress (Locker 1983).

Family relations

There is clear evidence that chronic illness can place intolerable strains on families. This can arise because of the necessity to provide high levels of care and support, the emotional connotations of giving and receiving help and changes in family roles and relationships. Even where families are able and willing to provide help, the person with a chronic disabling condition may feel that he/she is a burden and may refuse the assistance that is needed. It is also the case that particularly distressing symptoms, such as chronic pain, may lead the individual to withdraw from family life altogether. In some instances, both individual and family become isolated from the wider world. Marital breakdown is not uncommon in these instances.

MacDonald (1988) provides insights into the effects of chronic illness on marital and family relationships in her study of people living with the sequelae of rectal cancer. Two-thirds of the people she interviewed had a colostomy, with the remainder having been treated by excision of the cancer and anastomosis. Most of the individuals reported a loss of sexual capacity and a decline in the quality of the marital relationship. This was partly due to the physical effects of surgery and partly due to feelings of shame and embarrassment. These feelings of stigma were most marked among younger men, who reported that the consequences of surgery and fears for the future had created a barrier between them and their wives.

The consequences of surgery also had a profound effect on social relationships in general. Again, shame and embarrassment about noise and odours from the stoma, worries about offending others and feelings of self-disgust caused many to avoid social contacts and to lead a far more restricted life.

Biographical work and the reconstitution of self

All chronic disabling conditions pose a threat to identity and self-concept. One of the reasons for this is that the onset of chronic illness constitutes a 'biographical disruption' (Bury 1982) and calls into question both past and future. It necessitates a fundamental rethinking of both biography and self-concept. Williams (1984) argues that people with chronic illness must indulge in a process he calls 'narrative reconstruction', in which the individual's biography is reorganized in order to account for the onset of illness. This identification of cause, which draws on lay theories concerning the aetiology of illness, is part of the process of coming to terms with chronic illness. It gives meaning and order to the individual's world.

Charmaz (1987) has described how chronically sick people are involved in a constant struggle to lead valued lives and maintain definitions of self which are positive and worthwhile. This can be difficult; cultural definitions of disability devalue the individual, and interactions with others may constantly undermine the individual's sense of self-worth. Charmaz (1987) considers the 'loss of self' to be a powerful form of suffering experienced by the chronically ill.

Managing medical regimens

People with chronic disabling disorders must learn to manage their symptoms and manifestations during everyday life. The person with rheumatoid arthritis, for example, rapidly learns how much activity is possible before pain rises to intolerable levels. Daily life is then planned and organized in ways which allow the individual to accomplish a few valued activities before pain intercedes and he or she is forced to rest. The individual must also learn to manage the medical regimens prescribed to control symptoms. These can include diet, drugs or the use of advanced technologies such as a dialysis machine. In some instances the treatment can be as bad as the disease, consuming time, energy and financial resources and requiring hard work (Jobling 1988). The whole life of the chronically sick person can become organized around treatment.

An illuminating example is provided by a study of people with post-polio respiratory impairment, whose capacity to breathe had deteriorated to such an extent that permanent connection to a positive-pressure ventilator by means of a tracheostomy became necessary (Locker & Kaufert 1988). This highly efficient form of mechanical ventilation substantially improved physical and psychological health, allowed for far greater mobility than older technologies and transformed the quality of everyday life. However, the use of this machine meant that the individual concerned, and those providing care and support, had to learn a wide range of skills in order to manage the machine, including recharging batteries, suctioning tubing and maintaining the humidification system. Because this machinery often malfunctioned, usually without warning, it had to be carefully monitored and strategies had to be developed to cope with sudden failure. The potential for respiratory crises left both sufferers and family members feeling vulnerable and insecure. As a consequence, the machine, and tending to the needs of the machine, became a central focus of everyday life.

A less dramatic example is provided by a study of people with psoriasis, a disfiguring skin disease (Jobling 1988).

(Treatment) involves strict conformity over weeks, months or even years, to a programme of repetitious, daily bathing, rubbing and scrubbing. This is followed by anointment with oils, creams, pastes or ointments, some of which may involve a subjectively noxious smell. Regular exposure to the sun's rays, or at least an equivalent produced by a machine, is another component. All of this may take up several hours a day. (p. 235)

If is often the case that any prescribed regimen is substantially altered by the person concerned. This allows them to exert control over their illness and to maximize their well-being by avoiding some of the negative aspects of medical treatments.

Information, awareness and sharing

For the chronically ill, information is a significant resource for managing their lives. It reduces uncertainty, helps the individual to come to terms with the illness and allows for the development of strategies for managing the illness in everyday life. Nevertheless, many people with chronic conditions express dissatisfaction with the amount of information they are able to obtain about their disorder. Difficulty with communication is a major problem in the relationships between people with chronic illnesses and their doctors. Many rectal cancer patients interviewed by MacDonald (1988) were dissatisfied with what they were told about their operation, and some felt inadequately prepared for dealing with the colostomy and its effects. Some reported not knowing what a colostomy was, even at the time of surgery, and many complained of inadequate follow-up care from their family doctor.

Given these problems in communication, information may be culled from a variety of sources: from books and publications, from self-help groups or from others with the same or similar illnesses. This information provides the basis for action and the feeling that it is possible to do something about and have some control over the illness.

THE DOCTOR–PATIENT RELATIONSHIP IN CHRONIC ILLNESS

Patients with chronic disabling disorders can be difficult for a medical practitioner to manage successfully. This is only partly due to the fact that medicine has relatively few interventions which make a real difference to the patient's condition. It also arises because the medical gaze is frequently a narrow one, concerned predominantly with disease to the exclusion of its social and emotional consequences for patients and families.

Anderson and Bury (1988) indicate the need for 'a reorientation of the focus for care from repairing damage caused by disease to education and understanding for living with chronic illness'. In this sense, information, advice and support are among the most important interventions a doctor has to offer, their goal being to help the patient live as normal and satisfying a life as possible within family and community. Such help needs to be approached with care and sensitivity; patients need to be offered choices, not have them made by others on their behalves. This means ensuring that individuals are helped to be independent and not encouraged into dependency.

By giving due attention to the particular handicaps associated with a chronic condition, the care that is offered to both the sufferer and the family can be made more appropriate and relevant to their social and emotional concerns. This presupposes that the professional is fully aware of the many meanings of chronic illness, the burdens carried by the individual and those who provide informal support, and the contextual factors which shape these meanings and burdens.

This, in turn, highlights the issues of communication and information (see Chapter 4) and the importance of a free exchange of information between doctors and those with a chronic illness. Each has much to teach the other in working together to maximize the patient's quality of life.

REFERENCES

Anderson, R. & Bury, M. (eds) (1988) *Living With Chronic Illness: The Experiences of Patients and Their Families.* London: Hyman Unwin.

Blaxter, M. (1976) *The Meaning of Disability.* London: Heinemann.

Bury, M. (1982) Chronic illness as biographical disruption. *Soc. Hlth Illness,* **4,** 167–82.

Bury, M. (1988) Meanings at risk: the experience of arthritis. In: *Living With Chronic Illness: The Experiences of Patients and Their Families,* ed. R. Anderson & M. Bury. London: Hyman Unwin.

Charmaz, K. (1987) Struggling for a self: identity levels of the chronically ill. *Res. Soc. Hlth Care,* **6,** 283–321.

Conrad, P. (1987) The experience of illness: recent and new directions. *Res. Soc. Hlth Care,* **6,** 1–31.

Goffman, E. (1963) *Stigma.* Englewood Cliffs, NJ: Prentice Hall.

Harper, A., Harper, D., Chambers, L., Cino, P. & Singer, J. (1986) An epidemiological description of physical, social and psychological problems in multiple sclerosis. *Journal of Chronic Diseases,* **39,** 305–10.

Jobling, R. (1988) The experience of psoriasis under treatment. In: *Living With Chronic Illness: The Experiences of Patients and Their Families*, ed. R. Anderson & M. Bury. London: Hyman Unwin.

Lemert, E. (1967) *Human Deviance, Social Problems and Social Control*. Englewood Cliffs, NJ: Prentice-Hall.

Locker, D. (1983) *Disability and Disadvantage: the Consequences of Chronic Illness*. London: Tavistock.

Locker, D. & Kaufert, J. (1988) The breath of life: medical technology and the careers of people with post-respiratory poliomyelitis. *Soc. Hlth Illness*, **10**, 24–40.

MacDonald, L. (1988) The experience of stigma: living with rectal cancer. In: *Living With Chronic Illness: The Experiences of Patients and Their Families*, ed. R. Anderson & M. Bury. London: Hyman Unwin.

Office of Population Censuses and Surveys (1988) *OPCS Surveys of Disability in Great Britain: The Prevalence of Disability Among Adults*. London: HMSO.

Parsons, T. (1951) *The Social System*. New York: Free Press.

Robinson, I. (1988) Reconstructing lives: negotiating the meaning of multiple sclerosis. In: *Living With Chronic Illness: The Experiences of Patients and Their Families*, ed. R. Anderson & M. Bury. London: Hyman Unwin.

Topliss, E. (1979) *Provision for the Disabled*. London: Martin Robertson.

Williams, G. (1984) The genesis of chronic illness: narrative reconstruction. *Soc. Hlth Illness*, **6**, 175–200.

Williams, S. (1989) Chronic respiratory illness and disability: a critical review of the psychosocial literature. *Soc. Sci. Med.*, **28**, 791–803.

Williams, S. & Bury, M. (1989a) Breathtaking: the consequences of chronic respiratory disorder. Unpublished paper.

Williams, S. & Bury, M. (1989b) Impairment, disability and handicap in chronic respiratory illness. *Soc. Sci. Med.*, **29**, 609–16.

Wood, P. (1980) The language of disablement: a glossary relating to disease and its consequences. *International Rehabilitation Medicine*, **2**, 86–92.

7

Dying, death and bereavement

Graham Scambler

The inescapable fact of death provides one of the principal parameters of the human condition. As Lofland (1978) writes, 'it can neither be "believed" nor "magicked" nor "scienced" away'. Increasingly in the twentieth century physicians and other health workers have been called upon to give treatment and support to the terminally ill and their first-degree relatives. This chapter focuses on problems of communication about dying between health workers, patients and relatives; various 'stages' of dying; alternative facilities for the care of the terminally ill in Britain; aspects of the treatment of dying persons; and processes of bereavement.

TALKING ABOUT DEATH

In the final quarter of the twentieth century a higher proportion of people than ever before experience 'slow' as opposed to 'quick' dying; that is, dying has typically become a more protracted process. The reasons for this have been well documented and are summarized in Table 1. For obvious reasons this change has enhanced the salience of communication around death. It is ironic, therefore, that there is a broad consensus among historians that death over the last 100 years or so has become more and more 'unmentionable'. Aries (1983) characterizes modern — demythologized and secularized — death as *invisible death*: 'we ignore the existence of a scandal that we

93

——— **Table 1** ———
Conditions facilitating 'quick dying' in the pre-modern era
and 'slow dying' in the modern era

Conditions facilitating quick dying	Conditions facilitating slow dying
Low level of medical technology	High level of medical technology
Late detection of disease- or fatality-producing conditions	Early detection of disease- or fatality-producing conditions
Simple definition of death (e.g. cessation of heart beat)	Complex definition of death (e.g. irreversible cessation of higher brain activity)
High incidence of mortality from acute disease	High incidence of mortality from chronic or degenerative disease
High incidence of fatality-producing injuries	Low incidence of fatality-producing injuries
Customary killing or suicide of, or fatal passivity towards, the person once he or she has entered the 'dying' category	Customary curative and activist orientation toward the dying with a high value placed on the prolongation of life

Source: Lofland (1978).

have been unable to prevent; we act as if it did not exist, and thus mercilessly force the bereaved to say nothing. A heavy silence has fallen over the subject of death'. According to Aries, death has grown fearful again, imbued with all its 'old savagery'.

This historical analysis can be criticized as too general or simplistic, but there is little doubt that death in modern Britain is something of a taboo subject. It is not surprising, therefore, that deciding whether or not to tell someone he or she is dying is often regarded as particularly problematic for health workers. When asked, most people anticipate that they would want to be told if they were dying; physicians are themselves unexceptional in this respect. But how much credibility should be attached to such responses? Can young, healthy individuals accurately predict how they will feel as death approaches?

Cartwright et al. (1973), who interviewed relatives of a national sample of people who had died in the preceding year in Britain, were told by relatives that 37% of those dying knew as much, and a further 20% 'half knew'. Nearly three-quarters of the relatives felt they had themselves known. It was also apparent from this study that the relatives received more information from all sources than did the people who were dying. If death occurred in a hospital less information was forthcoming than if it occurred at home; in both contexts, however, the general practitioner was the key informant.

Herd (1990), in a study of terminal care in a semi-rural part of Britain, also found principal lay carers to be less aware and knowledgeable about what was happening if death took place in hospital than if it took place in the home.

Awareness of dying

Glaser and Strauss (1965) found there to be four common types of 'awareness contexts' in relation to the dying. They define 'awareness context' as: 'what *each* interacting person knows of the patient's defined status, along with his recognition of others' awareness of his own definition'. The four types are:

1. *Closed awareness:* the situation in which the patient does not recognize his or her impending death even though everyone else does.
2. *Suspected awareness:* the situation when the patient suspects what others know and attempts either to confirm or to invalidate his or her suspicions.
3. *Mutual pretence awareness:* the situation where each party defines the patient as dying but each 'pretends' that the other has not done so.
4. *Open awareness:* the situation where health workers and patient are each aware that the latter is dying, and where they act on this awareness fairly openly.

Some commentators have assumed that 'closed', 'suspected' and 'mutual pretence' awareness contexts are intrinsically undesirable and that health workers, especially physicians, are exclusively to blame for the fact that they frequently exist. As a study by McIntosh (1977) suggests, however, such assumptions can be naive and misleading. Interviewing physicians and selected patients with diagnosed but undisclosed cancers, McIntosh focused on how both physicians and patients cope with the *uncertainties* that often attend talk about dying.

The physicians told McIntosh that decisions to tell or not to tell rested on their assessments of individual cases; many added that these decisions were often complicated by clinical uncertainties concerning diagnosis and prognosis and by uncertainties about whether or not patients really wanted to know. These policy statements, however, did not seem to accord with actual medical practice. In fact, there were *no* disclosures unless they were deemed absolutely necessary: that is, unless patients were adamant and unyielding in their demands for 'the truth'. Physicians, in short, were biased against telling: 'the cornerstone of the doctors' philosophy on telling was the belief that the great majority of patients should not be told'. Most patients spoken to suspected malignancy. The majority sought information from members of the hospital team but, according to McIntosh's estimate, two out of every three did not 'really' want their diagnostic suspicions confirmed, and fewer still 'really' wanted to know their prognosis. They sought exclusively information which would reinforce an optimistic conception of their condition: uncertainty afforded hope. Most patients also felt that physicians would tell them everything *if asked*.

In a later Canadian study of 118 encounters during which 17 male surgeons disclosed the results of biopsies to women with breast cancer, Taylor (1988) found that each surgeon appeared to have adopted a favoured 'strategy' which he used routinely, thus 'bypassing the individuality of each case'. Four techniques were discerned. The first, *communication*, was deployed by some surgeons when they were in a position to make a reasonable and definite prognosis of the condition in terms comprehensible to the patient. Many surgeons claimed to use this technique, but in fact few did. Only 10% of the 118 disclosures were of this type. The second, *admission of uncertainty*, was used by a small minority of surgeons when no clinical prognosis was justified; 15% of the disclosures took this form. The third technique, *dissimulation*, or the pronouncement of a prognosis which could not be clinically substantiated, occurred when surgeons were reluctant to share the extent of their uncertainty with their patients; 30% of the disclosures fell into this category. The final technique, *evasion*, or 'the failure to communicate a clinically substantiated prognosis', was used by a number of surgeons who preferred not to respond directly to patient questions. 'For those surgeons whose patients asked direct questions to which the appropriate technical response might reveal a low chance of long-term survival, repressing information was a favoured policy'. Not infrequently, replies to specific questions drew on general statistics not easily applicable to the individual case. In 45% of disclosures surgeons used evasion as a means of coping with direct questions posed by women.

If one thing is clear it is that there is no easy, general answer to the question 'To tell or not to tell?'. Hinton (1967) offers physicians the following counsel: 'although it is not an infallible guide as to how much the dying patient should be told, his apparent wishes and questions do point the way. This means that the manner in which he puts his views should be closely attended to — the intonations and the exact wording may be very revealing. It also means that he must be given ample opportunity to express his ideas and ask his questions. If the questions are sincere, however, then why not give quite straight answers to the patient's questions about his illness and the outcome? It makes for beneficial trust'.

A study by Hinton (1980) himself highlights the importance of giving dying patients the opportunity to talk. He interviewed 80

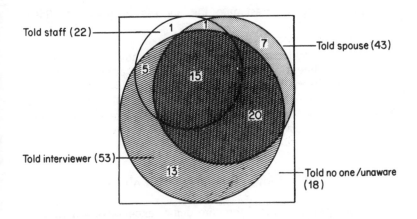

Told staff (22)

Told spouse (43)

Told interviewer (53)

Told no one /unaware (18)

1 1 7 5 15 20 13

Fig. 1. Awareness of the possibility of dying as shown by different people by 80 patients with terminal cancer. The square represents the 80 patients and the three shaded circles their communicated awareness to staff, spouse and interviewer. (Source: Hinton (1980).)

patients with terminal cancer at a mean of 10 weeks before death; 66% told him that they recognized they might or would soon die, 8% were non-committal, and 26% spoke only of improvement. Some patients spoke of dying to either their spouse or the staff and not to the interviewer, but they tended to say less to their spouse than to the interviewer and less still to members of the staff. This tendency is illustrated in Fig. 1. Hinton concludes that people are often ready to share their awareness *if someone is prepared to listen.*

STAGES OF DYING

How people come to terms with the prospect of imminent death depends on many factors (Hinton 1984). Of obvious importance is the nature of the physical and mental distress experienced. In a randomized national survey of terminal illness, Cartwright et al. (1973) reported the following symptoms occurring to a 'very distressing degree' during the last year of life: pain 42%, breathing troubles 28%, vomiting 17%, sleeplessness 17%, loss of both bladder and bowel control 12%, loss of appetite 11%, and mental confusion 10%. It has regularly been found that, when compared with lay carers, health workers tend to under-estimate patients' symptoms and to over-estimate the success of treatment (Herd 1990).

Among the many factors which can influence how individuals cope with terminal illness are age, family intimacy and support, and religious convictions. There is enormous individual variation and hence unpredictability in any given case. Kubler-Ross (1970) has claimed, however, that people who know they are dying *typically* pass through five 'stages'.

First stage: denial and isolation

Many people, on being told they are dying, experience a temporary state of shock. When the numbness disappears, a common response is: 'No, it can't be me'. One's own death is all but inconceivable. 'Denial' is usually a temporary defence, but some take it further, perhaps 'shopping around' for a more amenable clinical opinion (only three of the 200 patients in Kubler-Ross' study attempted to deny the approach of death to the very end). A deep feeling of 'isolation' is normal at this stage.

Second stage: anger

When the initial stage of denial can no longer be maintained, it is often replaced by feelings of anger, rage, envy and resentment. The question 'Why me?' is posed. The anger can be displaced and at times projected onto the environment almost at random (although it can of course be justified as well as unjustified). The hospital team, especially the nursing staff, frequently bear the brunt of these outbursts.

Third stage: bargaining

The third stage of 'bargaining', Kubler-Ross argues, has only rarely been acknowledged. The point is that terminally ill people will sometimes negotiate — openly with health workers or secretly with God — to postpone death: postponement will be the reward for a promise of good behaviour. For example, many patients in the study promised to donate parts of their bodies to medical science if the physicians undertook to use their knowledge of science to extend their lives.

Fourth stage: depression

When terminally ill patients can no longer deny their illness, when they are compelled to endure more surgery, when they grow weaker, the numbness or stoicism or anger gives way to a sense of great loss. This 'depression' may be *reactive,* for example a woman with cancer of the uterus may feel she is no longer a woman, or what Kubler-Ross calls *preparatory, that is,* based on impending losses associated with death itself.

Fifth stage: acceptance

The final stage of 'acceptance' is one in which dying patients commonly find a sort of peace, a peace which is largely a function of weakness and a diminished interest in the world. 'It is as if the pain has gone, the struggle is over . . .'. Kubler-Ross adds that this is also the time during which the family usually needs more help, understanding and support than the patient.

Several writers have criticized Kubler-Ross' specification of discrete stages of dying, usually on the grounds that it represents an over-generalization based on subjective data. There have, however, been few attempts to evaluate Kubler-Ross' theory empirically, and none have been decisive.

PLACE OF DEATH

Those like Aries who argue that death has become increasingly invisible during the twentieth century attach considerable significance to the fact that, since the 1930s and 1940s, death has been substantially removed from the community or 'hospitalized'. In the hospital, according to this thesis, death is no longer an occasion of ritual ceremony over which the dying person and his or her kin and friends hold sway. The physicians and hospital team are the new 'masters of death', of its moment as well as its circumstances. This interpretation of changing events is once again open to criticism, but there is no doubt that the hospitalization of death has continued. About two-thirds of those who die in Britain do so in hospital; a quarter die at home; and the remainder die elsewhere (e.g. in a hospice or public place). It does not follow, however, that the role of *home or lay care* for the dying has correspondingly diminished. Ward (1974) studied the last days of 279 people in Sheffield who died of cancer and found that, although most of them died in

———— **Table 2** ————
Worrying aspects of home care identified by lay carers.

	Number (%) of respondents
Anxiety about medication	26 (49)
Inability to leave patient unattended	22 (42)
Not knowing what to expect	18 (34)
Inability to help	15 (28)
Fear of being alone when death took place	11 (21)
Anxiety about what to do when death took place	5 (9)
Anxiety about calling the doctor	3 (6)
Other	5 (9)

Source: Herd (1990).

hospital, during their final month they only spent a mean of 8.7 days in hospital.

There is a growing feeling that the hospital is too frequently an inappropriate place in which to die. In his essay on *The Loneliness of Dying,* Elias (1985), who is fully aware of how emotionally taxing, as well as rewarding, a death in the family home can be, nevertheless stresses that in modern hospitals 'dying people can be cared for in accordance with the latest biophysical specialist knowledge, but often neutrally as regards feeling; they may die in total isolation'. Most hospitals are designed to provide for acute illness, and terminally ill people in acute wards can both disturb other patients and members of ward staff and be disturbed by them; most hospitals do not set aside a whole or part of a ward for dying patients because they are anxious to avoid the stigma of a 'death ward'. Several alternative locations exist in Britain, including special units within conventional hospitals, but the most discussed are the home and the hospice.

The home

For many health workers and lay persons alike, despite the statistical trend to hospitalization, the home remains the 'natural' and 'proper' place in which to die. As Bowling and Cartwright (1982) discovered, however, the care of dying people at home imposes severe physical, financial and psychological strains on relatives. In Herd's (1990) study, 74% of lay carers (four out of every five of them female relatives) mentioned 'emotional strain' as a problem, and 51% mentioned 'physical strain'. Table 2 ranks those aspects of home care that Herd's lay carers defined as 'worrying'. Lay carers are also likely to find their own activities restricted: Bowling and Cartwright report 26% describing their activities as 'severely restricted' and a further

19% as 'fairly restricted'. The extent to which professional and other support is at hand is likely to be contingent upon *ad hoc* factors affecting local planning and provision. Currently in Britain hospitalization is typically a function of the absence of local planning and provision. There are shortages of helpers ranging from Macmillan nurses to home helps and providers of meals-on-wheels.

The hospice

The hospice movement was founded in the mid-nineteenth century and was largely pioneered in Britain, although in-patient hospices still deal with less than 4% of dying people. The favoured pattern in Britain is to build small units in the grounds of general hospitals, using their facilities but remaining administratively independent. The range of care provided in a hospice is intermediate between that of a long-stay hospital and that of an acute hospital. The staffing ratios are similar to those of an acute hospital, but the call for diagnostic and other 'support' services is much less. The average length of stay is also closer to that of patients in an acute hospital than that of patients in a long-stay hospital, and costs are in keeping with this.

Central to the philosophy of the hospice is the view that the whole professional caring team should work in unison to develop the skills the dying person needs. Dramatic improvements in care have originated in hospices in the last quarter of the twentieth century, for example in standards of palliative medicine: hospice teams have reduced levels of uncontrolled pain to 8% and less (Parkes 1984). It should not be assumed, however, that, given the choice, everybody would opt for death in a hospice. In one study the care given in four radiotherapy wards of an acute hospital, in a Foundation Home visited by two general practitioners and in a hospice were compared (Hinton 1979).

Little difference was found between the acute hospital and the Foundation Home, but there was some evidence that patients were less depressed and anxious in the hospice and preferred the more frank communication available there. It was also found, however, that patients gave most praise to the out-patient system of care, *despite experiencing more anxiety or irritability at home*. The author concluded: 'treatment cannot be judged solely by the mental quiet it brings; freedom or hope may be preferred even if they bring worry'. It has been found that home-centred patients tend to experience more pain than hospital-centred patients, and their relatives more stress; but it does not follow that, even knowing this, patients and their relatives would necessarily choose to leave home. It should not be concluded that because adequate support for home care is rarely available the hospitalization of death should be accelerated.

Patterns of Death in Hospital

Sudnow (1967) has drawn a distinction between biological and social death. The problem of how to define biological death has been resolved by the medical profession for the time being in favour of the irreversible cessation of higher brain activity. Sudnow uses the term 'social death' in a general sense to refer to how organizations deal with different modes of dying and death. More specifically, social death is marked, within the hospital setting, by that point at which a patient is treated essentially as a corpse, although still perhaps biologically alive. He gives an example of social death preceding biological death. A nurse on duty with a woman she explained was 'dying' was observed to spend two or three minutes trying to close the woman's eyelids. After several unsuccessful attempts she managed to shut them and said, with a sigh of relief, 'Now they're right'. When questioned, she said that a patient's eyes must be closed after death, so that the body will resemble a sleeping person. It was more difficult to accomplish this, she explained, after the muscles and skin had begun to stiffen. She always tried to close them *before* death. This made for greater efficiency when the time came for ward personnel to wrap the body. It was a matter of consideration toward those workers who preferred to handle dead bodies as little as possible.

Glaser and Strauss (1968) distinguish seven 'critical junctures' in what is sometimes called the 'career' of the dying patient:

1. the definition of the patient as dying;
2. staff and family then make their preparations for the patient's death, as the patient may do if he or she knows that death is near;
3. at some point there seems to be 'nothing more to do' to prevent death;
4. the final descent, which may take weeks, days or merely hours;
5. the 'last hours';
6. the death watch; and finally,
7. death itself.

When these critical junctures occur as expected — as it were, on schedule — then all those involved, including sometimes the patient, are prepared for them. When, however, critical junctures occur unexpectedly, hospital staff and the patient's family alike may be unprepared. If a patient is expected to die quite soon, for example, but vacillates sufficiently often, then both staff and family are likely to find the experience stressful.

Predictability, then, makes the work of hospital teams easier. Miscalculations in forecasting can play havoc with the organization of work. When crises do occur, the staff attempt to regain control as quickly as possible, but sometimes the disruption of work is accompanied by a shattering of what Glaser and Strauss (1965) have called a ward's characteristic 'sentimental mood' or order. They cite an example: 'in an intensive care unit where cardiac patients die frequently, the mood is relatively unaffected by one more speedy expected death; but if a hopeless patient lingers on and on, or if his wife, perhaps, refuses to accept his dying and causes "scenes", then both mood and work itself are profoundly affected'.

Glaser and Strauss (1968) differentiate between a number of patterns of death, 'dying trajectories', paying special attention to the distinction noted earlier between 'quick' and 'slow' dying. Quick dying, they claim, may take three forms: 'the expected quick death'; 'unexpected quick dying, but expected to die'; and 'unexpected quick dying, not expected to die'. They report that, in general, unexpected quick deaths are more disturbing for staff and families than expected quick deaths. Even expected quick deaths, however, can give rise to distinctive difficulties. Glaser and Strauss focus on staff–family interaction and note, for example, that the likely presence of the family at the bedside when death occurs requires careful handling by the staff, since a 'scene' will disrupt ward order and worry other patients. Slow dying 'is fraught with both hazard and opportunity'. On the one hand, the dying may take 'too long', be unexpectedly painful or unpleasant, and so on; on the other hand, a slow decline may allow time for wills to be made or families to come together, and may provide the setting for quiet and dignified endings. All these consequences are less likely to occur with quick dying. It has been estimated that 50% of deaths in Britain are sudden and unexpected and 20% follow prolonged terminal care, the remaining 30% taking various other forms (Fry et al. 1984).

Bereavement and mourning

Just as experiences of impending death vary from person to person, so does the experience of losing a relative or friend. Much depends on the nature of the relationship. However, a sudden, unexpected death is often harder to get over than one where there was time to grieve before the occurrence of death: this is known as 'anticipatory' or 'pre-bereavement mourning'.

In his anthropological study of death in Britain, Gorer (1965) argues that mourners typically pass through three stages:

1. a short period of shock, usually lasting from death until the disposal of the body;
2. a period of intense mourning, accompanied by withdrawal of

attention and affect from the external world and by physiological changes like disturbed sleep, vivid dreams, failure of appetite and loss of weight; and

3. a final period of re-established social and physical homeostasis, with sleep and weight stabilized and interest again directed outwards.

Gorer's principal thesis is that, in an increasingly *secular* Britain, only the first of these three periods is socially acknowledged and surrounded by ceremony and ritual. After the funeral or post-funeral meal mourners are frequently abandoned to cope alone. To counter this social isolation during a time of continuing need for succour and support (periods 2 and 3) he advocates the creation of new secular rituals to replace now defunct religious ones.

Kamerman (1988) suggests that this twentieth-century process of 'deritualization' has been accompanied by a process of 'rationalization'. By this he means that death has increasingly come to be subsumed under conventions or routines which render it non-intrusive. Responses to death have become more 'business-like'. Both deritualization and rationalization are epitomized by the growing preference for cremation over burial. Approximately two-thirds of bodies are now cremated in Britain.

As if in affirmation of the need for continuing support after the funeral, several studies have shown elevated rates of morbidity and mortality and of visits to general practitioners amongst samples of recently bereaved persons.

It remains the case that many health students and workers receive minimal preparation for coping with terminal care and bereavement. Glaser and Strauss argue that much non-technical conduct in relation to the dying and bereaved is influenced by common-sense assumptions, 'essentially untouched by professional considerations or by current knowledge from the behavioural sciences'. The argument for the provision of a good grounding in those aspects of care — psychological, social, organizational and ethical — which are now relatively neglected is a strong one.

REFERENCES

Aries, P. (1983) *The Hour of our Death.* London: Penguin.

Bowling, A. & Cartwright, A. (1982) *Life After Death: A Study of the Elderly Widowed.* London: Tavistock.

Cartwright, A., Hockey, L. & Anderson, J. (1973) *Life Before Death.* London: Routledge & Kegan Paul.

Elias, N. (1985) *The Loneliness of Dying*. Oxford: Basil Blackwell.

Fry, J., Brooks, D. & McColl, I. (1984) NHS Data Book Lancaster: MTP Press.

Glaser, B. & Strauss, A. (1965) *Awareness of Dying*. Chicago, IL: Aldine.

Glaser, B. & Strauss, A. (1968) *Time For Dying*. Chicago, IL: Aldine.

Gorer, G. (1965) *Death, Grief and Mourning in Contemporary Britain*. London: Cresset Press.

Herd, E. (1990) Terminal care in a semi-rural area. *Br. J. gen. Practice,* **40,** 248–51.

Hinton, J. (1967) *Dying*. London: Penguin

Hinton, J. (1979) Comparison of places and policies for terminal care. *Lancet,* **ii,** 29–32.

Hinton, J. (1980) Whom do dying patients tell? *Br. med. J.,* **281,** 1328–1330.

Hinton, J. (1984) Coping with terminal illness. In: *The Experience of Illness,* ed. R. Fitzpatrick, J. Hinton, S. Newman, G. Scambler & J. Thompson. London: Tavistock.

Kamerman, J. (1988) *Death in the Midst of Life: Social and Cultural Influences on Death, Grief and Mourning*. Englewood Cliffs, NJ: Prentice Hall.

Kubler-Ross, E. (1970) *On Death and Dying*. London: Tavistock.

Lofland, L. (1978) *The Craft of Dying: The Modern Face of Death*. Beverly Hills, CA: Sage Publications.

McIntosh, J. (1977) *Communication and Awareness in a Cancer Ward*. London: Croom Helm.

Parkes, C. (1984) 'Hospice' versus 'hospital' care: a re-evaluation after 10 years as seen by surviving spouses. *Postgrad. med. J.,* **50,** 120–124.

Sudnow, D. (1967) *Passing On: The Social Organization of Dying*. New York: Prentice Hall.

Taylor, K. (1988) 'Telling bad news': physicians and the disclosure of undesirable information. *Soc. Hlth Illness,* **10,** 109–132.

Ward, A. (1974) Terminal care in malignant disease. *Soc. Sci. Med.,* **8,** 233.

PART III

Social structure and health

8

Inequality and social class

David Blane

In Bethnal Green in the year 1839 the average age of death in the several classes was as follows: 'Gentlemen and persons engaged in professions, and their families ... 45 years; tradesmen and their families ... 26 years; Mechanics, servants and labourers, and their families ... 16 years' (Chadwick 1842). The average age of deaths in these social classes was found to vary somewhat from area to area, but similar differences between the classes were found in all areas of Britain.

Although 'the average age of death' would be criticized today as a measure which is over-sensitive to high childhood mortality, Chadwick's study provided some of the first evidence that health varies with social class. The population's general level of health has improved dramatically since the first half of the nineteenth century, but subsequent investigations have shown that a relationship between mortality rates and social class remains. This has been repeatedly confirmed and shown to apply to morbidity measures as well (DHSS 1980). It is important, therefore, to understand both what is meant by 'social class' and why it should be related to health indicators of many kinds. With this in mind, this chapter starts with details of some modern inequalities and of different ways of accounting for them, the most influential of which draws on concepts of social class. It then goes on to examine the relationship between social class and health.

SOME DIMENSIONS OF INEQUALITY IN THE UK

Wealth and income

Wealth, defined in terms of marketable assets, is very unequally distributed. In 1985 the richest 1% of the population aged 18 or over owned 20% of the country's total personal wealth, and the richest 10% over half. The poorest 75% of the population owned approximately the same as the richest 1% (CSO 1989). The form of this wealth varied with its distribution. Some two-thirds of the wealth of those owning £50 000–100 000 in 1984 consisted of homes and life insurance policies, while land and company shares contributed a mere 6%. In contrast, land and company shares accounted for 50% of the wealth of those owning more than £300 000, and homes and life-insurance policies 17% (Board of Inland Revenue 1989). It can be argued that the wealth which is owned by the majority of the population is used in an attempt to guarantee the necessities of life, while the wealth of the rich also brings with it social power, in the sense of ownership of land and voting rights in the decisions of financial and industrial corporations.

Income, which mainly consists of earnings from employment but also includes investment income and the various state benefits, is more equally distributed than wealth. After income tax had been deducted, the top 10% of 'taxable units' (married couples are counted as one unit) received over one-quarter of total personal income in 1985, and the top 50% nearly three-quarters. The bottom 50% of taxable units received approximately the same as the top 10% (CSO 1989). Access to state facilities such as the education system and health service can also be seen as part of income, as can benefits in kind which are received on top of earnings from employment. Whilst those on low incomes derive marginally greater benefit from the former, benefits in kind disproportionately go to those with high incomes and tend to be greatest for those with the highest salaries. Thus, large inequalities in income remain despite the redistribution achieved by mechanisms such as income tax, state benefits and access to state facilities.

Living conditions

As would be expected in a market economy, the differences in income and wealth result in differences in such things as diet, possessions and housing. Compared to that of the better paid, the diet of the low paid contains far less fresh fruit, significantly less fresh vegetables, fresh fish and cheese, and more white bread, potatoes, sugar, lard and margarine (MAFF 1989). A car was owned by 92% of households whose weekly income in 1988 exceeded £350, central heating by 87%, a washing machine by 94% and a telephone by 95%; in contrast, a car was owned by only 34% of households receiving less than £100 per week, central heating by 67%, a washing machine by 80% and a telephone by 78% (CSO 1990). In 1986, 2.9 million dwellings in England, or 15% of the total stock, were inadequate in one or more of the following respects: unfit for habitation (0.9 million); lack of basic hygienic amenities (0.45 million); in need of urgent repairs costing more than £1000 (2.4 million). Living in poor housing was strongly related to income. Households with an annual income of less than £6000 accounted for 69% of dwellings which were unit for habitation, 76% of those which lacked basic hygienic amenities and 55% of dwellings in poor repair; the comparable figures for households with an annual income of over £15 000 were 2%, 1% and 4%, respectively (Department of the Environment 1988). In addition, the homes of families on low incomes were more likely to be in areas where the air was polluted with industrial waste and, lacking gardens, their children were more likely to have to play in an already overcrowded flat, or in the street.

Working conditions

An individual's income is strongly tied to the nature of their work. Sixty percent of male manual workers were paid a basic hourly rate of £5 or less in 1989, compared with 20% of non-manual workers, and virtually no manual workers were paid more than £11 per hour, compared with 20% of non-manual workers. For a number of reasons the difference in total weekly pay is not as great as the difference in the hourly rate. Manual workers work a greater number of hours per week, with three-quarters in 1989 having a basic working week of more than 38 hours, compared with one-quarter of non-manual workers, and 60% working overtime compared with 25% of non-manual workers. Manual workers are also more likely to work shifts, which attract additional payment, and to be paid some form of production bonus. Approximately one-third of manual workers' earnings are derived from overtime, shift payments and production bonuses and, in 1989, if these had been removed, the proportion of manual workers earning less than £200 per week would have increased from half to four-fifths (Department of Employment 1989). As these additional sources of income are likely to vary from week to week, it is more difficult for manual workers and their families to make financially sound plans, a disadvantage which is reinforced by manual workers' greater likelihood of being made redundant. Of considerable financial importance after retirement, manual workers are less likely to be members of an occupational pension scheme than non-manual workers; in 1987, 80% of professional workers were members of such schemes, compared with less than 50% of manual workers (OPCS 1989).

Manual work is usually more physically demanding, noisier and more dangerous than non-manual work (Hunter 1975), as well as being more likely to involve the physical and social disruption of shift work. Despite its more hazardous nature, manual work lasts longer than non-manual work. Manual workers enter the work-force at an earlier age and, as has been noted, their basic working week is likely to be longer and they are more likely to work overtime. In addition, their holidays are shorter, with non-manual workers being more likely to receive in excess of 5 weeks holiday per year. Manual work is also more likely to be repetitive than the work of professionals and managers, to offer little autonomy and to be experienced as boring. Perhaps as a result, manual workers are subject to closer supervision and tighter discipline; most have to clock in to work, automatically lose money when late for work, face dismissal if continually late, and many need a supervisor's permission to use the lavatory or obtain a drink outside of the set work-breaks.

POVERTY

The inequalities so far documented have been illustrated in terms of manual compared with non-manual, professional compared with unskilled, and so on. Such comparisons are useful because they indicate the direction and size of the general trends, but they can create the misleading impression that the work-force is divided into homogeneous blocks whose members share the same income and living and working conditions and that these, in turn, are clearly higher or lower than those of the next block. In reality there is considerable variation in income and conditions within each block and considerable overlap between them. As a result there is always room for debate about where it is appropriate to draw lines on this continuous distribution in order to identify specific groups. This problem complicates the definition of poverty, and attempts to identify those who are exposed to poverty first need to be clear about the sense in which the term is being used.

The term 'poverty' has been used in two ways. Absolute poverty refers to a standard of living which is incapable of sustaining life. When the term is used in this sense it could describe, for example, destitute people in the drought-stricken areas of the Sahel. One problem with this definition, however, is its failure to specify how long people can live before their standard of living is judged incapable of sustaining life. As the experience of hunger-strikers demonstrates, no standard of living is so low as to kill instantaneously, and low-grade malnutrition may only influence mortality after many years. In addition, because very few people in the rich countries of the world are starving, using the term poverty in its absolute sense fails to address the hardships which are endured by many members of these societies.

Relative poverty refers to a standard of living below that which is considered normal or acceptable by the members of a particular society. 'The resources (of those in relative poverty) are so seriously below those commanded by the average individual or family that they are, in effect, excluded from ordinary living patterns, customs and activities' (Townsend 1979). Using the term in this relative sense allows the concept of poverty to be applied to rich societies such as Britain, although for research purposes it does pose the problem of how to establish empirically what is considered normal or acceptable in a particular society. This relative 'poverty line' can be established by means of surveys, but a less expensive method which is frequently used in research is to equate relative poverty with an income below the State's Supplementary Benefit rate.

The most recent classic study of poverty in the UK found that 7% of households, containing 3.3 million people, received an income below the Supplementary Benefit rate, and that a further 24% of households which contained 11.9 million people were on the margins of poverty, defined as an income less than 40% above the Supplementary Benefit rate. When those in poverty were analysed according to their labour market, personal and other characteristics, the three largest groups were those employed on low wages or in casual work, the disabled and long-term sick and the elderly retired, with the unemployed and one-parent families being the next largest groups (Townsend 1979). While the numbers living in poverty have probably increased since this survey was made, there is no reason to believe that the characteristics of those who are most vulnerable to poverty have changed.

A potential shortcoming of such cross-sectional data is the extent to which they obscure the association between poverty and certain phases of the life cycle. In societies where incomes are primarily derived from the labour market and where human reproduction predominantly occurs within nuclear families, there is an in-built tendency for an individual's standard of living to be lowest during childhood, active parenthood and old age, and to be highest during the intervening phases. This longitudinal approach has certain advantages: it draws attention to the association between poverty and childhood; it reminds us that those who are not currently living in poverty may have experienced it in the past or may realistically expect to experience it in the future; and it enables us to see that it is often the same individuals whose standard of living will dip below the poverty line during the low phases of the life cycle. Thus, the child reared in poverty is educationally handicapped and is likely to be an early entrant to the unskilled sector of the labour market, where low wages and insecure employment will make family formation financially difficult and where the lack of an occupational pension scheme will predispose to poverty after retirement. Some idea of the proportion of the population which is likely to experience relative poverty at some stage during their lives is given by combining those who were found to be in poverty with those who were on its margins in the study quoted earlier; that is, 31% of households or 15 million people. Rather than being a marginal problem, therefore, poverty or the realistic fear of it is a fact of life for a substantial proportion of the population.

There is a considerable overlap between medical problems and poverty or the phases of the life cycle where the standard of living tends to dip. The size of this overlap is illustrated by the 75% of prescriptions which are exempt from charges, a figure which can rise to 90% in some areas. The medical consequences of poverty start before birth, with poor maternal nutrition contributing to prematurity and low birth weight. During childhood, poor nutrition inhibits normal growth and development, lack of hygienic facilities pre-disposes to infestations with scabies, head lice and intestinal worms, damp housing increases the incidence of upper-respiratory-tract infections which may lead to chronic ear disease, partial deafness and a poor educational record, and lack of play facilities hinders psychological development and increases the risk of accidents. During active parenthood the health hazards stem from attempts to maximize income. Men may seek the premiums attached to shift work, or the 'danger money' associated with hazardous jobs, as well as working overtime, taking a second part-time job on top of their main employment or working in the informal economy where poor health-and-safety conditions predominate. Such strategies increase income, but at the cost of physical exhaustion, risk of accidents, disrupted family life and increased vulnerability to depression in the mothers alone at home with their young children. Other, psycho-logical, effects include exhaustion by the ceaseless struggle to 'make ends meet' and low self-esteem because of failure in this struggle, shame because one's children cannot have the same things as other children and fear lest the furniture is repossessed, the gas or electricity is cut off or one is made homeless because of insufficient money to pay hire purchase installments, energy bills and rent. During old age the health effects of poverty reflect both immediate problems and the accumulation of past effects. Malnutrition ('tea and toast syndrome') and hypothermia are obvious examples, although the large increase in mortality during the winter compared with the summer months is probably a more important effect.

In summary, then, relative poverty affects a sizeable proportion of the British population. Because of the relationship between poverty and ill health, an even larger proportion of the patients whom doctors treat are likely to be affected in some way by its associated problems.

SOCIAL STRATIFICATION

Many other areas of inequality could have been documented in addition to those considered above, including, for example, education, career prospects and leisure activities (Reid 1989). These inequalities tend to go together in such a way that an individual who is disadvantaged on one dimension is likely to be disadvantaged on the others, and someone who is advantaged on one is likely to be advantaged on the others. The term 'social stratification' refers generally to this kind of socially structured inequality, and the concept of social class describes the form which social stratification takes in societies such as contemporary Britain. Most societies to date have been hierarchically structured in some way. Historical forms of stratification have included, for example, the Hindu caste system and the various estates of feudal society. Some social theorists, drawing on the work of the early German sociologist Max Weber, consider that the stratification of modern industrial societies involves three main dimensions: social class, social status or honour, and the political power of organized groups. Although class, status and power are usually related, so that, for example, unskilled labourers generally have low social status and little political influence, they are analytically distinct and can vary independently of one another. While it is generally agreed that social class is the most fundamental dimension of stratification, sociologists often differ in their precise definition and treatment of class and there are thus a number of competing theories.

The theory most commonly used involves the division of the population into two stereotyped groups of roughly equal size. 'Middle class' people are characterized as earning monthly salaries in non-manual jobs, borrowing money to buy their own houses and encouraging their children to get as much formal education as possible. 'Working-class' people, in contrast, are described as earning weekly wages in manual jobs, renting their homes from a Local Authority and trying to get their children started in a good job as soon

Table 1
Registrar General's classification of social classes

Social class	Description	Examples	% of economically active and retired Males	Females
I	Professional	Accountant Doctor Lawyer	5	1
II	Intermediate	Manager School teacher Nurse	22	21
IIIN	Skilled non-manual	Clerical worker Secretary Shop assistant	12	39
IIIM	Skilled manual	Bus driver Coal-face worker Carpenter	36	9
IV	Semi-skilled manual	Agricultural worker Bus conductor Postman	18	22
V	Unskilled manual	Labourer Cleaner Dock worker	7	7

Source: Reid (1989: Tables 2.6 and 3.1).

as they are allowed to leave school. Most of the population appear to have little difficulty in placing themselves in one or other of these two classes. One study which included an unprompted question about self-rated social class found that 40% of the population spontaneously described themselves as middle class and 48% as working class, a distinction which was mainly based on differences in life-style, but also influenced by considerations of family background, job and money (Townsend 1979). While this class scheme is primarily based on general life-style, a second, deriving from the work of Marx, is based on a group's relationship to the processes which produce society's wealth. This results in a division of the population into two social classes of markedly different size: a small 'capitalist class' which receives the profits derived from its ownership and control of the land, factories and financial institutions, and a 'working class' consisting of the overwhelming majority of the population, whose possessions are limited to necessities and whose members have to sell their mental or physical labour power in order to live.

For research purposes a more precise definition of social class is generally necessary. Many scales have been devised to meet this need, although each of these has its own particular strengths and weaknesses. The Registrar General's classification (Table 1), which is the most widely used, divides the population into five social classes, I–V, with social class III being further subdivided into non-manual (IIIN) and manual (IIIM). This system of classification is based on occupation, and it groups occupations into social classes according to their general social standing in the community. Men are allocated to a particular social class on the basis of their occupation, married women on the basis of their husband's occupation, children on that of their father and the retired and unemployed on that of their last significant period of employment. Single women are classified on the basis of their own occupation (OPCS 1980).

Certain characteristics of the Registrar General's classification need to be appreciated. Because it is based upon the general social standing of different occupations, it is primarily a measure of status rather than economic class or living standards. This, for example, allows certain professions whose low pay is notorious to be placed in social class I alongside the other professions. As the earlier comments on Weber indicate, however, status is, in general, sufficiently strongly linked to economic class for the classification to act as a reasonable indicator of such factors as lifetime earnings and conditions of life. Secondly, each of the Registrar General's social classes is far from being internally homogeneous. Social class II, for example, contains both tenant farmers working a few dozen acres and farmers who own thousands of acres; similarly, it contains both the corner shopkeeper and the senior manager in a multinational company. Finally, the Registrar General's classification deals inadequately with women's employment, which, among other things, weakens its power as an indicator of living standards. Married women are classified by the occupation of their husband, although the standard of living of the family's members can be decisively affected by whether or not the wife/mother has paid employment; for example, it has been calculated that the number of families living in poverty would double if they were deprived of these earnings. Despite these problems, the classification is widely used in research. It is convenient to use, having clear decision rules which allow virtually every member of the population to be placed into one of five classes, and its long-standing use in a wide range of research areas facilitates the comparison of findings from different studies. It also has proved capable of identifying social differences in most areas of life, although, as the earlier comments indicate, its use is likely to provide conservative estimates of the size of these differences.

——— **Table 2** ———
Social class and deaths due to all causes
(England and Wales; 1979–80, 1982–83).

Social class	Still-birth rate*	Infant mortality rate†	Mortality rate 1–15 years‡	Standardized mortality ratio§
Males				20–64 years
I	5	9	0.3	66
II	6	10	0.2	74
IIIN	6	10	0.3	93
IIIM	7	12	0.3	103
IV	9	15	0.4	114
V	9	18	0.6	159
Females				20–59 years
I	4	7	0.2	68
II	5	8	0.2	76
IIIN	6	8	0.2	86
IIIM	7	9	0.2	97
IV	8	12	0.3	108
V	8	13	0.4	130

Source: OPCS (1986, 1988).
* Number of deaths per 1000 live and dead births; rounded to the nearest integer.
† Number of deaths in the first year of life per 1000 live births; rounded to the nearest iteger.
‡ Number of deaths per 1000 population aged 1–15 years; rounded to one decimal place.
§ The ratio of the observed mortality rate in a social class to its expected rate from the total population, multiplied by 100.

SOCIAL CLASS AND HEALTH

As the quotation from Chadwick in the opening paragraph of this chapter illustrates, it has long been recognized that the various positions in the social hierarchy are associated with different chances of premature death. Good quality data on the relationship between social class and mortality in England and Wales have been published each decade for most of the twentieth century. The data reproduced in Table 2 are the most recently available, but the general pattern which they reveal has been a constant feature of all the earlier reports. The mortality rates increase as one moves from the Registrar General's social class I to social class V, with the mortality rate of the latter being approximately twice that of the former. This social-class gradient in total deaths due to all causes is found among both men and women and within all age groups up to age 65 years, although the differences tend to narrow with increasing age.

——— **Table 3** ———

Social class and main causes of death (England and Wales; 1979–80, 1982–83): standardized mortality ratios.

Cause of death	Social class					
	I	II	IIIN	IIIM	IV	V
Males 20–64 years						
Ischaemic heart disease	69	81	102	106	110	137
Lung cancer	42	62	78	117	125	175
Cerebrovascular disease	61	70	88	105	114	171
Bronchitis	34	49	84	109	134	208
Motor-vehicle accidents	64	75	79	101	114	175
Pneumonia	34	49	80	89	121	211
Suicide	86	78	94	84	110	190
Females 20–59 years						
Ischaemic heart disease	41	55	69	106	119	152
Breast cancer	107	103	105	100	99	94
Cerebrovascular disease	58	69	79	105	117	144
Bronchitis	33	54	71	100	119	165
Motor-vehicle accidents	76	89	102	63	94	114
Pneumonia	37	51	67	86	110	140
Suicide	77	81	99	55	76	84

Source: OPCS (1986).

The specific causes of death listed in Table 3 are the most prevalent for each sex, and they jointly account for some 50% of all deaths in this age group. In most cases the mortality rates increase as one moves from social class I to class V, and thus show the same gradient as deaths due to all causes. There are exceptions, however, which show no social-class gradient, and breast cancer in women is the most prevalent of these. Also, unlike the gradient for deaths due to all causes, the social-class gradient for some causes of death has changed during this century. Coronary heart disease is the most prominent of these; its mortality rate was highest in social class I and lowest in class V for the first half of the century, this gradient flattened out in the third quarter and reversed in the final quarter so that its mortality rate is now highest in social class V and lowest in class I.

The data presented so far have been mortality rates, and their use as a measure of health has certain advantages. In the vast majority of cases death is an unambiguous event which can, therefore, be recorded with high reliability. Death is also one of the few times that an individual is legally obliged to be seen by a doctor, with the result that the recording of death is virtually complete. Mortality rates, therefore, are reliable and complete measures. They are not perfect measures of health, however, because the term 'health' implies something more than simply the absence of premature death (see

Chapter 18). As a result, attempts to understand the relationship between social class and health have recently begun to examine the way in which morbidity (illness) varies with social class.

For a variety of reasons, the measurement of morbidity is less reliable and complete than that of mortality. Manual workers consult doctors more frequently than non-manual workers (OPCS 1989) but this measure, like all measures which depend upon consultation patterns, is more precisely a measure of illness behaviour (see Chapter 3) than of morbidity; indeed, the class gradient reverses when 'use/need ratios' are used to relate consultation rates to the prevalence of illness in the various social classes. Manual workers are also found to report more illnesses of all types (acute, long-standing, and limiting long-standing) than non-manual workers, with the differences tending to widen in the older age groups (OPCS 1989). These measures, however, like all measures which depend upon self-reported morbidity, involve subjective judgements about illness and its severity. The observed class differences on these measures may thus be reflecting systematic variation in these judgements due, for example, to the more physically demanding nature of manual occupations. Finally, some studies have used clinical measures of morbidity on samples of the whole population, and these studies should, therefore, provide results which are free from possible contamination by illness behaviour and systematic subjective variation. Among middle-aged men in the British Regional Heart Study, for example, manual workers were more likely to experience angina than non-manual workers, and similar social-class differences were also found in obesity and, to a lesser extent, in blood pressure (Pocock et al. 1987; Weatherall and Shaper 1988; Shaper et al 1988). Among men and women of working age in the Health and Lifestyle Survey, manual workers were more likely to experience psychological malaise and to have poorer respiratory function and, to a lesser extent, higher blood pressure than non-manual workers (Cox et al. 1987). Unfortunately, studies of this type are relatively expensive and are thus rarely conducted. When they are undertaken, they are often primarily concerned with a particular disease, and their results therefore give an incomplete picture of social-class differences in overall morbidity. In addition, like all surveys, they suffer from non-responders who are selected but choose not to take part, and their results therefore are not based upon the complete coverage achieved by mortality data.

In summary then, for many decades reliable and complete data have revealed social-class differences in mortality, with members of social class V having approximately twice the chance of dying at any particular age as members of social class I. More recently, attention has turned to morbidity which is a more valid measure of health than mortality, although more difficult to measure with comparable reliability and completeness. Social-class differences have nevertheless been found in various measures of morbidity, although the size of these differences may vary considerably and may be absent in particular age groups. This lack of a perfect match between social-class differences in mortality and in morbidity is not surprising. Not only is the measurement of morbidity in its comparative infancy, but some major causes of death, such as accidents and violence, need not be preceded by illness and disease, and some common serious diseases, such as arthritis and depression, rarely cause death.

INTERPRETATION OF THE RELATIONSHIP BETWEEN SOCIAL CLASS AND HEALTH

The association between social class and health shows that death and disease are socially structured, as opposed to being randomly distributed throughout the population, and that they vary in line with the differences in living standards which were documented earlier. However, correlation does not imply causation, and the relationship needs to be examined further in order to establish the status and direction of causality. This can best be achieved by using the explanatory framework which was first developed by the Department of Health's Research Working Group on Inequalities in Health (DHSS 1980). Their report, which has become eponymously known as the Black Report, suggested four types of explanation of social-class differences in health: artefact, social selection, behavioural/cultural and materialist.

Artefact

The artefact type of explanation examines the possibility that observed social-class differences in mortality may be an artefact of the process by which these two variables are measured. An example of this type of explanation is numerator–denominator bias. The Black Report had to rely on the conventional mortality rates which are derived from two sources; death registration which provides the number of deaths and the Decennial Census which provides the number of people in the population. It is possible that an individual's occupation may be described sufficiently differently at these two events for them to be assigned to one social class at census and another at death. The higher mortality rates of social classes IV and V could, in consequence, result from semi-skilled and unskilled manual occupations being more precisely described at death registration than on the census form. The OPCS Longitudinal Study (LS), which is following a 1% sample of the 1971 census population, was partly designed to eliminate this potential bias. It achieved this aim by categorizing individuals at death according to their social class at the 1971 census, and found social-class differences in mortality which are similar to, although smaller than, those which depend upon death registration and the census (Fox & Goldblatt 1982). This exercise thus both confirmed that social-class differences in mortality are not an artefact of registration and raised the question of the size of these differences.

Although eliminating numerator–denominator bias may narrow the size of social-class differences in mortality, other aspects of the conventional measures of social class and mortality have the opposite effect. The wide range of living standards within each of the Registrar General's social classes has already been noted, and the differences in mortality which appear when this measure of social class is used can be compared with those found in particular industries, where each employment grade is much more homogeneous in terms of its standard of living. Such comparisons are only available in the case of deaths due to coronary heart disease, but these reveal differences between the top and the bottom of the social hierarchy which are considerably wider than those found between social classes I and V on the Registrar General's classification (Davey Smith et al. 1990). The other side of the relationship between social class and mortality is conventionally expressed in terms of the standardized mortality ratio, which has been criticized for failing to give due weight to differences in the age at which death occurs. When a measure of mortality is used which does weight deaths in this way, the resulting class differences are found to be wider than those revealed by the standardized mortality ratio (Blane et al. 1990). The artefact explanation, therefore, is unable to account for class differences in mortality, although its various forms do have countervailing implications for the size of these differences. On balance, though, the differences shown in Table 2 are probably conservative estimates.

Social selection

The social selection explanation accepts that social class and health are causally related, and hypothesizes that health determines social class through a process of health-related social mobility in which the healthy are more likely to move up the social hierarchy and the unhealthy to move down. There is little doubt that chronically sick and disabled people may be additionally disadvantaged in this manner, although they have a range of other options from which to choose such as early retirement, unemployment or a move to a similar but less demanding job none of which involve downward social mobility on the Registrar General's scheme, although all are likely to entail a reduction in income. Similarly, those who are taller than average, and in this context height is taken as an indicator of good health, have been found to have a greater than average chance of upward social mobility (Power et al. 1986). Health-related social mobility is, therefore, a real phenomenon which could, in theory, account for social-class differences in health. Whether or not it does so has become an important question for research.

Two pieces of evidence relevant to this question come from the OPCS Longitudinal Study (LS). Firstly, the LS has been able to follow individuals after retirement and so for the first time produce data on social-class difference in mortality at ages over 65 years. These show that class differences at ages 65–74 years and at ages 75 years and over are virtually identical to those found during the years of working life (Fox et al. 1985). The post-retirement differences, unlike those during working life, could not be due to health-related social mobility because, in the Registrar General's scheme, a retired individual's social class is fixed by their last significant period of employment and thus social mobility is no longer possible. Secondly, as most deaths during the years of working life occur at ages 45–64 years, the LS examined mortality in this age group in relation to the social mobility which occurred between the 1971 and 1981 censuses. This analysis failed to identify any clear relationship between mobility and mortality. The upwardly mobile in some cases had higher mortality rates than the class they left and in others lower mortality rates. The downwardly mobile, similarly, in some cases had lower mortality rates than the class they left and in others higher mortality rates. In aggregate the mortality of those changing social class was not found to differ markedly from those whose social class did not alter, and the movement of individuals between social classes was found to have little effect on class mortality differentials (Goldblatt 1989). These findings from the LS indicate that social mobility plays little part in accounting for social-class differences in mortality at ages over 45 years.

If health-related social mobility makes a significant contribution, therefore, its effect on mortality differentials will be confined to the years between birth and age 45 years. Between birth and labour-market entry a young person is assigned to one of the Registrar General's social classes on the basis of their father's occupation. In consequence, a young person's health can only indirectly influence their social position. A father, for example, might be forced into downward mobility as a result of the time needed to care for a chronically sick child. Alternatively, the children of a sick, downwardly mobile father might suffer worse health because of either an inherited disease or reduced living standards. At present these remain theoretical possibilities, although judgements about their plausibility need to take account of the likelihood that the health of fathers will influence their social mobility between labour-market entry and age 45 years.

Studies of social mobility have found that it most commonly occurs during the early years of working life and that mobility between the middle class and the working class becomes unusual after men have passed their mid-twenties. These more general studies have also found that educational achievement, the type of secondary school attended, and the cultural and material background of the family of origin are the main influences on social mobility, which implies that the effect of health on social mobility at these ages is likely to be small. This conclusion is supported by the age distribution of morbidity. The age groups between labour-market entry and 45 years experience relatively low mortality and morbidity, and the prevalent chronic diseases do not start to impair health seriously until after this period. This is thus a mismatch between the ages at which social mobility is common and those at which impaired health is prevalent, which makes it unlikely that the latter can have a significant impact on the former. The social selection explanation, therefore, is potentially applicable to the first half of life only, and at these ages its contribution to social class differences in health is probably small.

Behavioural/cultural and materialist

The next two types of explanation suggested by the Black Report both accept that social class and health are causally related, and that social class in some way affects health. They differ, however, in the level at which they hypothesize this effect. Behavioural/cultural explanations stress social class differences in behaviours which damage or fail to promote health and which, at least in principle, are subject to individual choice. Materialist explanations, in contrast, concentrate upon hazards which are inherent in society and to which some people have no choice but to be exposed, given the present distribution of income and opportunity.

Social class differences in the consumption of tobacco, alcohol and highly processed foods are examples of behavioural/cultural explanations, as are class differences in leisure-time activities and the use of preventive medical services such as immunization, contraception and antenatal surveillance. Considerable weight is given to this type of explanation by the evidence which has accumulated as a result of medicine's long interest in such issues. However, the social and economic context in which these behaviours occur also needs to be recognized. Diet, for example, is influenced by both cultural preferences and disposable income, and the ability of nicotine to maintain a constant mood in situations of stress and monotony may predispose towards cigarette smoking in repetitive and highly supervised occupations. Other evidence further cautions against a one-sided emphasis on behavioural factors. Earlier this century, for example, cigarette smoking was more prevalent among the middle class than the working class, but class gradients in respiratory and all-causes mortality were similar to the present. Similarly, intervention studies have rarely produced the clear-cut improvements in health which would be predicted by the behavioural/cultural approach, despite achieving reduction in the hazardous behaviours. The behavioural/cultural type of explanation, therefore, can go some way towards accounting for social-class differences in health, although such behaviours need to be seen in their material context and uncertainty remains about their importance relative to materialist explanations.

The Black Report judged that materialist explanations were the most important in accounting for social class differences in health. The health-damaging effects of physico-chemical exposures in certain occupations have long been recognized, while more recently the additional importance of income and psycho-social factors in this respect have also been demonstrated. Damp housing has been shown to be associated with worse health and, particularly, with higher rates of respiratory disease in children. Both the men who were recorded as unemployed at the 1971 census, and their wives, have been found to have higher mortality rates than employed men and their wives. Finally, small-area studies have found a strong ecological correlation between material deprivation and both raised mortality and morbidity. Each of these factors could contribute to class differences in health because hazardous work, poor quality housing, unemployment and material deprivation are all more likely to be experienced by the working class than the middle class.

There is thus a certain amount of evidence which supports the materialist type of explanation, although most medical researchers would probably judge behavioural/cultural factors, and cigarette smoking in particular, to be of greater importance. The primacy assigned to materialist explanations by the Black Report can, nevertheless, be defended on the grounds that research so far has ignored the accumulation of advantage or disadvantage which is associated with social class. As the earlier sections of this chapter have indicated, inequalities are found on many dimensions of existence and social class is the concept which stresses the likelihood that disadvantage on any one dimension will be associated with disadvantage on others. Thus the psycho-social disadvantages of many manual occupations are likely to be combined with noisy, physically demanding work as well as disadvantages in the domestic sphere such as inadequate rest, dampness and family anxiety over financial matters. It will not be possible to make a secure judgement about the relative importance of behavioural/cultural and materialist

explanations until the effect on health of such combined disadvantages has been established.

THE OVERALL PICTURE

As a result of the work of social researchers such as Chadwick, the
Victorians became aware of the vicious circle of 'poverty causes
disease which causes poverty'. Despite the subsequent development
of the welfare state, those in poor health, and particularly the chronic
sick, are still at risk of relative poverty and downward social mobility.
This side of the Victorian's vicious circle, however, would now
appear to be of lesser importance overall than the side which stresses
the effect of material well-being, or the lack of it, on health. In other
words, class differences in mortality are primarily due to the
combined effect of class differences in exposure to factors which
promote health or cause disease.

This was the conclusion reached by the Department of Health
Working Group which produced the Black Report. The Report went
on to suggest measures for starting to eliminate these inequalities in
health. There are 37 of these recommendations; a few of them are
designed to ensure better information about class differences in
health, but most were carefully targeted at a limited number of issues
where class differences in health were thought to be both widest and
most likely to respond to relatively small sums of money. Disability,
for example, was the subject of six recommendations which
attempted to break its links with poverty. These covered prevention
(fetal screening for neural tube defects and Down's syndrome),
welfare procedures (a comprehensive disablement allowance, with
the severity of disablement assessed in terms of limitation of activities
rather than loss of faculty or type of handicap), housing (expand
specialist housing for disabled people) and community-care services
(shift resources towards home-help and nursing services for disabled
people). This set of recommendations appears designed to prevent
disability where this is presently possible (fetal screening) and, where
it is not, to ensure that the lives of working-class people with
disabilities are not markedly disadvantaged in terms of income
(welfare procedures) and living conditions (housing and community
services) compared with those of people with disabilities in the
middle class.

In addition to disability, equally detailed recommendations were
made concerning infant and child health, cigarette smoking, occupational health and safety, and Local Authority housing. Particular
priority was given to the abolition of child poverty by means of a new
infant-care allowance, increased child benefit and the provision of
free school meals. These recommendations, in common with the rest

of the report, were described by the Government as 'unrealistic' and the report was published 'without any commitment by the Government to its proposals'. Nevertheless, subsequent research has greatly increased our understanding of the relationship between social class and health and the Government, through its involvement in the World Health Organization's campaign for 'Health for All by the Year 2000', has since committed itself to narrowing class differences in health by that date. A subsequent authoritative review of changes in this area during the 1980s, however, found that child poverty, for example, was increasing rather than decreasing and suggested that on present policies the Government was unlikely to succeed in attaining its target (Whitehead 1987).

REFERENCES

Blane, D., Davey Smith, G. & Bartley, M. (1990) Social class differences in years of potential life lost: size, trends and principal causes. *Br. med. J.,* **301,** 429–432.

Board of Inland Revenue (1989) *Inland Revenue Statistics 1989.* London: HMSO.

Central Statistical Office (1989) *Social Trends 19.* London: HMSO.

Central Statistical Office (1990) *Family Expenditure Survey 1988.* London: HMSO.

Chadwick, E. (1842) *Report on the Sanitary Condition of the Labouring Populating of Great Britain 1842.* Edinburgh: Edinburgh University Press, 1965.

Cox, B.D., Blaxter, M., Buckle, A.L.J., et al. (1987) *The Health and Lifestyle Survey: Preliminary Report.* London: Health Promotion Research Trust.

Davey Smith, G., Shipley, M.J. & Rose, G. (1990) The magnitude and causes of socio-economic differentials in mortality: further evidence from the Whitehall study. *J. Epidem. Commun. Hlth,* **44,** 265–270.

Department of Employment (1989) *New Earnings Survey 1989.* London: HMSO.

Department of the Environment (1988) *English House Condition Survey 1986.* London: HMSO.

Department of Health and Social Security (1980) *Inequalities in Health: Report of a Research Working Group (The Black Report).* London: HMSO.

Fox, A.J. & Goldblatt, P.O. (1982) *Longitudinal Study: Socio-demographic Mortality Differentials.* London: HMSO.

Fox, A.J., Goldblatt, P.O. & Jones, D.R. (1985) Social class mortality differentials: artefact, selection or life circumstances. *Journal of Epidemiology and Community Health,* **39,** 1–8.

Goldblatt, P.O. (1989) Mortality by social class 1971–85. *Popul. Trends,* **56,** 6–15.

Hunter, D. (1975) *The Diseases of Occupations,* 5th edition. English Universities Press.

Ministry of Agriculture, Fisheries and Food (1989) *Household Food Consumption and Expenditure 1988.* London: HMSO.

Office of Population Censuses and Surveys (1980) *Classification of Occupations 1980.* London: HMSO.

Office of Population Censuses and Surveys (1986) *Occupational Mortality: Decennial Supplement 1979–80, 1982–83.* London: HMSO.

Office of Population Censuses and Surveys (1988) *Occupational Mortality: Childhood Supplement 1979–80, 1982–83.* London: HMSO.
Office of Population Censuses and Surveys (1989) *General Household Survey 1987.* London: HMSO.
Pocock, S.J., Cook, D.G., Shaper, A.G. et al. (1987) Social class differences in ischaemic heart disease in British men. *Lancet,* **ii,** 197–201.
Power, C., Fogelman, K. & Fox, A.J. (1986) Health and social mobility during the early years of life. *Q. J. soc. Aff.,* **2,** 397–413.
Reid, I. (1989) *Social Class Differences in Britain,* 3rd edition. London: Fontana Press.
Shaper, A.G., Ashby, D. & Pocock, S.J. (1988) Blood pressure and hypertension in middle-aged British men. *J. Hypertens.,* **6,** 367–374.
Townsend, P. (1979) *Poverty in the United Kingdom.* London: Penguin.
Weatherall, R. & Shaper, A.G. (1988) Overweight and obesity in middle-aged British men. *J. clin. Nutr.,* **42,** 221–231.
Whitehead, M. (1987) *The Health Divide: Inequalities in Health in the 1980s.* Health Education Council.

9

Women as patients and providers

Sheila Hillier

The special issues surrounding women's health are important for several reasons: firstly, epidemiological evidence shows that there are differences in the disease patterns of women and men; secondly, female symptomatology and what is defined as illness in women are particularly good examples of the introduction of *social* definitions into what are often thought of as the purely scientific exercises of diagnosis and treatment; thirdly, looking at the way women are treated as patients is informative not only about how medical practices incorporate many of the socially derived stereotypes of sex and gender, but also how this helps to confine women to certain limited and limiting roles in society; fourthly, women form the major part of the health-care labour force, although they are under-represented in the higher echelons of the medical and administrative hierarchies.

THE HEALTH OF WOMEN

Mortality

In modern industrialized societies like Britain or the USA, women live longer than men and at every age there is an excess of male over female mortality. Life expectancy for both males and females has steadily increased over the last 100 years, but the average life expectancy of women is longer: at present in the UK it is 78 years for females and 72 years for males.

These differences appear to be related to social factors. For example, in less-developed countries female life expectancy is lower than that of males, and women are more likely to be malnourished and to have less access to health care. Moreover, there is little difference in female and male rates of death from the epidemics which afflict developing societies or which have occurred in the past in developed ones. The major change affecting the mortality of women over the last 100 years in Britain has been the change in patterns of child bearing and the consequent decline in maternal mortality. The average woman married in 1880 would expect to bear about five live children, whereas a woman married in 1990 will probably have only two. The other side of the coin, the excess of male mortality, seems to be related, at least partly, to the different living patterns of men and women. Typically, men are more likely to engage in activities which are injurious to health, both at work and during leisure activities: they drink more, smoke more, drive faster and work in more physically hazardous occupations than women (Waldron 1976). Men are more likely to commit suicide and to murder. In trying to live up to a stereotyped self-image of one's own sex, vulnerability to certain causes of death are increased, for example cirrhosis of the liver due to excessive drinking.

The excess of male over female mortality might be even greater were it not that a considerable number of women die of cancers of the breast, cervix and uterus. Thirty-nine per cent of deaths in women aged 25–44 years are from cancer, a third of these being malignant cancers of the breast. Even after the age of 44 years, when diseases of the circulatory system take over as the major cause of death in women as in men, breast cancer accounts for one in ten female deaths.

One important development needs to be noted, however. Since 1970, mortality/sex ratios have remained virtually unchanged and the advantage that females have over males has become stabilized and is not increasing. This does not represent a deterioration in the health of women, but a marked improvement in the rate of decline in mortality for men.

Women have not modified their smoking habits as dramatically as men. Whilst more men (35%) than women (31%) smoke, there was a 14% drop in the number of male smokers between 1972 and 1982, but only an 8% drop among women (OPCS 1984). As increasing numbers of women smokers enter the older age groups, when most smoking-related diseases occur, the lung-cancer deaths among women will rise. By 1988 they were over 50% higher than in 1974 (OPCS 1990). A quarter of all female deaths are from lung cancer. In the UK, women in social class V are one and a half times as likely to smoke as those in social class I.

There has been an increase in the number of mental-hospital admissions for alcoholism among women (OPCS 1984), but this may merely reflect a decline in the stigma associated with the condition. There is no evidence overall that women's drinking patterns are converging with those of men, but there is an increase in the number of women who are moderate to heavy drinkers. Between 1978 and 1987 women's average weekly consumption of alcohol increased by 14%. Consumption fell by 4% for men over the same period. It is still three times higher than for females (OPCS 1990) but the risks of cirrhosis for women are considerably greater than those for men. Single females drink more than married, divorced, widowed or separated women.

There are also iatrogenic risks of disease for women, and perhaps the most well known is that associated with the oral contraceptive pill, with dangers of cardiovascular disease being greatest for women over 40 years who are also heavy smokers. The administration of post-menopausal oestrogens also carries risks, as do hysterectomies.

It has been suggested that the mortality patterns of women will come to resemble men as differences in life-styles diminish, and this is particularly related to the growing participation of women in the labour market and their entry into a 'man's world'. In the UK at present about 50% of married women work full time, and 83% part time. This suggests that in addition to entering the work-force most women are doing two jobs, inside and outside the home, for sharing all domestic tasks equally between males and females is still unusual (OPCS 1984). It is estimated that, internationally, women work on average some 80 hours per week compared with their husbands' 50 hours per week and a recent survey showed that even when parents work full time the woman still takes on most of the child-care and household tasks (Jowell et al. 1988).

Occupational stress is thought to be a contributory factor in coronary heart disease and rates continue to rise in the UK. Women are hormonally protected prior to menopause. A study of women working inside and outside the home showed no difference in incidence between them and the rates remained lower than those for men (Haynes & Feinleb 1980). One particular group, however, were at greater risk — clerical and non-manual workers with children in a traditional female work role. It seems clear that it is not working as such that is a risk factor — women in high status work have fewer problems. It is rather the multiple stresses of relatively low status jobs, role expectations at work (e.g. pliability, submissiveness and suppression of anger) and heavy domestic burdens which are a source of danger.

A recent publication summarizing occupational risks to women indicates that most of the occupations which women have traditionally undertaken — nursing, sales, secretarial and clerical work — all carry environmental risks, but interest in improving occupational health has concentrated mainly upon the risks associated with conception and pregnancy. Environmental factors, as well as behaviour and situations related to employment, are all in some sense 'toxic', and these problems are most likely to occur among women manual workers and those in traditional female occupations (Denning 1984).

Overall, however, women still enjoy a more favourable mortality experience than men and social changes have, on the whole, been beneficial to them. Men, on the other hand, largely for cultural and social reasons, are less fortunate. However, the class dimension should not be ignored: men of social class I still have a lower overall mortality than women of social class V.

Morbidity

Much illness and suffering is occasioned by diseases which do not in themselves kill, but are often chronic and disabling. Because women live longer than men they are likely to experience the greater morbidity associated with age. At almost every age, however, more women than men report with chronic sickness. Women are more likely, for example, to suffer disability from strokes, rheumatoid arthritis, diabetes and varicose veins. In fact, two-thirds of the 4 million disabled and handicapped population in the UK are women. This fact, compared with women's relatively favourable mortality experience, requires some explanation.

Figures on morbidity are collected from general practitioners, from hospital, from the DHSS and occasionally from community studies or surveys like the *General Household Survey*. All these suggest higher morbidity among women, but difficulties in interpretation exist. For example, statistics from general practice indicate that women are more likely than men to consult their doctors: on average women visit their general practitioners six times per year, men four times (General Household Survey 1987). The average for both sexes has been rising, with the current average for men now approaching that for women of 10 years ago. Working women have a slightly lower consultation rate than housewives. These visits cannot be regarded as a true measure of illness, however, since not every symptom leads to a consultation (see Chapter 3). Contrary to the view that it is somehow 'easier' for a housewife to visit the doctor, there could equally be under-reporting of female morbidity because of women's domestic responsibilities. Data suggest that, as a group, housewives are less likely to regard themselves as being 'in excellent health' (Waldron 1976). It may be culturally more acceptable for women than for men to admit 'weakness' and seek help from others, which would suggest an under-reporting of *male* morbidity. It remains likely that the various statistics on morbidity do not afford a complete picture, but rather an approximation of actual sex differences in morbidity.

Because of this, one should beware of drawing too strong conclusions. For example, it is sometimes asserted that women have more mental illness than men. To attribute more to women than to men carries with it greater opportunities for making judgements, often of a stigmatizing kind, about the nature of women. As Standing (1980) says, 'an illness such as "depression" carries a much greater load of [these] messages and judgements than does, say, tonsillitis or malaria'.

If the effects of age and marital status are combined with sex, single males aged 35 years upwards have higher rates of admission to psychiatric hospitals than single women of the same age group. After the age of 65 there are twice as many women as men in psychiatric beds, but this reflects the greater number of women in that age group, as well as the possibility that men are more likely to be cared for by their spouses than women. 'Mental illness' is usually taken to mean psychosis and neurosis. Women are more frequently diagnosed as neurotic than men (although 'neurosis' is a less stable and reliable diagnostic assessment), but not as schizophrenic. If both diagnoses are aggregated — as they usually are — there is a bias in the combination which shows women to have a higher overall prevalence. Mental illness generally does not include alcoholism, personality disorders or acting-out behaviour more often displayed by men.

The causes of mental illness are sometimes attributed to women's social role, which is deemed to be more stressful than that of men, but a study of Camberwell women showed that five-times as many *working-class* women as middle-class women were chronically depressed, so clearly the class factor is important (Brown & Harris 1980). Studies of men's mental illness and social class show a similar concentration of morbidity in the lower social classes.

Some popular stereotypes exist to the effect that women are either intrinsically weaker or less stoical than men and unreasonably fussy about their physical condition. It is plausible, however, to suggest the opposite: that women are more sensitive to and commonsensical about matters of health and sickness, and that there are social pressures on men which lead them to take risks with their health and to fail to protect themselves.

THE SPECIAL PROBLEMS OF WOMEN

Sex and gender

In all known societies assumptions are made about what is
appropriate behaviour for men and for women. These assumptions
cover not only behaviour but also personal attributes. Social scientists
refer to them as sexual stereotypes. Such stereotypes are extremely
powerful, deriving much of their strength from the belief that
behaviour is biologically based, and that the most fundamental aspect
of any person's identity is his or her sex. From this it is but a short
step to deduce that the behaviours that men and women are
expected to exhibit, for example competitiveness and aggression in
men, passivity and nurturance in women, somehow reflect basic
differences between the sexes and are biologically determined.
Evidence from other cultures, however, shows that the personality
traits and behaviour stereotypes attributed to men and women in
societies like Britain are not always similarly attributed elsewhere, nor
do they necessarily accord with objectively observed behaviour in
Britain. Thus it seems that, whatever the ultimate biological basis for
the behaviour of males and females may be, the stereotypes result
mainly from cultural values.

It may be useful at this stage to distinguish between the biological
and the cultural by using the word *sex* to refer to those elements of
the male and female which are indisputably biological, and the term
gender to refer to the socially assigned meanings given to sexual
differences. For example, differences in sex determine who has
menstrual periods and who nocturnal emissions; but it is gender
assignment to regard tender loving care as a female characteristic and
skill with a surgeon's knife as a male one.

While it may be easy to realize that gender and sex are not the
same thing, what is more difficult to recognize is that they may not be
coincidental. 'A biological male may not necessarily be a social male
and a biological female a social female' (Clarke 1983). One study has
shown that 'feminine' social characteristics are associated with poorer
mental health and poorer self-asserted physical health than 'masculine' ones — for both male and female subjects (Annandale and
Hunt 1990). The strong distinctions between male and female
identities result in women being seen as 'other', with normality
residing in men, and women as a deviant minority who are judged on
the degree to which they approximate 'normality'. This also means
that 'women' are falsely regarded as a homogenous group, whose
similarities far outweigh their differences.

Some writers would argue that this adds further confirmation to the view that masculine conduct, whether by men or women, has more social power, and is valued more.

Bearing these issues in mind, it is appropriate to turn to a discussion of women as patients, and to consider how far the medical management of their illnesses incorporates socially derived sexual stereotypes.

SEXUAL STEREOTYPES IN MEDICAL PRACTICE

One of the commonest stereotypes of women is that they are 'by nature' more delicate and more susceptible to illness because of their reproductive function. This view was often expressed by male doctors in the nineteenth century, who argued that women's physiology made them more prone to hysteria (a term itself derived from the Greek for womb). Some writers have even suggested that doctors contributed to the debate on women's political and legal rights by suggesting that they were biologically unfit to participate in national affairs because of their propensity to 'nervous excitation'. Furthermore, it was argued that women should not be admitted to medical school because they would faint in anatomy lectures and their reproductive organs would be damaged by study, rendering them 'repulsive and useless hybrids'.

Although such ideas would be thought silly today, others possibly as pernicious but less obvious are still around. For example, teaching in medical schools today rarely covers psycho-sexual development, and recent evidence concerning the nature of female sexuality appears to have had little consideration; lectures tend to limit themselves to female hormonal reactions and the 'mechanisms' of pregnancy and childbirth.

The sexual stereotypes of the woman as potentially sick — 'the product and prisoner of her reproductive system' — and emotionally unstable have militated against a rational approach to women's illnesses. Cystitis, premenstrual tension, pelvic pain dysmenhorroea, and menopausal symptoms have sometimes been written off as 'not real' illnesses.

A series of studies in Aberdeen contain some fairly damning evidence of the treatment of 'womens complaints' (Porter 1990). Side-effects of contraceptives were dismissed as minor: patients whose physical complaints could not be explained or satisfactorily treated were labelled as neurotic, and those who could not find a type of contraceptive that suited them as 'unreasonable'.

Labelling womens complaints as 'psychogenic' is sometimes a polite way of saying imaginary. Unfortunately, there has been too little application of accepted scientific methods to the study of disorders of allegedly psychogenic origins. Many of the studies which purport to explain infertility or pregnancy complications were carried out on small groups of patients and lacked controls. They were usually retrospective, or, if prospective, did not assess personality variables before pregnancy (Oakley 1979).

It is useful to remember that many findings are reported in such a way as to create a picture of women that is congruent with social stereotypes of weakness and instability. The consequences of this can be two-fold: either symptoms will not be taken seriously, or they will be dealt with in a way which reinforces and reflects women's lack of control over their own health. Some examples might be appropriate here; they relate exclusively to those aspects of women's health which are associated with being female, because it is these aspects, many researchers feel, which demonstrate most clearly the essentially oppressive use of sexual stereotypes.

Pregnancy and childbirth

Over the last 20 years, evidence has continued to accumulate about the lack of control which many women experience over an essentially natural and healthy process — that of giving birth. Many sociologists have written about the 'medicalization' of reproduction (see Chapter 12). Some have argued that the historical shift from female-dominated midwifery to male-dominated obstetrics was related to the largely male medical profession's expansionist tendencies (Oakley 1979), and that this resulted in the transformation of a normal process into a pathological one, over which doctors exercise control.

Antenatal care

The ceding of control begins with the 'diagnosis' of pregnancy. Women are believed by doctors to be unreliable observers of their menstrual cycles and, therefore, it is the doctor who must make the initial pronouncement of pregnancy (Oakley 1979). Not until this has happened can a woman feel free to communicate the news. Access to antenatal care and confinement is largely controlled by medicine, and it is here that the woman is introduced to a view of childbirth as something that is likely to entail pathology for mother and child. Women will also be given advice on their personal habits, especially smoking, with the warning that smoking can result in a low-birth-weight baby. In one study, few modified their habits, but not because they were unaware of the evidence (Oakley 1990). Women had high levels of anxiety related to previous traumatic births, or after trying to give up smoking experienced serious life events which precipitated a return to the habit. Almost none of this was understood by the staff. One woman described how 'The consultant came down and he said, tut, tut, smoking!, he kept on and on about smoking. That's all he said' (Oakley 1990). And after the initial moral lecture it seemed as if most women were given up as a lost cause.

Antenatal clinics have been criticized for long waiting times, brief examinations, cursory treatment and lack of information (O'Brien & Smith 1981). The 'production line' procedures are such that women's own views and knowledge are ignored. In one absurd, but possibly revealing, consultation (Oakley 1979) the following exchange took place.

> *Doctor* (reading case notes): Ah, I see you've got a boy and a girl.
> *Patient:* No, two girls.
> *Doctor:* Are you sure? I thought it said . . . (checks in notes). Oh no, you're quite right, two girls.

The 'are you sure' could only have been uttered by a doctor who had learned to treat women's experiences as irrelevant and hence not worth listening to. Studies of antenatal consultations in a working-class area of Aberdeen (MacIntyre & Porter 1989) showed that doctors and paramedical workers seemed to have a low opinion of their largely working-class clientele. Women were deemed to be unreliable in keeping appointments, although a follow-up study revealed that very few women failed to turn up, and that those who did not had very good reasons. Only 37% of patients asked questions in antenatal clinics, and those who did were likely to be labelled as 'anxious'. Persistent questioners, or those who seemed to display interest in their routine tests were likely to be seen as 'neurotic'. Repeated studies in many parts of the UK over 20 years have produced similar findings.

Delivery

Today, there is widespread use of technological devices in childbirth. Ninety-eight percent of births take place in hospital. There has been much criticism of the lack of choice and involvement in decisions over procedures. A particular focus of criticism was the use of induction in labour. Although the rate is now declining, it reached a peak of over 40% in the mid-1970s. It is unpopular with women. One study showed that only 17% of mothers who experienced it would have it again (Cartwright 1977). Intervention in labour remains a contentious issue. In 1985, over 20% of births used forceps, caesarian section or vacuum extraction (OPCS 1988). While intervention techniques can be of positive benefit, the style in which they are managed is often open to criticism. The long-term consequences of feeling devalued when giving birth are not always considered. Oakley (1979) has shown that having a technologically managed birth is one factor precipitating post-natal depression.

Women may vary in their responses to childbirth, depending upon their social class or ethnic group. One of the objections raised to campaigns to improve maternity services was that they were led by 'vocal' white middle-class women. Porter's study of working-class women showed that one of their concerns was time, and that they were less likely to question the medical model of childbirth. But she was unsure, finally, whether or not women simply did not feel it worthwhile to pursue issues or felt 'unqualified' to argue with doctors. In any case, whether concerns are the same or vary between women, usually little attempt is made to establish what these actually are.

New reproductive technologies

In a society which expects that couples should produce children, the realization of infertility is painful for women and men. The number of infertile couples in the UK is *estimated* at about 10%, and in one-third of cases the husband suffers sterility. Most information on infertility is derived from clinic-based studies, and so only includes those who have come for treatment. It has been suggested that perhaps around 40% of people do not come for treatment. New reproductive technologies (NRT), for example artificial insemination (AID) and *in vitro* fertilization (IVF) seem to offer a way out, but there are social costs as well as benefits. New reproductive technologies are expensive and elaborate procedures. It has been estimated that each child born from an IVF procedure costs about £30 000. The service is not widely available and most patients must use the private sector; therefore access is unequal. Furthermore, IVF has a low success rate — many people leave an IVF programme without a baby.

Writers who have looked at the problems, as well as the solutions, posed for women by the NRT, usually consider the following issues. Firstly, a proportion of female infertility is due to untreated pelvic inflammatory disease — a condition which is often ignored, overlooked or whose symptoms are described as 'psychosomatic'. If women had appropriate treatment earlier on, infertility problems might be reduced. Secondly, although many women may subscribe to 'marriage-motherhood', not all will. The existence of NRT, and the social expectations of women may pressurize them into treatment. Being in an infertility programme is very stressful both physically and mentally. In IVF the woman is exposed to risks like powerful hormonal treatment and surgical intervention.

Thirdly, NRT has legal and ethical implications. For example, when an embryo is fertilized *in vitro* but cannot be replaced in the mother's womb, another woman must carry the baby. This arrangement, known as surrogacy, gave rise to the famous 'Baby M' case in 1986, where the surrogate mother refused to give up the baby when she was born. In that case, money had been paid. Commercial surrogacy is outlawed in this country, but the fear exists that poor women might be under commercial pressure to 'womb-lease' or perhaps donate eggs for IVF. Other writers have said that a woman's body is her own to use as she wants, and this should include commercial surrogacy arrangements.

Finally, some writers fear that NRT has the power to subordinate women, and envisage the application of eugenic policies, the rejection of female embryos, and selection of women for breeding. They regard NRT as finally wresting control over reproduction from women. The question as to who controls NRT is seen as central to its potential for good or evil (Arditti et al. 1984).

Abortion

Views about the social role of women as wives and mothers, or about their sexuality may be incorporated in judgements about abortion. There are inequalities that exist in the provision of abortion in different parts of the UK which cannot be explained solely in terms of facilities available. In a study of a clinic which gave antenatal care and also referred patients for abortion, different responses to the pregnancies of single and married women were noted (MacIntyre 1977). For the former, pregnancy was assumed to be a disaster, for the latter a 'happy event'. For single women, abortion was assumed to be the most likely outcome of pregnancy, for married women, childbirth. No attempt was made to verify these assumptions.

The common assumption that there is 'nothing to it' as far as abortion is concerned under-estimates the physical pain and mental distress involved, particularly in second trimester abortions. The belief that women regard the fetus as 'a nuisance' which must be 'got rid of' assumes that grief can attend a miscarriage, but not a legally terminated pregnancy.

Menopause

The menopause marks the end of fertility. Physical changes occur and ovarian functions decline, culminating in the cessation of the menses. However, these physical changes occur in a socio-cultural context which reflects how far the value attached to women is associated with their ability to reproduce. This, in turn, shows what the menopause may mean to women in a particular society.

Although there is a clear *medical* definition of menopause, this is beguiling, because symptoms, including absence of menstruation are open to different interpretations. Kaufert (1982), writing in a North American context, noted two competing views about menopause. First, the medical view, which characterizes the menopausal woman as relatively wealthy, from a happy conventional home, with time on her hands, succumbing to the temptation to become a hypochondriac. The recommendation is that she takes firm advice from her doctor, who will protect her against over-reaction to her bodily state, will advise her on whether or not she needs hormone replacement, and will monitor for cancer. The potentially pathological character of the menopause and need for medical guidance is emphasized.

Opposed to this view is what Kaufert calls the 'feminist' view, which locates some menopausal symptoms in the suppressed rage that women feel at having given so much of themselves to their families, and so little to themselves. Therapies, somewhat holistic in character, include better diet and exercise, and self-help rather than reliance on doctors is recommended. The use of hormones is usually opposed.

One view sees the woman as passive, the other as active. In one, women's knowledge of their bodies is held to be irrelevant or dangerous, in the other as valuable. There are obvious parallels with the literature on childbirth. However, both agree that the menopause is a problematic life event. How far this is correct remains somewhat questionable. Labelling symptoms as 'menopausal' ignores the fact that some may have a different origin. Research has suggested that depressed mood in middle-aged women is related less to the menopause than to particular life events. No excess of depressive disorder at the menopause has been detected (Gath 1987). Whether menopause is interpreted as dangerous obsolescence or a chance for active new growth and new selfhood, both views have similarities which have the potential of defining women largely in terms of their reproductive capacities and familial relationships, in ignorance of how women from different backgrounds or cultures, single or married, with or without children, may experience this development.

These examples suggest that stereotypes of women's roles and allied beliefs about the causes of women's diseases perhaps serve to divert attention from the serious consideration — as well as the research still needed for a proper understanding — of women's health problems. A change in emphasis which treats the health problems of women as worthy of the same kind of *scientific* attention as is afforded to the pathological problems which are not confined to women is clearly desirable.

WOMEN AS HEALTH WORKERS

In the National Health Service (NHS), approximately 70% of the work-force are women. There are nurses, doctors, domestics, physiotherapists, occupational therapists, technicians and midwives, but the great majority work in the more subordinate positions and are relatively poorly paid. Women have struggled to be allowed to train as doctors and to have nursing recognized as an important and integral aspect of health care. These struggles still continue.

Women doctors

In medieval times, both women and men attended medical schools, but from the late Middle Ages onwards attempts to professionalize medicine by basing it in the universities led to their exclusion. Women were still expected to be skilled in the treatment of minor ailments, and female bonesetters and surgeons continued to practise until their work was outlawed by the professional associations of apothecaries and barber surgeons in the time of Henry VIII. The first woman to be trained at a 'modern' medical school was Elizabeth Blackwell, an American who went to the medical faculty at the University of Geneva and graduated in 1849. During the remainder of that century a tiny number of women were admitted to medical school against enormous opposition. The Medical Press of 1874 stated 'no-one who knows what the course of study of a medical student is can doubt that a woman must be of a very exceptional character if she can pass through those scenes and still remain undimmed in those characteristics that are the beauty and ornament of a woman's life'. It was not until 1944 that it was recommended that women should be admitted to the previously single-sex London medical schools, and not until 1978 that restrictions on the admission of women students were outlawed by the Sex Discrimination Act. Women now form an increasing percentage of medical school entrants (47% in 1989).

Much has been made of the problems of 'wastage' of women doctors, although the wastage of male doctors through migration, disability disqualification and death should not be forgotten. A study done in the 1960s showed that only one-fifth of women with young

--------- **Table 1** ---------
Female hospital medical staff by grade, as a percentage of all hospital medical staff at each grade in 1976 and 1986.

	1976	1986
Total women in hospital posts	18.5	25.0
Consultants	9.1	13.5
Associate specialist (formerly medical assistant)	41.0	44.2
Senior registrar	18.7	23.7
Registrar	17.4	23.1
Senior House Officer	21.4	33.4
House Officer	31.2	39.7
Paragraph 94 appointment*	24.0	28.7

Source: DHSS (1987: Table 3.4).
* Mainly those carrying out part time work.

children and one-third of women with older children were working full time (Elliott & Jeffreys 1966). However, most were eager to work and between 1965 and 1976 the proportion of women active in medicine rose from 66% to 83%. Nowadays, women doctors are more likely than other professional women with family responsibilities to continue working, but in 1988 District Health Authorities provided only 1197 nursery places for children under 5 years of age.

One traditional solution for women doctors has been to undertake part-time work which can be combined with family, and the number of part-time doctors in hospitals has increased since 1976, but they comprise a relatively small proportion. Most women doctors in hospital, particularly at the junior levels, are unlikely to be able to pursue their careers as effectively as men, or may be regarded as lacking commitment if they attempt part-time arrangements. For most, it is not an option anyway, since such opportunities are limited below consultant level.

A recent survey of a small number (8%) of female junior hospital doctors showed that, in addition to experiencing the stresses which are reported by all juniors (overwork, long hours and poor relations with consultants), they face additional hazards, including sexual harrassment and conflicts between personal or family and work responsibilities. The study found 46% to have scored as clinically depressed (Firth-Cozens 1990). However, there was no comparison made with males.

One particular problem which younger women doctors experience is the lack of women in senior positions who could act as role models. In part, this reflects earlier, discriminatory policies of admission to medical school. The number of women consultants is rising slowly: in 1963, 5.3% of all consultants were women, in 1987 the proportion was 13.5% (see Table 1).

At present only 6% of consultants in general medicine and less than 1% in general surgery are women (Godlee 1990). Women are still more likely to find consultant posts in the 'shortage' specialities like public-health medicine, mental subnormality or geriatrics. It has been argued that this serves to reinforce the ideas that such specialities are 'second class', and that women, who are seen as 'second class' doctors are the ones most suitable to work in them. It remains to be seen whether the greater proportion of women entrants to medicine will alter the balance. Certainly in general practice, where 27% of doctors are women, they comprise 40% of those aged under 30 years, compared with 20% in the 40–44 years age group.

Unpaid lay carers

Developments in community care, especially in the care of the elderly, chronically sick or handicapped, are often seen as a better and cheaper alternative to expensive hospital care. However, such care may well have 'hidden costs'. In the absence of trained staff, and where resources are stretched, the unpaid volunteer labour of women who care for sick members of the family on a long-term basis is usually forgotten (see Chapter 16).

Although the *proportions* of women and men caring for a sick person are not very different (15% women, 12% men) because there are more women than men, about 3.5 million women compared with 2.5 million men are caring for someone who is not a child. Women are more likely to be the main carers, to care for someone outside the home, and to spend longer hours caring. Single women aged 45–64 years carry the heaviest burden. One-quarter of women, compared with only 8% of men are caring single-handed. Women are also likely to be given less professional help with the job — 66% of men compared with 48% of women were receiving assistance from outside agencies (Green 1985).

Women form the majority of the patients and providers of health care. As patients, they suffer rather than benefit from views which presume their physical and/or psychological weakness. Such views affect not only what will happen to them as patients, but serve to reinforce existing social attitudes towards women. As workers, they suffer from inequality of opportunity, low-status positions and poor pay, for within the health service the distribution of power and the social relationships which exist often mirror the general relationships of inferiority and superiority between women and men in society. The position is slowly changing, however, and it remains to be seen whether increasing numbers of women doctors, coupled with increasing self-confidence on the part of women patients, will fundamentally alter the picture described in this chapter.

REFERENCES

Annandale, E. & Hunt, K. (1990) Masculinity, feminity and sex: an exploration of their relative contribution to explaining gender differences in health. *Soc. Hlth Illness*, **12**, 24–47.

Arditti, R., Klein, R. & Minden, S. (eds) (1984) *Test Tube Women: What Future for Motherhood?* Boston: Pandora Press.

Brown, G. & Harris, T. (1980) *The Social Origins of Depression*. London: Tavistock.

Cartwright, A. (1977) Mothers' experiences of induction. *Br. med. J.*, **2**, 745–749.

Clarke, J. (1983) Sexism, feminism and medicalisation: a decade review of the literature on gender and illness. *Soc. Hlth Illness*, **51**, 62–81.

Denning, J. (1984) *Womens Work and Health Hazards: a Selected Bibliography*. London: Department of Occupational Health, London School of Hygiene and Tropical Medicine.

Department of Health and Social Security (1987) *Hospital In-patient Inquiry: Hospital Medical Staff*. London: HMSO.

Elliott, P.M. & Jeffreys, M. (1966) *Women in Medicine*. London: Office of Health Economics.

Firth-Cozens, J. (1990) Sources of stress in women junior house officers. *Br. med. J.*, **301**, 89–92.

Gath, D. & Isles, C. (1990) Depression and the menopause. *Br. med. J.*, **300**, 1287–8.

General Household Survey 1987, Morbidity No. 17. London: HMSO.

Godlee, F. (1990) Stress in women doctors. *Br. med. J.*, **301**, 76–77.

Green, H. (1985) *Informal Carers. OPCS GHS 15. Supplement A*. London: HMSO.

Haynes, S.G. & Feinleb, M. (1980) Women, work and coronary heart disease: prospective findings from the Framingham heart study. *Am. J. publ. Hlth*, **70**, 137–141.

Jowell, R., Witherspoon, S. & Brook, L. (eds) (1988) *British Social Attitudes: the 5th Report*. Aldershot: Gower.

Kaufert, P.A. (1982) Myth and the menopause. *Soc. Hlth Illness*, **4**, 141–161.

MacIntyre, S. (1977) *Single and Pregnant*. London: Croom Helm.

Macintyre, S. & Porter, M. (1989) Problems and prospects in promoting effective care at the local level. In *Effective Care in Pregnancy and Childbirth*, ed. M. Enkin, M. Keirse and I. Chalmers. Oxford: Oxford University Press.

Oakley, A. (1976) Wise woman and medicine man: changes in the management of childbirth. In *The Rights and Wrongs of Women*, ed. J. Mitchell & A. Oakley. Harmondsworth: Penguin.

Oakley, A. (1979) *Becoming a Mother*. London: Martin Robertson.

Oakley, A. (1990) Smoking in pregnancy: smokescreen or risk factor? Towards a materialist analysis. *Soc. Hlth Illness*, **11**, 311–335.

O'Brien, M. & Smith, C. (1981) Womens views and experiences of antenatal care. *Practitioner*, **225**, 123–126.

Office of Population Censuses and Surveys (1984) *Social Trends: Health*. London: HMSO.

Office of Population Censuses and Surveys (1988) *Hospital Inpatient Inquiry 1987*. London: HMSO.

Office of Population Censuses and Surveys (1990) *Social Trends: Health*, pp. 112–113. London: HMSO.

Porter, M. (1990) Professional–client relationship and women's reproductive health care. In *Readings in Medical Sociology*, ed. S. Cunningham-Burley & N. McKeganey. London: Tavistock Routledge.

Standing, H. (1980) Sickness is a womans business. In *Alice Through the Microscope*, ed. L. Birke & S. Best. London: Routledge & Kegan Paul.

Waldron, I. (1976) Why do women live longer than men? *Soc. Sci. Med.*, **19**, 349.

10

The health and health care of ethnic minority groups

Sheila Hillier

Identifying and caring for the special or distinctive needs of ethnic minorities is a test of the flexibility of the National Health Service (NHS). This chapter will try to illustrate some of the conditions to which ethnic minority groups are susceptible, and to examine the part played by the experience of migration, and the social conditions in the host society. It will also consider minorities' own perceptions of illness, the use that is made of health services and the quality of care received. Much literature has accumulated over the past decade, including large surveys, particularly census data, case studies of clinical conditions and surveys of attitudes and utilization. The work is mixed: some stresses the importance of particular life-styles which incorporate risk factors for disease, while other research draws attention to the relationship between patterns of disease in ethnic groups and health inequalities in general, together with added experiences of racism.

The term *ethnic minority* is thought by some to be contentious, since it seems to imply that there is an homogeneous 'majority' somewhere in British society. It can also imply an homogeneity amongst ethnic groups — for example, to talk simply about the 'Asian' ethnic minority belies the variety of religions, geographical origins and languages that exist. Sometimes the term is used to mean the same as *migrants* — those not born in the UK; but to confuse it in this way ignores the many British born members of ethnic minorities. Finally, not everybody is happy at being described as a member of an ethnic minority. For some groups at least, this is thought to have overtones of racism. Such was the difficulty experienced by the census takers in trying to produce suitable definitions of origin that the 1980 census omitted a question on ethnicity. After extensive research, a formula has now been produced, and questions on ethnic origin will be included in the next census.

A working definition of ethnic minority is 'a social group with distinctive language, values, religion, customs and attitudes'. The diversity of Britain is shown when we consider the wide variety of such groups — Turks, Greeks, Poles, West Indians, Irish, Chinese, Jews, Bangladeshis and Sikhs, to name only some. The last census data on ethnic minorities reflected only 'migrants', those born outside the UK. The largest group are from the New Commonwealth and Pakistan (NCWP) the bulk of whom have settled in Britain over the last 40 years.

Recently, data have appeared on the population of ethnic minority communities, which includes children born here. Data from the Labour Force Survey analysed by Haskey (1990) suggest that the NCWP population stands at 2.58 million, or 4.7% of the population. This is in line with earlier predictions. Fifty-one per cent of the ethnic minority population is described as Indian, Pakistani or Bangladeshi and 19% are West Indian. the numbers of West Indians have declined since 1981, while the Pakistani population has grown by 50% and the Bangladeshi population by 100%. Thirty per cent of Pakistanis and 34% of Bangladeshis are under 10 years old. It is clear that policies have to be constructed to care for the health needs of these particular groups. Most research has concentrated upon ethnic populations of Indian, Pakistani, Bangladeshi or West Indian origin, and what follows reflects this, although not to the exclusion of all other ethnic groups.

GENERAL PATTERNS OF MORTALITY AND MORBIDITY

The 1971 census provides the major data on the patterns of mortality (Marmot et al. 1984). It gives data on those who migrated to the UK from abroad. At its broadest, the picture can be summarized thus. People who migrate are usually healthier, with lower death rates standardized for age than those who remain in the country of origin. The only exception is Ireland, where death rates are higher for migrants than for Irish people in Ireland (Adelstein et al. 1986). However, migrant mortality from all causes, compared with the population of England and Wales, is higher at every age. Although evidence is difficult to summarize, it appears that migrants tend to bring with them the disease risks of their own country (e.g. early malnutrition), but these risks generally approximate, within one or two generations, to those of the country in which they have settled.

Broadly speaking, the major killers for people who settle here are the same as for the indigenous population (cancers, ischaemic heart disease, disorders of the circulatory system and diabetes), but there are also problems which seem to be concentrated in particular ethnic groups, for example rickets and osteomalacia (different Asian minority groups), sickle cell anaemia (Caribbean born), lung cancer (Irish), thalassemia (Cypriot community), and Tay-Sacks disease (Jews of Eastern European origin). If we compare ethnic groups within the broad categories of mortality we can find a wide variety of causes of death, and this must reflect a complex intermingling of influences of the old country, the new country, selective migration and the process of migration and settlement. There are many theories to account for observed differences; for example, it is argued that diet may change, or that relationship patterns may be altered or disrupted, or that the new country may be unwelcoming if not outright hostile; we can only sort out the factors when finer comparisons, for example between different groups of migrants from the same country, can be made.

It is worthwhile, however, to consider the groups in more detail. One interesting finding has been that standardized mortality ratios of female migrants are, in many cases, higher than those of males. This is the opposite of the case for the population of England and Wales as a whole.

Migrants to the UK from the Indian subcontinent (India, Pakistan and Bangladesh) have a high mortality from liver, mouth and oesophageal cancer, and from ischaemic heart disease, especially among women. They also suffer high death rates from hypertension, stroke and diabetes. In general, the major killing cancers in England and Wales (lung, stomach and bowel) have low mortality rates among this group. People born in the Caribbean or Africa have high rates of mortality from hypertension, stroke and blood disorders; like those from India stomach cancer rates are low.

Irish groups have higher mortality (even than in Ireland) for lung and cervical cancer, cirrhosis of the liver, and tuberculosis but show little evidence of diabetes.

Maternal and infant mortality

Mortality rates of mothers from NCWP are consistently higher than those of UK mothers. The picture for children is even more striking

——— **Table 1** ———

Mortality statistics:* perinatal and infant social and biological factors
in England and Wales, 1987

	Still births	Perinatal	Neonatal	Post-neonatal	Infant deaths
All	5.0	8.9	5.0	4.0	9.0
UK	4.8	8.6	4.9	4.0	8.9
Irish Republic	7.1	11.1	5.3	4.2	9.5
Australia/Canada/New Zealand	4.0	6.0	3.2	2.4	5.6
NCP (all)	6.9	12.2	6.8	4.1	10.9
Bangladesh	9.4	12.5	4.1	4.3	8.5
India	6.8	11.5	6.2	2.5	8.7
East Africa	5.7	9.0	4.5	2.5	7.0
Rest of Africa	5.8	14.3	10.8	4.8	15.6
Caribbean Commonwealth	8.7	15.9	8.1	3.3	11.4
Mediterranean Commonwealth	5.1	8.8	4.8	3.3	8.1
Remainder of the New Commonwealth	3.7	8.5	5.9	3.3	9.3
Pakistan	8.2	14.9	8.7	6.5	15.2
Remainder of Europe	4.0	7.9	5.2	4.3	9.4

Source: OPCS (1987: 26–30).
* Numbers and rates per 1000 live births.

(see Table 1). There are important and unexplained differences
between ethnic groups. For example, still births are highest amongst
Pakistani, Bangladeshi and Caribbean babies. It is sometimes argued
that perinatal mortality is related to low birthweight — about 11% of
Indian and Bangladeshi babies have a low birthweight compared with
6.7% nationally (OPCS 1984, 1985). In general, white babies are
heavier than others, but studies in variations of size at birth do not
always consider the heterogeneity of the Asian population, and one
study found that in healthy areas with low birthweights, those with a
high number of ethnic births had *lower* perinatal mortality (Kurji &
Eduard 1984). Another attributed cause of death is congenital
malformation, and in Pakistani babies this is particularly high, due to
both structural and metabolic problems.

The predisposing factors which cause ethnic babies to have low
birthweights have not been fully investigated. However, it is clear that
the risk factor of *poverty*, which is associated generally with infant
mortality, must provide the background to many of these deaths.
Stress factors like poor housing may well be augmented by relatively
lower levels of antenatal care. Evidence is ambiguous: one study
showed more Asian than white women in Bradford had only short
periods of antenatal care (Barnes 1982), being likely to start antenatal

care later, and another found that they were more likely to have a general practitioner not on the obstetric list (Clarke & Clayton 1983). However, comparisons of infant mortality rates for all ethnic groups between 1980 and 1988 show important declines in still-birth, perinatal neonatal and post-neonatal mortality (OPCS 1987) and the rate of improvement appears greater than for UK born babies of non-ethnic groups.

One factor that might explain some of the Caribbean infant deaths is sickle cell disease in mothers. This is a serious condition which provides antenatal complications, and is associated with spontaneous premature birth and low birthweight. The estimated mortality rate for mothers is about 6%. From a position where there was relatively little research or attention paid to the condition, neonatal screening for sickle cell disease and trait is now becoming standard practice in inner cities.

Childhood rickets

Children and young adults in Asian ethnic minorities are thought to have particular problems with rickets. A study done in Glasgow (Geol 1976) found 5% of Asian children had rickets, and a study in Bradford found 40% of the children studied had some evidence of the disorder (Ford 1976). The condition is caused by vitamin D deficiency. In its extreme form the growing skeleton is damaged and there is pain and swelling. The levels of vitamin D in the Asian diet, which is largely based on chapatis made from refined flour and ghee, is low, although it has been suggested that in other respects the high-fibre diet of the Asians is healthier. As yet prophylactic measures have been poorly organized, although in Glasgow free vitamin D supplements were introduced. By 1979, 74% of the children were using the supplements regularly and the prevalence of rickets was reduced. A comprehensive programme for all young people was subsequently set up.

Some writers have interpreted the rickets campaign as a 'moral panic', underpinned by the misleading view that the main health problems which ethnic minorities have are specifically related to their own cultural practices. An example of this is the statement that 'The long term answer to Asian rickets probably lies in health education and a change towards Western diet and lifestyle' (Geol 1976). There are conflicting views over whether or not chapati flour should, like margarine, be fortified with vitamin D. The Department of Health recommends that 'soft planning' by health education and vitamin supplements should continue, and has made these a matter of local rather than central initiative.

The elderly

Norman (1985) has characterized the situation of the ethnic elderly as one of 'triple jeopardy', by virtue of their age, economic and social disadvantage, and racial discrimination. The demographic projections suggest a two- to six-fold increase in the number of those of pensionable age in the next 10 years. At present, those aged over 60 years form 5% of the ethnic population. Those born in Asia will form the largest group, but we know little about what special kinds of intervention may be necessary for them to maintain health and fitness in old age. At present only 46% of Asian born people of pensionable age are receiving state benefits and a high number, 88%, most of whom are women, are unable to speak English. Some studies have suggested that elderly Asians enjoy greater respect and support in their families. Only 5% live alone, and the majority of Asian ethnic minority households have an average of five people (Haskey 1989). However, the ethnic elderly complain of loneliness and social isolation, and mention in particular the fear of racial harassment as a factor preventing casual outdoor social contacts. They often feel trapped in an alien society.

Ethnic groups and mental illness

Migration to another society is commonly held to be a stressful experience and, although it may be undertaken in a spirit of hopefulness, not all migrants have come to Britain because they wanted to. Many are here as a result of poverty, civil strife or deliberate policies of expulsion in their countries of origin. East African Asians who were forced to depart are an example.

It is not easy to gauge the true state of psychiatric morbidity amongst ethnic minorities. Most of the figures on mental illness are derived from *psychiatric-hospital admissions*, but it is difficult to draw significant conclusions from these since they may only reflect what beds are available, what particular admissions policies are operating, how ethnic minorities react to the mental illness or 'deviant behaviour' of one of their members, or how doctors diagnose symptoms presented to them. Inevitably, they give a picture of gross pathology rather than less serious conditions.

An early study by Cochrane (1977) found West Indians to have an almost equivalent, and Asians a lower rate of admission than the indigenous population. Data from the Mental Health Enquiry now suggest that more young West Indian men are admitted to mental hospitals than whites. There is a roughly four-fold excess of admissions in the 20–34 and 35–55 year age groups (Glover 1989). This could not be explained by social-class differences in the comparison group of whites as the class composition of both groups was similar. The majority of patients are diagnosed as schizophrenic and are more likely to be hospitalized as a result of compulsory admission. Littlewood and Lipsedge (1981) noted the number of admissions involving police activity or social workers rather than relatives, and the over-representation of black patients in secure units and special hospitals.

Compulsory detention may be influenced by diagnostic criteria. Studies of the West Indian admissions have shown that the type of schizophrenia presented was not typical of Britain, and was characterized by confusion, religious references and paranoia — a response to stress. Acute psychotic reactions are widely recognized in developing countries, but the category is not used much by British psychiatrists who may therefore be more likely to 'section' patients. On the other hand, a study of minor psychiatric disorders (Burke 1984) showed higher rates of depression and psycho-somatic conditions than among whites, but one in five were undiagnosed. For all these reasons, the picture of mental illness is likely to be somewhat inaccurate, with over-representation at the psychotic end of the spectrum, and perhaps a failure to diagnose minor psychiatric illness.

As to the prevalence of mental illness among Indians, Pakistanis and Bangladeshis, the evidence is somewhat uncertain. One study has shown higher rates of first-time admission to hospital among Indians, than among the British or Pakistani populations (Dean et al. 1981). There appear to be differences in symptomatology among men and women, and between different ethnic groups. Some writers suggest that psychological morbidity is lower in Asian groups than in the British population, others that it is higher. A community study of Bangladeshis and their British neighbours on a London housing estate (MacCarthy & Craissati 1989), showed the former to be experiencing more serious life events and chronic difficulties, with symptoms of distress.

Yet seeking help may be difficult, because contact with psychiatric services may be seen as stigmatizing. Much mental illness, especially of a minor sort, and particularly affecting women and children, may simply be contained within the family. Fear of a psychiatric hospital admission may inhibit contact with a general practitioner. When help is finally sought, doctors may misunderstand symptoms, because of the way they are expressed by patients. Indian and Pakistani patients may complain of pain, feelings of weakness and impotence and discomfort in the chest ('my heart feels pressed') as ways of expressing depression and anxiety, using these descriptions as metaphors.

Clearly, more detailed analyses on larger samples which consider differences in economic circumstances, sex and religion will be important in gaining a better understanding of ethnicity and mental illness. This should help to elucidate whether or not particular cultures have a protective effect, as some suggest, or whether ethnicity combined with poverty, isolation and discrimination puts people at greater risk.

HEALTH INEQUALITIES AND ETHNIC EXPERIENCES

Social class

The most robust indicator of health inequalities is social class, and an inverse relationship between social class and most causes of death has been found for UK populations (see Chapter 8). For ethnic populations, the relationship between social class and death is more complex. In the case of Ireland the gradient is the same as for England and Wales, but the mortality rate is *higher* for every class. Migrants from the Indian subcontinent exhibit the highest mortality in social class IIIA, and for those from the Caribbean the highest mortality is in class I, with non-manual classes generally having a higher mortality than manual ones. In those from Africa, the relationship is curvilinear with high rates in social classes I and V. Therefore it seems that social-class position is only a partial explanation of the higher mortality rates of migrants. Reasons as to why this is vary. One proposed reason is that people bring with them their 'old country' patterns — for mortality rates reflect the country of origin, if at lower levels. Deaths from ischaemic heart disease of men in social class III non-manual from the NCWP are the highest of all social classes. It seems unlikely, however, despite some differences in the 'classic' patterns of health inequality, that social-class position does not have some effect on the mortality rates of ethnic minorities.

Migration

Various theories discuss the stressful nature of migration and its possible effects on health. One can distinguish between 'push' factors like unemployment and poverty and 'pull' factors – the demand for labour in the post war UK economic expansion being particularly significant. Migrants were actively sought, but whether they were welcomed once arrived is another matter. Initial curiosity on the part of the receiving society can be replaced by antagonism during times of stress, especially economic crises. Initially, many NCWP migrants were single men, hoping to earn money and return home but, as conditions in the home countries worsened, they settled, brought over wives and started families. A study of Greek and Punjabi women migrants to Canada showed how women in particular were not only trapped in menial jobs (many working outside the home for the first time), but also lacked the English which would provide them with a broader network of social supports. They had been admitted to the country as 'dependents' of their husbands. Their lives were concentrated within the family, yet the family was often their husband's. They lacked the previous support of their own mothers and sisters (Anderson 1987).

People coming to Britain may also retain many aspects of their own cultural identity and their customary way of life may conflict with the society that receives them. Particular religious observances, family structures and beliefs about the relationship between the sexes or between old and young may come under strain. The values of a rural peasant society, where the family comes first, are not always adaptable to an industrial society. 'Host' communities usually either *assimilate* ethnic groups, when the migrant group is dispersed and absorbed, or *accommodate* them. In the latter case the migrant group retains its own culture, but is accepted. It is doubtful that either accommodation or assimilation has taken place. Although illegal, there is considerable racial discrimination in jobs and housing. For some groups this propounds the disadvantages they already suffer in education.

Employment

Most black people are concentrated in semi-skilled and unskilled jobs (social classes IV and V). The position of black citizens in Britain largely remains, geographically and economically, that allocated to them as immigrant workers in the 1950s and 1960s. While 19% of white men occupy professional or managerial positions, the respective proportions for ethnic minorities are West Indians 5%, Indian 11%, and both Pakistani and Bangladeshi 10%. Only 16% of white men have unskilled jobs, while the figures for ethnic groups are West Indian 35%, Indian 42%, Pakistani 43%, and Bangladeshi 75% (Ohri & Faruqi 1988).

People in ethnic minorities tend to earn less for similar jobs and are more likely to be unemployed. Young blacks coming off Youth Training Schemes are less likely to find jobs. Being well qualified is no protection — twice as many Asians as white graduates are unemployed. Only one-third of male Asian graduates are working in professional and managerial jobs compared with almost two out of three white graduate men.

Racist attitudes

A survey in the UK (CSO 1985) found 90% of people saying that prejudice exists against Asians, and 31% of the sample described themselves as prejudiced. The survey found sympathy for provision for minority cultures, but not cultural diversity. Very few thought that the 'mother tongues' of ethnic minorities should be actively encouraged, and the clear message was that they should adapt as much as possible. Legal measures which affect black people are also important in producing a climate where the receiving society is seen as hostile. Immigration Acts, and the 1983 Nationality Act, have particularly affected ethnic minorities. But the law does not necessarily protect them. Between 1976 and 1981 there were 31 documented racist murders, including stabbings by white youth gangs and the burning to death of a mother and her three children (Fryer 1985).

USING HEALTH SERVICES

Some services for ethnic minorities are unaccessible or unacceptable. For example, few facilities exist to deal with patients suffering from sickle cell anaemia, which affects the West Indian community. As the mortality figures show, ethnic minorities retain the patterns of their country of origin, including high death rates from diabetes. Ten years ago a Radio London 'phone in' on ethnic health problems found 11% of calls were concerned with diabetes, 13% with 'breathlessness' and asthma (see Depression above) and psychosexual problems, including infertility. In many cases men called on behalf of their wives with particular requests for the services of women doctors. This suggested that patients were experiencing some difficulty at that time in obtaining adequate attention for complaints which were uncommon or had less significance to the indigenous population. In contrast, two recent studies of general-practice consultations (Gillam et al. 1989; Balarajan et al. 1989) found that consultation rates were higher for NCWP groups. Particular concerns were diabetes, diseases of the circulatory system and upper-respiratory-tract infections.

Interest in, and use of, preventive services among some ethnic minority households has been found to be significantly higher than for the indigenous white population (Johnson 1986). A study of children's immunization found that Pakistani and Indian groups had a better rate of uptake than whites (Baker et al. 1984). A study in Nottingham of the use mothers made of maternal and child welfare services found that Asian mothers were as likely to use the services as British-born mothers (Ronalds et al. 1977). Yet, although the maternal and perinatal death rates of ethnic minorities are falling they still remain higher than those of the indigenous population. The fact is that the environment seems to have had some impact on death rates, which are lower than in the country of origin, but what particular *feature* of the environment has contributed — fewer babies and better health services — is not clear.

Generally speaking, it seems that there is less reluctance by ethnic minorities to use some of the health services than might be supposed, and it is of interest that community-based outreach services, which have attempted some understanding of the needs, language and culture of ethnic minorities, have been successful (Watson 1984). However, studies on ethnic minorities' utilization have so far concentrated on socially deprived inner-city communities, where the use made by the indigenous population of the health services was below average.

Contact with hospitals raises a new set of problems. For most people, entering hospital is a stressful experience; for people brought up in rural areas of the India subcontinent with little or no experience of hospitals before coming to England the prospect can be very frightening. A mother gives birth to her baby not in her own bed surrounded by her female relatives, but in a strange room full of machinery and men. When this experience is augmented by linguistic difficulties, fear on the part of the mother, and frustration and irritation on the part of health workers, is the inevitable consequence. The embarrassment of many Asian women during vaginal examination by a male doctor cannot be over-emphasized, and women doctors should carry out this procedure wherever possible.

Hospitals have been ill-prepared for the communication or reception of information in a variety of languages, and interpreters are still a rarity. Language difficulties can undoubtedly affect the understanding of symptoms and treatment compliance. Record clerks and receptionists are still often unable to pronounce and record Asian names. The food served in hospital takes little note of the dietary laws of Islam and Hinduism and there is almost no recognition of the need to observe particular rituals after childbirth amongst Chinese, Indian, Pakistani and Bangladeshi women.

The brisk approach of hospital staff geared towards 'getting the patient up and out of bed' may be experienced as harshness by those who believe that a long period of rest and recuperation after illness or childbirth is necessary. The inhibited expression of distress in the face of pain or worry, characteristic of British patients, is unknown in almost any ethnic group. Most feel able to express themselves openly and this may be regarded as attention-seeking behaviour by hospital staff. One Asian woman describes a bad experience after surgery. She relates: 'when I came round I felt sick . . . one nurse was very mad and angry. She said "Why are you being sick and saying you feel dizzy and this and that? Nothing is happening to you. You are pretending that you are being sick. You are making yourself sick!"' (Eyles & Donovan 1990).

TRADITIONAL BELIEFS ABOUT HEALTH

Traditional beliefs about illness may persist after migration. Those of Asian descent may perceive health in terms of their traditional theory of the importance of the bodily balance of 'hot' and 'cold'. Therefore temperature is seen as an important indicator of the state of health. One study reported the suspicion that Asian ethnic minorities have about the food available in Britain. It is regarded as unhealthy and full of preservatives. Frozen meat is particularly bad: 'all the goodness goes into the ice'. The use of ghee (clarified butter) is recommended as a healthy pure food. Traditional views about weight challenge those of British health educators, since a certain amount of fatness is seen as a sign of health. When ill, certain foods are avoided — for example a 'hot disease' like measles will mean the avoidance of 'hot' foods like chicken, meat or eggs. Pregnant women may refuse to take iron tablets on the grounds that they are too 'hot'. 'Bhye baddi' is a Punjabi term that describes illness caused by a food imbalance.

Traditional remedies may be used, especially in the West Indian community, e.g. herbal teas and 'bay rum', a poultice of bay leaves, nutmeg, ginger and lime. Herbs and spices may be used in the Asian community, and there is occasional use of a traditional practitioner, the Hakim, who practices Unani or Ayurvedic medicine. Hakims may well have special insight into the problems of ethnic migrants and have a better knowledge of family background. They may be playing a less important role as time goes on, which is perhaps an illustration that cultures are not static but adaptive entities.

The research on ethnicity, health and health care, although increasing, still remains fragmentary. Some of the work can be described as 'culturalist', emphasizing the special beliefs and customs of particular ethnic groups. It is important to remember that many behaviours attributed to 'cultural differences' may in fact be a reflection of migrants' need to survive in a new society. Whilst a 'culturalist' approach can be valuable to health workers, it can sometimes reinforce stereotypes or give a picture which is out of date. It is perhaps more important to remember that members of ethnic groups may be at risk in relation to their health because of early disadvantage at 'home' and current disadvantage in the labour and housing markets. We live in a multi-ethnic community and the provisions of the NHS should seek to reflect this diversity.

REFERENCES

Adelstein, A.M., Marmot, M.C. & Dean, G. (1986) Comparison of mortality of Irish immigrants in England and Wales with that of Irish and British nationals. *Ir. med. J.*, **79**, 7, 185–89.

Anderson, J. (1987) Migration and health: perspectives on immigrant women. *Soc. Hlth Illness*, **9**, 4, 410–439.

Balarajan, R., Yuen, P. & Soni Rahleigh, V. (1989) Ethnic differences in G.P. consultations. *Br. med. J.*, **299**, 958–961.

Baker, M.R., Bandaranayke, R. & Schweiger, M.S. (1984) Differences in the uptake of immunisation among ethnic groups. *Br. med. J.*, **88**, 1975–1978.

Barnes, R. (1982) Perinatal and mortality rates in Bradford. In *Obstetric Problems of the Asian Community in Britain*. London: Royal College of Obstetricians and Gynaecologists.

Burke, A. (1984) Racism and psychological disturbance among West Indians in Britain. *Int. J. soc. Psych.*, **30**, 50–68.

Central Statistical Office (1985) *Social Trends 15*, pp. 14–15. London: HMSO.

Clarke, M. & Clayton, D. (1983) The quality and organisation of medical care provided to immigrants in pregnancy in Leicestershire. *Br. med. J.*, **286**, 261–262.

Cochrane, R. (1977) Mental illness in immigrants in England and Wales: an analysis of mental hospital admissions. *Soc. Psychiat.*, **12**, 25–35.

Dean, G., Walsh, D., Downing, H. & Shelley, E. (1981) First admissions of native born and immigrants to psychiatric hospitals in S.E. England. *Br. J. Psychiatr.*, **139**, 506–512.

Eyles, J. & Donovan, J. (1990) *The Social Effects of Health Policy*. Aldershot: Avebury.

Ford, J.A., McIntosh, W.B. & Butterfield, R. (1976) Clinical and subclinical vitamin D deficiency in Bradford children. *Arch. Dis. Child*, **51**, 939.

Fryer, P. (1985) *Staying Power*. London: Pluto Press.

Geol, K. (1976) Florid and subclinical rickets among immigrant children in Glasgow. *Lancet*, **i**, 1141.

Gillam, S.J., Jarman, B., White, P. & Law, R. (1989) Ethnic differences in consultation rates in urban general practice. *Br. med. J.*, **299**, 953–958.

Glover, G. (1989) The pattern of psychiatric admissions of Caribbean born immigrants in London. *Soc. Psychiat.*, **24**, 49–50.

Haskey, J. (1989) Families and households of the ethnic minority population of Great Britain. *Population Trends, 57, OPCS*. London: HMSO.

Haskey, J. (1990) The ethnic minority population of Great Britain — estimated by ethnic group and country of birth, *Population Trends 60, Summer 35–38, OPCS*. London: HMSO.

Johnson, M.R.C. (1986) Inner city residents, ethnic minorities and primary care in the West Midlands. In: *Health, Race and Ethnicity*, eds T. Rathwell and D. Phillips, pp. 192–212. London: Croom Helm.

Kurji, K.H. & Eduard, L. (1984) Ethnic differences in pregnancy outcome. *Public Hlth London*, **98**, 205–208.

Littlewood, R. & Lipsedge, M. (1981) *Aliens and Alienists: Ethnic Minorities and Psychiatry*. London: Penguin.

MacCarthy, B. & Craissati, J. (1989) Ethnic differences in response to adversity. *Soc. Psychiat.*, **24**, 196–201.

Marmot, M.G., Adelstein, A.M. & Bulusu, L. (1984) Immigrant mortality in England and Wales 1970–78. *Studies in Medical and Population Subjects, No. 47, OPCS.* London: HMSO.

Norman, A. (1985) *Triple Jeopardy: Growing Old in a Second Homeland*. London: Centre for Policy on Ageing.

Ohri, S. & Faruqi, S. (1988) Racism, employment and unemployment. In: *Britain's Black Population*, ed. A. Bhat, R. Carr-Hill and S. Ohri, pp. 61–69. London: Radical Statistics Race Group/Gower.

OPCS (1984) *DH3 84/5 Birthweight Statistics*. London: HMSO.

OPCS (1985) *DH3 85/6 Birthweight Statistics*. London: HMSO.

OPCS (1987) *DH3 No. 21 Mortality Statistics: Perinatal and Infant Mortality Social and Biological Factors in England and Wales*. London: HMSO.

Ronalds, C., Vaughan, J. & Sprackling, P. (1977) Asian mothers' use of general practitioner and maternal child welfare services. *J. R. Coll. gen. Pract.*, **27**, 281–284.

Watson, E. (1984) Health of infants and use of health services by mothers of different ethnic groups in East London. *Commun. Med.*, **6**, 127–135.

11

Elderly people and health

David Blane

Elderly people are major users of health services. Half the patients in non-psychiatric National Health Service (NHS) hospitals are more than 65 years of age and their greater use of general practitioner services is financially recognized in the form of a higher capitation fee for those over retirement age. As a group, therefore, the elderly are of major concern to all who work in the health services. This chapter examines the proportion of elderly people in the population, their social situation and the help they receive.

PROFILE OF ELDERLY PEOPLE

Changes in the age structure of the population have resulted in elderly people forming an increasingly large proportion of the total population. Those over retirement age have increased from 8% to 21% of the population during this century (Table 1) and numbered 11 900 000 people in 1991.

Four million people, or about 1 in 14 of the population, were aged 75 years or more in 1991, and the very elderly are increasing as a proportion of those of pensionable age. Between 1981 and 1988, for example, the size of the age group 65–75 years fell by 3%, while the number aged 85 years or more increased by 33%. Although the size of the elderly population as a whole is expected to remain fairly stable over the next 25 years, the numbers aged 75 and over and 85 and over are projected to increase by 16% and 66%, respectively, between 1988 and 2011.

——— **Table 1** ———
The elderly as a percentage of the total population.

	1901	1951	1991	2015
Over retirement age	7.6	15.7	20.7	22.8
Over 75 years	1.3	3.6	7.0	7.6

Source: CSO (1987: Table 1.1).

Increased life expectancy is one reason for this change. During this century, life expectancy at birth has improved from 50 years (1906) to 75 years (1986). Much of this increase, however, has been due to a reduction in infant and childhood deaths. Improvement in life expectancy at 40 years has been more modest, having increased from 28 years (1906) to 37 years (1986). Increased life expectancy, therefore, predominantly reflects the greater proportion of people who survive childhood.

A more important reason for the increasing proportion of elderly people is a corresponding decrease in the proportion of the population which consists of infants and children. The birth rate in England and Wales fell from 35 per 1000 population in 1870 to approximately half that level in 1930, since when it has fluctuated, although the size of these fluctuations has been small compared with the earlier fall. This change from a high-mortality/high-fertility society to one characterized by low mortality and fertility is referred to as 'the demographic transition'. As the total fertility rate in England and Wales at present is still below replacement level, the population is still ageing, although more slowly than during the first half of the twentieth century.

It is important to bear the demographic transition in mind when considering the standard of living of elderly people, because it is sometimes suggested that the working age groups will be unable to support the growing population of elderly people. Fortunately this fear is unfounded because it ignores those at the other end of the life cycle, the infants and children, who are also dependent on the working population. When these two groups of dependants are combined, the 'dependency ratio' (the proportion of the population which is outside the working age groups) is found to have changed little during the twentieth century. Infants and children together with those over retirement age amounted to 40% of the total population of England and Wales in both 1901 and 1991, and this proportion is expected to be little changed by 2015 (CSO 1987). The relatively stable dependency ratio, moreover, has occurred against a background of greatly increased industrial productivity. In other words, the working population now produces far more goods, yet has a similar number of dependants. There is, thus, no absolute material reason why old age should not be a time of plenty.

——— **Table 2** ———
Changing life expectancy (years) by sex.

Life expectancy		Male	Female	Male–female difference	Percentage growth in difference 1906–1986
At birth:	1906	48	52	4	
	1986	72	78	6	50
At age 40:	1906	27	29	2	
	1986	34	39	5	150

Source: CSO (1990: Table 7.2).

So far, the figures used have referred to men and women combined. More women than men survive into old age, however, and this sex differential tends to widen with increasing age. Women's life expectancy at birth in 1986 was 78 years compared with 72 years for men and, whereas 69% of the over-75s were women, they comprised 80% of the over-85s. The very elderly as a group are, thus, predominantly women. Partly for this reason, but also because women tend to marry men who are older than themselves and because elderly women are less likely to remarry than men of the same age, widowhood is now the most common way for a woman to spend the last years of her life.

Women's greater life expectancy is often explained in terms of the physiological differences between the sexes; for example, the effect of hormonal fluctuations during the menstrual cycle on the development of atherosclerosis. The difference between men's and women's life expectancy at birth, however, has increased by 50% during this century and at age 40 years it has increased by 150% (Table 2). Relatively rapid changes of this size are unlikely to be due to physiological or genetic factors. A more plausible explanation lies in the differential social experience of men and women during this century; while women's lives have been transformed by fewer pregnancies and smaller families, changes in the lives of men have been much more modest (Jefferys & Thane 1989) (see Chapter 9).

SOCIAL SITUATION

Whereas the biological process of ageing involves progressive, but individually variable, physical deterioration, *old age* is a label which tends to be applied abruptly to all individuals at a certain age, irrespective of their physical abilities or personal wishes. The age at which this usually happens is that of retirement from work and an important part of the popular image of 'old age' is derived from the consequent loss of work income. Various negative connotations may be associated with this; for example, the elderly are sometimes seen as 'a burden on society' or objects of charity. The negative stereotypes attached to old age in industrial societies are in marked contrast to the honour and high status traditionally accorded to elderly people in predominantly agricultural societies.

All human societies need special arrangements for the physical reproduction of the next generation and for the distribution of the necessities of life. In contemporary Britain the former is achieved mainly by means of the nuclear family, by which is meant a household consisting of parents and children as opposed to the extended family household which also includes grandparents and more distant kin such as cousins and aunts. The distribution of the necessities of life in contemporary Britain takes place predominantly through work incomes. In old age, however, an individual becomes marginal to both of these social institutions. The consequences of this are felt by nearly all elderly people and, for a large minority, pose a serious threat to their well-being.

The nuclear family can be isolating. The process starts at marriage when the partners often begin to see less of their friends; it is consolidated during the years of child-rearing when the parents' energies are likely to be directed inwards towards their children; and it may become acute when the children leave home, especially when the children's search for work, housing, freedom or education takes them a long way from their parents. Elderly couples may thus be extremely dependent on one another, and when one dies the survivor may be left living alone and feeling isolated.

The proportion of elderly people living alone increases with age. In 1985, 29% of those aged 65–74 years were living alone, as were 47% of those over 75 years (CSO 1987). The high frequency with which elderly people currently live alone appears to be a relatively recent phenomenon and there is some evidence that changes in this respect since World War II have been more profound than during the two centuries before 1945 (Wall 1989). The reasons for this change are still uncertain, but the fall in the birth rate, the low marriage rate in the years after World War I and the increase in childless marriages are probably all contributory factors.

Social isolation is not an inevitable consequence of living alone. Those who live alone may be active members of organizations, such as church congregations or the constituency branches of political parties, and they can maintain relationships with neighbours, friends and family. A recent survey, for example, found that 90% of those over retirement age and living alone reported seeing friends or relatives each week (OPCS 1988). A somewhat older study, however, found that only one-third of the elderly people who lived alone had taken part in more than 20 10-minute conversations during the previous week (Tunstall 1966), which shows that much of this social contact is relatively infrequent and suggests that it may not be particularly confiding or supportive. The risk of social isolation is highest among those who are over 70 years old, single or widowed, infirm or chronically sick and have no children or other relatives living near by (Shanas et al. 1968).

While the nuclear family seems to entail a substantial number of elderly people living alone and being socially isolated, the distribution of resources through work incomes seems to ensure that many also have to live in poverty or on its borderline (see Chapter 8). This remains the case in spite of financial provision such as the statutory retirement pension, occupational pensions, and Income Support. Everyone over retirement age is automatically entitled to a statutory retirement pension. However, this often falls below the official poverty line, as defined by the income below which a person is entitled to Income Support. The statutory retirement pension for a single person in 1990, for example, was £46–90 per week; at the same time the lowest rate of Income Support for a single pensioner was £48–50 per week to which would be added rebates to cover rent and residential taxes (Child Poverty Action Group 1990). Thus, in order to avoid poverty the statutory retirement pension needed to be supplemented by Income Support, which is means-tested, or by an occupational pension.

The size of an occupational pension is related to income during working life, and occupational pensions therefore vary greatly in value. Most, however small, raise their recipients above the poverty line, although as many of these are not inflation-proofed their recipients move closer to poverty as they age. While most managers and white-collar workers receive an occupational pension, many manual workers do not. It is mostly manual workers, therefore, who will need income support when they retire. Unfortunately, the intricacies of income support and other welfare schemes mean that many old age pensioners do not receive the benefits which would be necessary to take their income above the official poverty line. At the same time, others fail even to apply for the benefits to which they are eligible, because they are ignorant of their rights, dislike the means-test or are afraid of being thought 'scroungers' (Atkinson 1975).

The most recent classical study of poverty in the UK found that approximately one in seven men and one in six women aged over 65 had an income which was lower than the state's minimum subsistance level (Table 3). As this is designed to ensure minimal housing, food and heating, the 1.5 million elderly people whose income fell below this level were likely to be at risk in terms of at least

──────── **Table 3** ────────
Poverty among the elderly (over 65 years).

	In poverty (%)	On margin of poverty (%)
Men	13.8	36.8
Women	16.8	42.9

Source: Townsend (1979).

──────── **Table 4** ────────
Housing amenities of the elderly.

| | Type of household (%) | |
| |-----------------------|---|
	One adult; aged 60 or over	Two adults; one or both aged 60 or over
No shower or bath	2	1
No sole use of indoor toilet	3	1
No central heating	37	32
No freezer	57	56
No washing machine	46	14
No telephone	26	12

Source: OPCS (1989: Tables 3.34 and 3.43).

one of these basic requirements. A further 37% of the men and 43% of the women in this age group were found to have incomes of less than 140% of the state's minimum and were thus at risk of poverty whenever extra expenses became necessary, such as house repairs, large heating bills or the replacement of furniture. In total, then, 50% of elderly men and 60% of elderly women either lived below the official poverty line or could be forced below it for varying periods of time by unexpected expenses. If the financial position of these elderly people has changed at all since the mid-1970s when this study was done, it is likely to have worsened rather than to have improved.

Poverty is not randomly distributed among elderly people. As has been shown, it is more common among women than among men; it also increases with age and is more common among those who held manual jobs during their working lives. Poverty is, therefore, most prevalent among very elderly ex-manual workers and their wives. Occupational pensions, or the lack of them, are particularly important in explaining this distribution, and in this sense income differentials in old age are merely the continuation of those established during working life (Victor 1989).

The social situation of elderly people is relevant in several ways to the health services. Social isolation may produce apathy, confusion

166   Social structure and health

——— **Table 5** ———
Health of elderly people.

Age (years)	Long-standing illness (%)	Limited long-standing illness (%)
65–74	61	44
≥75	72	58

Source: OPCS (1989: Table 4.1).

and loss of self-care skills, and delay the arrival of assistance in medical emergencies. Poverty will tend to raise morbidity due to inadequate nutrition and warmth as well as depriving many elderly people of basic household amenities (Table 4). Lack of a telephone, for example, can isolate and may make contacting the health services difficult; lack of a washing machine makes basic hygiene onerous; and the alternatives to central heating make accidental fires more likely. The social and material situation of the elderly, therefore, influences both their health and the resources with which they can cope with their ill-health.

STATE OF HEALTH

The elderly population has the highest morbidity rates, and these rise with age. Sixty-one percent of those aged 65–74 years, for example, report that they suffer from a long-standing illness, a proportion which increases to 72% among those aged over 75 years (Table 5). Multiple disabilities often combine to limit physical activity severely. One study found that 4% of the over-65s had disabilities which were sufficiently severe to confine them to their beds or their homes, while a further 10% could leave their homes only when aided (Hunt 1978). Approximately 1.25 million elderly people, therefore, suffer disabilities which render them house-bound, while many more experience great difficulty with tasks such as taking a bath, getting into bed, putting on shoes or cutting toe nails. The poor or inappropriate housing occupied by many elderly people both magnifies the handicapping effect of such disabilities and increases the likelihood of injury as the result of accidents and falls.

Some of the disabilities experienced by elderly people are caused by diseases which, although they affect all age groups, occur more frequently among the elderly. Some of these are incapacitating but not fatal, such as joint disease, visual defects, foot disabilities, dental problems and hearing defects, while others such as chronic bronchitis and ischaemic heart disease may also cause death. Other incapacitating conditions, however, are largely confined to elderly people, for instance osteoporosis, senile dementia and partial paralysis following a stroke. It is known that only a proportion of the disease in the community reaches the health services (see Chapter 3) and that this clinical iceberg is as likely to be found among the elderly population as among younger age groups (Williamson et al. 1964).

The existence of a clinical iceberg among the elderly population is particularly unfortunate because comparatively simple treatments can often alleviate their disabilities and improve their quality of life. For example, chiropody can improve the mobility of those with foot disabilities, spectacles or medical or surgical treatment can restore effective sight to many with visual defects, hearing aids can transform the lives of the partially deaf, properly fitting false teeth can improve nutrition by eliminating painful eating and widening the range of foods which can be chewed, and physiotherapy can restore mobility and independence after strokes. Conversely, failure to identify and treat such conditions may produce a vicious circle of deteriorating health. For example, poor vision combined with foot disabilities make a fall more likely; fear of a fall in traffic may make the person housebound; being housebound can result in social isolation and an inadequate diet; this in turn may lead to apathy and nutritional deficiencies; and if a fall does occur, osteoporosis makes a fracture and prolonged hospitalization likely. This chain can be broken by early detection and treatment of physical disabilities, allowing elderly people to continue leading an independent life.

Concern that the disabilities suffered by elderly people should receive early and energetic treatment has developed in the context of falling mortality rates at elderly ages. Since the 1950s the fall in mortality among those aged over 75 years has been steeper than in other adult age groups with, for example, life expectancy at age 85 having increased during the 1970s by some 6 months to 4.6 years for men and 5.6 years for women (Grundy 1984). Optimism about this change, however, has been tempered by the realization that this increase in length of life is often accompanied by considerable morbidity. If for no other reason, therefore, steadily increasing resources will be needed to care for the growing numbers of the very old.

SOCIAL SUPPORT

Elderly people often become progressively less able to lead an independent life and rely increasingly on others for help. Most of this help comes from 'informal carers', who are most often family members but sometimes friends and neighbours, with varying degrees of assistance from the health and social services ('formal carers'). Usually one informal carer provides all or the great majority of the care which is needed by a particular elderly dependent. The importance of informal care is well illustrated by a 30-year-old study of East London which found that 70% of elderly people received regular help from their families, and that for 15% their family's support alone allowed them to remain out of hospital; only 10% received no help from their families (Willmott & Young 1957). Increased geographical mobility since the 1950s has probably reduced the level of assistance which elderly people receive from their families, although a study of elderly people in 1980 found that around 50% of those living alone and needing help with cooking, shopping and bathing obtained these services from their relatives (Evandrou et al. 1986). As well as maintaining independence, such informal care also seems to affect psychological well-being. Elderly people who live alone and have little contact with others are consistently found to have poorer psychological health than those elderly people who have extensive contact with others despite living alone (Grundy 1989).

Many informal carers receive less help from the health and social services than they need, and the effects of this may be felt by both informal carers and their elderly dependants. Only one-half of those dependent on informal care, for example, receive regular visits from any branch of the welfare services and over 50% of informal carers report that it would be very difficult or impossible for them to take a 2-day break from this work (OPCS 1988). For the elderly person, inadequate assistance may mean unnecessarily curtailed independence or premature admission into institutional care. For the informal carers, inadequate support can have widespread repercussions, including loss of the primary carer's paid work, household financial difficulties, family discord, loss of social life and holidays, and an adverse effect on the health of carers and other members of their family.

Some elderly people's need for help increases beyond the point at which the informal carers can cope on their own, although reaching this point can be delayed by the provision of official assistance from the health and social services such as the various discretionary allowances, domestic help and nursing care. Home helps and district nurses are the most frequently used formal helpers (Table 6), although they, like the other services, are extremely short-staffed and only serve a small minority of elderly people. This shortfall in community-care staff was identified in the mid-1970s (DHSS 1976), and the situation since then has probably worsened rather than improved, if only because the number of over-75s, who are high users of community care services, have increased faster than the

——— **Table 6** ———
The elderly's use of health and welfare services.

Service	Percentage using in past month	
	All people aged 65 years and older	All people aged 85 years and older
General medical practitioner	33	37
Home help	10	31
District nurse or health visitor	8	23
Chiropodist	9	14
Meals-on-wheels	3	15
Day centre	5	7

Source: OPCS (1986: Tables 8.23 and 8.25).

number of staff to care for them (Grundy 1987). The under-staffed service which results can appear impersonal and thus deter those who need its assistance. For informal carers the shortage of community-care staff is often compounded by difficulty in obtaining information about the types of official help available, and there is a tendency for more services to go to those who are already in contact with some part of the welfare system. In addition, there is a chronic shortage of accommodation suitable for those with disabilities. As a result, many elderly people at present do not get the social and nursing support services which they need.

Attempts are usually made to admit into an institution those who can no longer manage in the community. Institutional accommodation is provided in an uncoordinated way from a number of sources. Local authorities provide sheltered housing through their housing departments, and Part III accommodation through their social services departments; the NHS provides geriatric hospitals and geriatric units in general hospitals; voluntary associations operate residential homes which often cater to those of a particular religious denomination; and the private sector offers wardened accommodation and nursing homes. The private sector is usually expensive, while in many areas sheltered housing, Part III accommodation, voluntary organization homes and hospital geriatric beds are in short supply and often have long waiting lists for admission. A lack of coordination between the various types of institutional care undermines the optimum usage of even these inadequate facilities. The private and voluntary sectors are largely unplanned, while the organization of the State sector is split between the NHS, which is responsible for the hospital beds, and the Local Authorities which provide the sheltered housing and Part III accommodation. In consequence, elderly people often experience difficulty in obtaining the type of institutional care which they need.

This situation can affect doctors in a variety of ways. General practitioners, for example, may attempt to admit their elderly patients who can no longer manage at home into acute hospital beds. The elderly people concerned are often happy with this arrangement, at least for a short time, but the staff of acute hospitals are likely to resist such admissions because they anticipate these patients staying a long time due to the difficulty of arranging alternative accommodation (see Chapter 5). The work of many doctors is therefore complicated by the shortage of facilities for elderly people, but these shortages have rarely been challenged collectively by the profession. A relatively low proportion of specialists in geriatric medicine, for example, receive merit awards and in the mid-1970s, when this information was last published, the weekly expenditure on a patient in the mainly geriatric long-stay hospitals was only 40% of that in acute hospitals (DHSS 1982). The profession's emphasis on curative medicine allows it to condone this situation, while the stereotype which it creates prevents many doctors from appreciating the significant curative component in geriatric medicine.

CONCLUSIONS

This chapter has concentrated upon those sections of the elderly population which are likely to be of particular concern to the health services. The growing numbers of the very elderly, those living alone and socially isolated, the high proportion of the elderly who receive inadequate incomes and those who are in poor health, together with informal carers and their families, are likely to need considerable assistance from the primary care sector, community care and the hospital services.

This situation can easily generate an unthinking stereotype of all elderly people as lonely, poor, sick and a burden on their families. A re-reading of the data in this chapter, however, will quickly reveal the inaccuracy of this stereotype. Over 70% of those aged 65–74 years do not live alone and more than half of those aged over 75 years still live with someone else. Even among those who live alone, and depending on how it is measured, at least one-third are not socially isolated. Nearly half the elderly population neither lives in poverty nor can be forced into it by extra expenses such as large heating bills or the need to replace consumer durables, and among this more affluent 50% are many who enjoy excellent incomes. Similarly, two out of every five people aged 65–74 years do not report long-standing illnesses and neither do some 30% of those aged over 75; 85% of elderly people can leave their homes unaided. Many informal carers can accommodate with minimal disruption the demands which these responsibilities entail and obtain considerable satisfaction from the experience. Finally, the community care services in some areas of the country are adequately resourced and effectively coordinated, and offer a range of imaginative services to both infirm elderly people and their informal carers. The stereotype is therefore inaccurate and, in fact, the elderly as a group show a wide range of health and living conditions whose distribution has its origins in the earlier phases of life. Old age thus accentuates earlier inequalities, rather than being a distinct social category whose members experience relatively homogeneous conditions.

The stereotypical view of the elderly as lonely, poor and sick can be seen as one element in a more general system of discrimination against elderly people which has been described as 'ageism'. This stereotype is not entirely negative, in the sense that it produces such financial concessions as exemption from NHS prescription charges, reduced transport fares and, at an informal level, the 'special offers' which many shopkeepers make to their elderly customers. Such concessions, however, tend to identify the elderly as requiring charity, a usually unwelcome status which is derived from the inadequate level of the statutory retirement pension.

Compulsory retirement, residential segregation and the need to apply for means-tested Income Support are other elements of ageism. With the notable exception of the politicians who legislate on these matters, most people have to retire from paid employment at 60 or 65 years of age, and this is resented by many who are physically capable of continuing and do not wish to be deprived of the satisfaction of work and the social contact it brings. Similarly, many elderly people do not wish their social life to be confined to people of their own age, and feel that segregated schemes of sheltered housing and institutional care deprive them of the company of younger people. Finally, many are critical of a statutory retirement pension the level of which consistently falls below the accepted minimum income and which thus forces them to apply for means-tested supplements, an invasion of privacy which most would prefer to avoid. Ageism, then, is a system of discrimination which deprives elderly people of dignity, maximum attainable independence and an interesting life. The challenge to those working in the health and welfare services is to avoid ageism whilst at the same time meeting the needs of elderly people.

REFERENCES

Atkinson, A. (1975) *The Economics of Inequality.* London: Oxford University Press.
Central Statistical Office (1987) *Social Trends 17.* London: HMSO.

172   Social structure and health

Central Statistical Office (1990) *Social Trends 20*. London: HMSO.
Child Poverty Action Group (1990) *National Welfare Benefits Handbook 1990–91*. London: CPAG.
Department of Health and Social Security (1976) *Priorities for Health and Personal Social Services in England: A Consultative Document*. London: HMSO.
Department of Health and Social Security (1982) *Health and Personal Social Services for England 1982*. London: HMSO.
Evandrou, M., Arber, S., Dale, A. & Gilbert, N. (1986) Who cares for the elderly?: Family care provision and receipt of statutory services. In: *Dependency and Interdependency in Old Age*, ed. C. Phillipson, M. Bernard & P. Strang. Beckenham: Croom Helm.
Grundy, E. (1984) Mortality and morbidity among the old. *Br. med. J.*, **288**, 663–664.
Grundy, E. (1987) Community care for the elderly 1976–84. *Br. med. J.*, **294**, 626–629.
Grundy, E. (1989) Living arrangements and social support in later life. In: *Human Ageing and Late Life Multidisciplinary Perspectives*, ed. A. Warner. London: Edward Arnold.
Hunt, A. (1978) The elderly at home. In: *Central Statistical Office. Social Trends 8*. London: HMSO.
Jefferys, M. & Thane, P. (1989) Introduction: an ageing society and ageing people. In: *Growing Old in the Twentieth Century*, ed. M. Jefferys. London: Routledge.
Office of Population Censuses and Surveys (1986) *General Household Survey 1984*. London: HMSO.
Office of Population Censuses and Surveys (1988) *Informal Carers*. London: HMSO.
Office of Population Censuses and Surveys (1989) *General Household Survey 1987*. London: HMSO.
Shanas, E., Townsend, E., Wedderburn, D. et al. (1968) *Old People in Three Industrial Societies*. New York: Atherton Press.
Townsend, P. (1979) *Poverty in the United Kingdom*. London: Penguin.
Tunstall, J. (1966) *Old and Alone: A Sociological Study of Old People*. London: Routledge & Kegan Paul.
Victor, C.R. (1989) Income inequality in later life. In: *Growing Old in the Twentieth Century*, ed. M. Jefferys. London: Routledge.
Wall, R. (1989) Leaving home and living alone: an historical perspective. *Popul. Stud.*, **43**, 369–389.
Williamson, J., Stokoe, I., Gray, S., et al. (1964) Old people at home: their unreported needs. *Lancet*, **i**, 1117–1120.
Willmott, P. & Young, M. (1957) *Family and Kinship in East London*. London: Harmondsworth.

PART IV

The social process of defining disease

12

The limits of
medical knowledge

Sheila Hillier

In Molière's play *Le Medécin Malgré Lui,* two doctors are talking:

> *1st doctor:* It seems to me you are locating them wrongly. The heart is on the left and the liver is on the right.
>
> *2nd doctor:* Yes, in the old days that was so, but we have changed all that and we now practice medicine by a completely new method.

Molière, who often satirized medicine in his plays was writing in the seventeenth century. He was showing, in a comical way, how ideas about health and disease and the understanding of the human body change, and that these changes are sometimes subject to fashion. Treatments alter too. Many of those used in the past — like rolling a small cannon ball on the abdominal wall to treat gastropsis — seem bizarre to us today, and no doubt methods and approaches in current use will become outmoded similarly. Changes take place, not only in a simple response to fashion, but because the understanding that underlies them alters. A different way of looking at disease may emerge, an easier technique may be discovered.

Although medicine has made important contributions to curing or alleviating some conditions, a questioning and evaluative approach to its achievements is important, indeed, it is the only truly scientific one. It is usually argued that medical knowledge has progressed over many thousands of years from a relatively primitive state to a scientific corpus of knowledge with well established boundaries. Medicine, it is held, has moved by slow and painful steps from a time when it was largely ineffective, tinged with elements of superstition and quackery to one where dramatic advances have been made in the scientific treatment and understanding of disease. It is because of such progress, it is suggested, that medicine now holds the superordinate position it does, defining states of health and disease and distinguishing legitimate treatments and practices. For the past 50 years medicine has been held in unprecedentedly high regard, whereas even in the fairly recent past it was treated with scepticism.

The reasons for this current predominance bear examination, for admiration is not unmixed. In the past decade the effectiveness of modern medicine has been questioned by those who argue that, although advances have been made in describing pathogenesis down to the level of the cell and sometimes beyond, understanding the *causes* of disease has been much more limited. This has meant that powerful medical interventions into the major killers of the developed world (cancer and heart disease) are limited. At the same time, the cost of providing health care escalates, and this has led some to wonder if the social and economic costs do not outweigh the benefits. It is further suggested that medicine exerts too much influence over our daily lives and, thereby, becomes an instrument of social regulation whose brief extends far beyond simple healing and caring for the sick. Medicine may, in both theory and practice, be highly contaminated with the social prejudices of its time. Some writers also maintain that the development of medical knowledge is thus coloured by the social environment, and that its claims to scientific objectivity are thereby rendered suspect.

CHANGING THEORIES OF DISEASE

It is possible here to give only the briefest outline of the development of medical thought. The written records go back to Ancient Egypt where the oldest surgical textbook dates to 1500 B.C. The Greeks contributed much to medical thought. Hippocrates, whose oath is taken by every doctor today, was a Greek physician. In particular, the Greeks developed the view that health and disease could be explained in terms of natural rather than supernatural forces, and in Hippocrates' writings, ill health was attributed to an imbalance of the body's four basic humours, the sanguine (yellow bile), the choleric (blood), the melancholic (black bile) and the phlegmatic (phlegm). This idea of the body's balance is found in many other ancient medical systems, notably in traditional Chinese medicine, and Ayurvedic medicine. The Roman physician Galen continued to use these ideas and his Latin texts together with translations of

Hippocrates and Aristotle survived to form part of the corpus of knowledge taught for many hundreds of years and given great respectability in the medieval universities of Europe. The works of Arabic, Spanish and Jewish physicians were also studied. Not much was added to the corpus that significantly changed its general reliance on humoral theory until the sixteenth and seventeenth century attacks on Galen by more empirically minded doctors. Their medicine was based on observations which they made. These observations were both clinical and anatomical and were based on dissection and post-mortem examination. As a result, doctors began to suggest that there was not one disease caused by an imbalance, but that disease took many different forms and could not be reduced to a single cause (Open University 1985).

These conflicts produced an enormous diversity in methods of treatment and, more importantly, the identification and classification of diseases as disturbances of particular organs, which began to develop during the eighteenth and nineteenth centuries, produced a view of disease as specific in character and cause. This meant that the earlier holistic view of the patients disease — as being caused by the particular balance of humours in the individual's body, which could be affected by feelings and life circumstances — was displaced. Instead, diseases themselves became the focus of study and the 'sick man' disappeared (Jewson 1976). The clinical and pathological observations of earlier years were greatly improved by advances in technology. The simple microscope in use in the seventeenth century was replaced by one with greater powers of magnification and this meant that not only organs but also cells could be examined and micro-organisms identified. By the end of the nineteenth century, many of the specific 'germs' causing a variety of diseases like cholera, tetanus, plague, anthrax and typhoid, had been identified.

However, these improvements in understanding were not accompanied by better cures. Surgery was heroic and hazardous. Doctors were unable to offer help in the face of the major cholera epidemics which swept Britain in the nineteenth century. Whilst the focus of medical inquiry had become narrower and more rigorous with a greater ability to describe illnesses, medical prevention and cure were less successful. As McKeown (1979) has demonstrated, the major reductions in mortality in the nineteenth century were due to the decline in deaths from infectious diseases, but the contribution of medical measures or discoveries was relatively small. Improvements in nutrition, sanitation, a purer water supply and the reduction in family size which reduced the pressure of population on food supply were the major factors contributing to the decline in mortality (see Chapter 1). The popular view throughout most of the nineteenth century of medical practice as being of dubious efficacy was mirrored in a divided profession, riven by factional disputes.

But change was occurring. Pasteur's ability, in 1881, to demonstrate the efficacy of his new anthrax vaccine is often regarded as the 'turning point' for the development of a credible scientific medicine (Shyrock 1936). From that time on, the developments of vaccines and a vast armamentarium of drugs, together with improved medical training incorporating the 'new' sciences of pharmacology and biochemistry all served to fix an image of medicine as the victorious outcome of progress in science.

As mentioned earlier, this view is now being tempered both within medicine and without. In a recent review of the state of medicine, Rose (1990) remarked 'Unfortunately most of the common and incurable diseases remain common and incurable. Our ability to control their underlying symptoms has grown impressively, but our ability to alter their natural course has not'. Equally, the medical profession has grown increasingly sensitive to criticism of its practice. It has been argued that the narrow focus of inquiry has led to a failure to recognize the social and psychological factors associated with becoming ill. This has led not only to a neglect of the causal importance of these factors but an arrogant disregard for the patient as well. These criticisms stress that the patient must be seen as a person with a biography, with feelings and with the right to exercise choice and participate in decisions about treatment.

Such a position, although critical of medicine, does not amount to a fundamental critique of its position in society. The legitimacy of medicine as the major source of expert care is maintained and restated, with an inclusion of newer forms of knowledge, derived from the social sciences as a further evidence of the rightness of the position which it holds.

Outside medicine, however, the criticisms are more far reaching, and various arguments are put forward. These include the 'medicalization' thesis, the 'social constructionist' view, and a broadly social structural approach. These arguments generally question the nature of medical knowledge, in particular, its claims to scientific objectivity and independence, and the extent and form of medical practice.

MEDICALIZATION

Stated simply, the medicalization thesis argues that there is an increasing tendency for medicine to expand its claims. As a result, more and more areas of life become subject to its jurisdiction and definition. Problems are defined in medical terms and medical treatments are seen as appropriate solutions. Most writers see this as a wholly negative practice (Zola 1975). Oakley (1980), in her studies on childbirth, shows how the medical profession has redefined childbirth as a potentially pathological process, requiring more medical intervention. Other examples include hyperactivity, obesity, violence, alcoholism and child abuse which have fairly recently become the province of doctors who have the final authority to label such conditions as illnesses, even if they do not take all the responsibility for dealing with them, but cooperate with professionals from other groups (Conrad 1976).

Critics suggest that social problems are redefined as medical ones. While most psychiatrists would argue that mental illness has a clear organic cause or is due to specific psychological disturbances, critical writers, like Szasz (1961) have suggested that the label of 'mental illness' is a convenient way of describing what are, fundamentally, problems of living. Therefore, the application of medical treatments — like drugs and electroconvulsive therapy — is a violation of human rights.

Szasz's position is at one extreme. Arguing against him, Halmos (1966), has described the substitution of medical treatments for legal punishments as a social advance. It is argued that it is better to attempt therapy with alcoholics, sex offenders, drug addicts and overdose patients, than to impose fines and prison sentences. It could also be suggested that doctors are not consciously expanding their work; they are just the most readily available 'catch all' for newly emergent problems.

It is clear, however, that medicine still holds a position of social power and influence. Part of that power rests on its claims to its effectiveness and scientific basis, and part of it on its position of professional dominance (Freidson 1970). It is not possible to understand the powerful position that medicine has achieved without realizing that professional *organization,* backed by powerful claims about knowledge, lies at the root. Therefore the medical profession itself is in a position to define its own areas of work, to extend, or direct its medical monopoly in response to professional interests of autonomy, control and reward (see Chapter 15). As Hughes (1958) succinctly puts it

> collectively they tell society what is good and right for the individual and society at large in some aspects of life . . . indeed they set the very terms in which people may think about it.

The medical profession therefore does not simply provide a service, but determines the conditions of service. This may include expanding areas of practice (as in the 'medicalization' view), but can also lead to a number of other consequences. For example, in health-care systems where fee-for-service payments are in operation, there may be a temptation to put material interests over the interests of patients. The profession can also define some types of work as more rewarding intellectually or materially than others, and can also control the type of practice and the work of other occupations which are defined as subordinate. What this adds up to is that the professional organization determines the nature of medical work and is, therefore, an intrinsic part of the monopolistic nature of medical practice. In turn, this monopoly as the only supplier of what has already been defined as essential, can set the limits of medicine, expanding or contracting as professional interest dictates.

It could be suggested that this is a somewhat out-of-date picture and that the medical profession, far from having such control over our daily lives, is in turn controlled by societal forces. Illich (1975) takes a broad view of the 'medicalization of life'. Modern industrial society he argues, is characterized by large bureaucracies and professional bodies. These types of organization are instrumental in creating dependence, since they remove so much of the individual's control over life. Nowhere is this more true than in the case of the medical establishment which has become a 'major threat to health'. It is, to use Illich's word *iatrogenic.* He describes three types of iatrogenesis. The first kind, *clinical,* describes the way in which medical interventions can be clinically damaging and irrelevant. Evidence is cited from the USA of the large numbers of unnecessary operations, with their associated fatalities. The second is *social;* the expanding nature of medicine accompanies the industrialization of society, and creates, like industry itself, an artificial need for its products. The third type is a consequence of the second. In *structural* iatrogenesis, the existence of medicine as it is currently organized, inhibits people's own autonomy by 'undermining their competence in growing up, caring for each other, and ageing'. They are deprived of confronting their own pain or death. Illich believes that people need to rediscover how to cope with life and death, and that medical knowledge should be demystified, and its exclusive control over practice removed.

Social construction

Implied in Illich's arguments is the idea that medical knowledge should be questioned, although he is not very precise about how this should be done. The writings of *social constructionists* have been more specific. The approach begins simply enough by arguing that concepts of disease are not necessarily universal, ahistorical or unrelated to the society in which they emerge. The French epistemologist Foucalt has been important in the development of social constructionist ideas. He shows how the development of the clinic as a base for medical training in eighteenth century France, itself a response to medical malpractice and quackery, laid an emphasis on clinical observation. Large numbers of patients could be observed, and the idea of the pathological localization of diseases, as *entities* distinct from sick individuals, was thereby developed. This change in emphasis, referred to earlier as the 'disappearance of the sick man' and his replacement by a catalogue of clearly defined diseases, also encouraged a view of the body itself as an entity distinct from a person which could be studied as an example of the general class of bodies.

Foucalt's work also lays great emphasis on the importance of medical techniques and practices as expressions of medical power. Even simple matters like palpating the patients abdomen, or listening to the chest with a stethoscope are examples of how clinical techniques, by their nature, dehumanize patients and render them passive and quiet (Armstrong 1987). They become objects of study. The patient's most intimate areas of the body are legitimate phenomena for examination, and the depersonalized nature of what is, in fact, very personal contact between two people, becomes that of 'patient' and 'doctor'. This depersonalization is achieved by the operation of the central rule of clinical medicine — that, first and foremost, correct knowledge is gained by physical examination of the patient. Such a tenet, Foucalt argues, gives the doctor legitimate physical power over patients, and its practices reinforce and sustain this. It also promotes intellectual power for, it seems, the doctor 'knows' the patients body, better than the patient herself (Foucault 1973).

The matter is not confined to physical examination. Writing about modern general practice in Britain, Armstrong (1983) has shown how developments in the work of general practitioners have created yet another way of looking at patients. General practice appears to represent a more humanistic approach to medical care than that purveyed by the high-technology hospital. Yet, Armstrong argues, by emphasizing patients' psychosocial needs, and events in their lives, general practice is simply another form of control, all the more subtle since patients are themselves urged to be 'willing partners' in detailing their personal troubles and difficulties. The general practitioner has become the 'Confessor' of present times, and there is no reason to regard the changes that have taken place as representing progress. As other writers have suggested, the doctor and patient are not equal partners in the consultation, and the consultation itself 'individualizes' health-care problems, preventing a more radical review of the health and social circumstances of a class, group or community (Waitzken 1976).

Social constructionists are sometimes accused of saying that medicine's claims to scientific objectivity are rendered suspect by the fact that one can identify the social circumstances under which certain ideas and practices have emerged. By implication, if circumstances had been otherwise, then the form of medicine, its areas of investigation and the corpus of medical knowledge might have been different. Most will not commit themselves so far; after all, if medicine's knowledge is relative to time and place, cannot one say the same of social constructionism (Bury 1986)? On the whole, social constructionists seem to be content to emphasize that medicine is a social *as well as* a scientific enterprise, and that the strands are closely interwoven even at the level of *apparently objective 'discoveries'*.

Social structure

Whilst social constructionists have tended to concentrate their argument on particular forms of medical knowledge techniques and practices (a micro-focus), other writers have considered how far the practice of medicine and the general propagation of the biomedical model of health and illness serves the interests of the State, the ruling class in society or society as a whole (a macro-focus). Such an approach suggests that medicine does not so much create its own objects (as in the medicalization view), but that it carries out certain activities on behalf of some other institution. Parsons (1951) was an American sociologist who regarded the health-care system as the means by which the threat posed to *society* by ill health was controlled (see Chapter 13). Parsons was generally uncritical of medicine, but argued simply that its shape was congruent with prevailing American values. It emphasizes 'doing', 'achievement' and 'progress'. He did not say that its claims to independence and objectivity were thereby compromised, but other writers are more trenchant.

Illich's (1975) argument is rehearsed again here; *industrialization* has caused medicine to take the form of an all-enveloping bureaucracy whose objective is to foster further growth and consumption of its products. Navarro (1976) goes further. He suggests that financial capital has invaded, transformed and dominated the health-care arena. Health care has thus become a *commodity* to be bought and sold and the effect is that decisions about health care will be made on the basis of their profitability. Activities where the result is unprofitable, or where profit cannot be measured, will never be given priority. For example, adequate legislation to protect workers' health will not be enforced if it affects an organization's level of profit. In individual consultations, finance may predominate over service and assistance to the patient. Capitalism may also influence the way in which medical definitions of disease are formulated. In the nineteenth century, tuberculosis was regarded as a 'constitutional weakness' rather than something resulting from poverty and bad working conditions. Today, diseases like cancer and heart disease are seen as problems of individual life-style rather than of pollutants, the efforts of advertisers and the powerlessness of people whose only release is simple affordable pleasure.

Navarro suggests that it is not only capitalism but the State itself which has a role in the control of medicine. While some regard the State in capitalist countries as merely a servant of the capitalist class, Navarro says that the State acts on behalf of capitalism but is not dominated by it. There are features of State organization that occur in capitalist and non-capitalist countries alike. Both socialist and capitalist governments have adopted a variety of strategies in relation to medicine. Often these strategies are an attempt to solve conflicts between various objectives. Governments might wish to have a healthy work-force but not want to endanger profitability or production levels. They might regard preventive health measures as an important objective but be reluctant to surrender the revenue obtained from tobacco and alcohol, or increase unemployment by reducing the number of cars sold. The State may wish to introduce certain types of health care to buy off political discontent, or to use medicine in the control of political dissidents. The role of the State in relation to medicine is a complex one, and it does appear that the State itself over and above classes or dominant interest groups potentially possesses great power over the form and direction of medical care and should not be ignored in an analysis of the limits of medical knowledge. It can promote expansion or set boundaries and priorities, particularly when central government finance is involved.

SUMMARY

Huge resources are invested in our systems of health care but, traditionally, these systems and their practitioners — doctors — have not been held accountable. This will not continue, however, as health-care systems are subject to increasingly rigorous financial control. In addition, the scientific evaluation of medicine, using broader, multidisciplinary criteria, is likely to grow. This will not bring about a Utopian situation where a well-regulated and caring health system addresses unchanging basic human needs — for needs themselves change.

Because the form that medicine takes has consequences beyond the immediate healing role, it is important that the claims made by medicine need to be evaluated and reviewed. Medicine, perhaps, is 'too important to be left to doctors'.

REFERENCES

Armstrong, D. (1983) *The Political Anatomy of the Body.* Cambridge: Cambridge University Press.

Armstrong, D. (1987) Bodies of knowledge: Foucalt and the problem of human anatomy. In: *Sociological Theory and Medical Sociology,* ed. G. Scambler. London: Tavistock.

Bury, M. (1986) Social constructionism and the development of medical sociology. *Soc. Hlth Illness,* **8,** 137–170.

Conrad, P. (1976) *Identifying Hyperactive Children: the Medicalisation of Deviant Behaviour.* Lexington, KY: D.C. Heath.

Foucault, M. (1973) *The Birth of the Clinic: an Archeology of Medical Perception.* London: Tavistock.

Freidson, E. (1970) *The Profession of Medicine.* New York: Dodd Mead.

Halmos, P. (1966) *The Faith of the Counsellors.* London: Constable.

Hughes, E. (1958) *Medical Men and Their Work.* Glencoe, IL: Free Press.

Illich, I. (1975) *Medical Nemesis.* London: Calder and Boyars.

Jewson, N.D. (1976) The disappearance of the sick man from medical cosmology 1770–1870. *Sociology,* **10,** 225–244.

McKeown, T. (1979) *The Role of Medicine.* Oxford: Oxford University Press/Nuffield Provincial Hospitals Trust.

Navarro, V. (1976) Social class, political power and the State and their implications in medicine. *Soc. Sci. Med.,* **10,** 437–457.

Oakley, A. (1980) *Women confined: Towards a Sociology of Childbirth.* Oxford: Martin Robertson.

Open University (1985) *Caring for Health: History and Diversity U205 7.* Milton Keynes: Open University Press.

Parsons, T. (1951) *The Social System.* Glencoe, IL: The Free Press.

Rose, G. (1990) Reflections on the changing times. *Br. med. J.,* **301,** 683–687.

Shyrock, R. (1936) *The Development of Modern Medicine.* First Edition. Wisconsin: University of Wisconsin Press.

Szasz, T. (1961) *The Myth of Mental Illness.* New York: Harper.

Waitzken, H. (1976) Medicine, superstructure and micropolitics. *Soc. Sci. Med.,* **13A,** 601.

Zola, I. (1975) In the name of health and illness. *Soc. Sci. Med.,* **9,** 83–88.

13

Deviance, sick role and stigma

Graham Scambler

Social norms are definite principles or rules which people are expected to observe in a given culture or milieu: 'Norms represent the "dos" and "don'ts" of social life' (Giddens 1989). Only a tiny minority of norms are likely to be codified as laws. *Deviance* can be defined as non-conformity to a norm, or set of norms, which is accepted by a significant proportion of local citizens or inhabitants. Deviant behaviour is behaviour which, once it has become public knowledge, is routinely subject to sanctions — to punishment, correction or treatment. Importantly, behaviour which is acceptable in one culture may be deviant in another. For example, smoking marijuana is deviant in British culture while consuming alcohol is not; the reverse is the case in some Middle Eastern cultures.

ILLNESS, DEVIANCE AND THE SICK ROLE

Few analysts before the 1950s regarded illness as a form of deviance. The term 'deviance' was reserved for behaviour for which individuals could be held responsible; infractions of the law were seen as paradigmatic. A significant change of outlook dates from the work of Parsons (1951), who defined illness as a form of deviance on the grounds that it disrupts the social system by inhibiting people's performance of their customary or normal social roles. If such disruption is to be minimized, then the behaviour associated with illness — which unlike other forms of deviant behaviour cannot be prevented by the threat of sanctions — must be controlled. Control is exercised through the prescription of social roles for the sick and for physicians (see Chapter 4).

According to Parsons, the *sick role* consists of two rights and two obligations. The rights are that sick people are exempted (1) from performing their normal social roles, and (2) from responsibility for their own state. Sick people are at the same time obligated (3) to want to get well as soon as possible, and (4) to consult and cooperate with medical experts whenever the severity of their condition warrants it. Failure to meet either or both of these obligations may lead to the charge that people are responsible for the continuation of their illness, and ultimately to sanctions, including the withdrawal of the rights of the sick role. Gerhardt (1987) describes Parsons' sick role as a social 'niche' where 'the incapacitated have a chance to recover from their weakness(es), and overcome their urge to withdraw from rather than actively tackle the vicissitudes of the capitalist labour market'. In fact, it can afford its incumbents a legitimate breathing space from a wide range of social demands, and not only from those associated with the labour market.

The sick role is a temporary role into which all people, regardless of their status or position, may be admitted. It is also 'universalistic', in that physicians are held to draw upon general and objective criteria in determining whether or not individuals are sick, how sick, and what kinds of sickness they are suffering from. Its main function is to control illness, and to reduce its disruptive effects on the social system by ensuring that sick people are returned to a healthy state as speedily as possible. Physicians serve as 'gatekeepers', policing access to the sick role by authoritatively determining who is sick and who is healthy. They also spur the urge to leave the sick role (Gerhardt 1987). Unlike some other commentators, Parsons is not at all critical of physicians functioning as *agents of social control*. Indeed, he sees the sick role, and physicians' policing of it, as important contributions to the stability and health of the social system.

Freidson (1970) is among those who are less sanguine about physicians' social control functions. He acknowledges Parsons' pioneering work in linking illness and deviance, but insists that the argument must be taken a step further: 'Unlike Parsons, I do not argue merely that medicine has the power to legitimize one's acting sick by conceding that he really is sick . . . I argue that by virtue of being the authority on what illness "really" is, *medicine creates the social possibilities for acting sick.* In this sense, medicine's monopoly includes the right to create illness as an *official social role*'. Freidson adds that it is in medicine's interests — because it enhances the demand for its practitioners' skills — actively to pursue 'the proliferation of situations that create deviant illness roles'.

It is not necessary to adhere to a thesis of 'medical imperialism' —

namely, to claim a conspiracy on the part of physicians to 'medicalize' society — to acknowledge either that a multiplicity of new deviant illness roles have in fact been created this century, perhaps most conspicuously as a product of the growth of psychiatry, or that this has accorded physicians greater powers and responsibilities as agents of social control. Freidson's contribution is to have pointed out that these powers and responsibilities have *social* — not merely scientific — origins, and require careful analysis and evaluation. After all, to diagnose disease is to define its bearer as in need of correctional 'treatment' of body or mind (even if in practice this often involves little more than recognizing a disease's self-limiting natural history). Contrary to Parsons, Freidson sees physicians' social control functions as extending far beyond the policing of the sick role and as possessing negative as well as positive potential for society.

THE FORCE OF A LABEL

In modern societies professionally trained physicians are generally responsible not only for (collectively) constructing but also for (individually) selecting and applying diagnostic labels. It is now recognized, however, that the application and communication of some diagnoses can have especially serious and unwelcome consequences for patients. This occurs most conspicuously when the conditions being diagnosed are personally or socially *stigmatizing*. Stigmatizing conditions can be defined as conditions that set their possessors apart from 'normal' people, that mark them as socially unacceptable or inferior beings. Thus people experiencing deafness, mental illness, severe burns, diabetes, psoriasis, acquired immunodeficiency syndrome (AIDS) and numerous other diseases or symptoms of disease have been in the past and continue to be avoided, rejected or shunned to varying degrees by others.

Another unhappy consequence of being labelled in this way is that people's stigma can come to dominate the perceptions that others have of them and how they treat them. In the vocabulary of sociology, an individual's deviant status becomes a *master status*: whatever else she may be — for example, mother, teacher or school governor — she is regarded primarily as a diabetic, cancer victim, or whatever. In other words, her deviant status comes to dominate and push into the background her other statuses. Even her past may be unsafe and subject to retrospective interpretation. Especially pertinent to this line of reasoning are the concepts of 'cultural stereotyping' and 'secondary deviation'.

Cultural stereotyping

Those afflicted with a stigmatizing condition may be expected to conform to a popular stereotype. An American study, for example, found that blind people are often attributed distinctive personality characteristics that differentiate them from sighted people: 'helplessness', 'dependency', 'melancholy', 'docility', 'gravity of inner thought' and 'aestheticism' (Scott 1969). However far-fetched or misleading such stereotyping may be, the blind person cannot ignore how others expect her to behave; to do so might well be to ignore key factors in her interaction with them. The author goes on to claim that blind people adapt to cultural stereotyping in five major ways: by simply concurring; by 'cutting themselves off' to protect their self-conceptions; by deliberately adopting a facade of compliance for expediency's sake; by making people pay something for a 'performance' (e.g. begging); or by actively resisting. It should be mentioned that they may also be obliged to respond to stereotypes of blindness held by physicians and other health professionals.

Secondary deviation

One distinction which has gained currency among those investigating links between *crime* and *deviance* is that between 'primary' and 'secondary' deviation (Lemert 1967). Study of the former focuses on how deviant behaviour — for example, stealing — originates; and study of the latter focuses on how people are symbolically assigned to deviant statuses — for example, thief or criminal — and the effective consequences of such assignment for subsequent deviation on their part. The importance of studying secondary deviation has been increasingly acknowledged since the 1960s. It is now accepted, for example, that disapproving cultural and professional *reactions* to deviant behaviour can often foster rather than inhibit a continuing commitment to deviance.

Similarly, some have claimed that a negative, stereotyped reaction to a stigmatizing illness or handicap can confirm individuals in their deviant status, can constrain them to see themselves as others see them and to behave accordingly. For example, a blind person who is expected to be and is consistently treated as 'helpless' and 'dependent' may actually become so; he or she may find it less exacting to concur with and ultimately adopt the prescribed role than to resist it. Those in institutional or custodial care for long periods are particularly vulnerable in this respect.

Perhaps the area in which 'labelling theory' has had the most controversial impact in relation to medicine has been that of mental illness. In the mid-1960s an American sociologist, Scheff (1966), claimed that labelling is the single most important cause of mental illness. He argued that there exists a residue of odd, eccentric and unusual behaviour for which the culture provides no explicit labels: such forms of behaviour constitute 'residual rule-breaking' or 'residual deviance'. Most psychiatric symptoms can be categorized as instances of residual deviance. There exists also a cultural stereotype of mental illness. When for some reason or other residual deviance becomes a salient or 'public' issue, the cultural stereotype of insanity becomes the guiding imagery for action. In time, contact with a physician is established, a psychiatric diagnosis made and, perhaps, procedures for hospitalization put into effect. Problems of secondary deviation follow with a degree of predictability.

Scheff's theory has been criticized by others, notably Gove (1970). Gove agreed that there is a cultural stereotype of mental illness, but not that people are treated as mentally ill because they inadvertently behave in a way that 'activates' this stereotype. If anything, he argued, 'the gross exaggeration of the degree and type of disorder in the stereotype fosters the denial of mental illness, since the disturbed person's behaviour does not usually correspond to the stereotype'. Scheff is also wrong, according to Gove, in suggesting that, once publicly noticed, the person will be routinely processed as mentally ill and admitted for institutional care; public officials, he argued, 'screen out' a large proportion of those who come before them. Finally, Gove claimed that Scheff overstated the degree to which secondary deviation is associated with hospitalization for mental illness. Although the dispute between Scheff and his critics continues, it seems reasonable to conclude that he fell foul of the temptation to explain too much in terms of a single, if important, insight.

LIVING WITH A STIGMATIZING CONDITION

Stigmatizing conditions vary in terms of their visibility and obtrusiveness and of the extent to which they are recognized. Not surprisingly, there is an equivalent degree of variation in their effects on individuals' lives. People who are 'discredited', to use Goffman's (1963) terminology, are those whose stigma is immediately apparent, such as amputees, or widely known, such as someone whose fellow workers know of his suicide attempt. The discredited will often find they have to cope with situations made awkward by their stigma: their problem will be one of *managing tension*. The physically handicapped, Davis (1964) found, typically pass through three stages when meeting with strangers: the first is one of 'fictional acceptance' — they find they are ascribed some sort of stereotypical identity and accepted on that basis; the second stage is one of 'breaking through' this fictional acceptance — they induce others to regard and interact with them normally; and the third stage is one of 'consolidation' — they have to sustain the definition of themselves as normal over time.

One major criticism of Davis' account is that it over-estimates people's strength of will and psychological stamina to engage in what he calls 'deviance disavowal'. It was noted earlier that some blind people regard it as less taxing to defer to than to contest cultural stereotypes of blindness. Higgins (1980) found that deaf people sometimes actually 'avow' their deviance, and even extend it by acting mute, in order to simplify and smooth their relations with the hearing: written messages can minimize misunderstandings and save time and embarrassment.

However, people who are discreditable are those whose stigma is only occasionally apparent, such as people with epilepsy who suffer infrequent seizures, or little known, such as someone whose status as human immunodeficiency virus (HIV) positive is known only to his doctor. The discredited will usually find they have to take care to manage information: to 'pass as normal' they will have to censor what others know about them. In Goffman's (1963) words, the main quandary is: 'To display or not to display; to tell or not to tell; to lie or not to lie; and in each case, to whom, how, when and where'. People with epilepsy frequently opt to pass as normal, and hence find themselves having to manage information with extreme caution. The following paragraphs illustrate this, and these and the succeeding section on rectal cancer afford some indication of the types of factors that affect adjustment to stigma.

Epilepsy

The adults with recurring seizures that Scambler and Hopkins (1986) studied clearly felt that, in an important sense, physicians had 'made them into epileptics' by selecting and communicating the diagnosis of epilepsy. It was a diagnostic label that most found unpleasant and threatening and some openly resented and contested, largely, it seems, because they saw the status of 'epileptic' as highly stigmatizing. Those who had been diagnosed in childhood often seemed to have learned to think of their epilepsy in this way as a result of their parents' behaviour: for example, well-intentioned advice never to use the word 'epilepsy', especially outside the home. Schneider and Conrad (1983), reporting the same finding in the USA, graphically refer to such parents as 'stigma coaches'. They add that careless or over-protective physicians can also function as stigma coaches.

Once applied, diagnostic labels tend to be difficult to shake off. Nevertheless, the stigma of people with epilepsy is dormant between seizures; for much of their time, therefore, they are discreditable rather than discredited. Scambler and Hopkins found that, fearing discrimination, people tended to conceal their epilepsy whenever possible. Witnessed seizures were often 'explained away' – for example, as faints — and 'stories' constructed to account for the fact that people could not drive, because of the law, or drink, because of their anticonvulsant medication. Two-thirds of those experiencing epileptic seizures at the time of marriage hid the fact from their partners, at least until after the ceremony. Of those with full-time jobs outside the home, 28% had disclosed their epilepsy to their employers, and only 1 in 20 — all of whom were experiencing seizures daily at the time — had done so before taking the job.

The same authors made a distinction between *felt stigma* and *enacted stigma*. The former refers to the shame associated with 'being epileptic' and, most significantly perhaps, to the fear of being discriminated against solely on the grounds of an imputed cultural unacceptability or inferiority; and the latter refers to actual discrimination of this kind. Scambler (1989) has utilized this distinction to formulate a 'hidden distress model' in relation to epilepsy. This states that the sense of felt stigma is so strong that people with epilepsy typically do their utmost to maintain secrecy about their symptoms and the diagnostic label: they disclose only when it strikes them as prudent or necessary. Non-disclosure, in turn, reduces the likelihood of encountering enacted stigma. Thus felt stigma leads to a policy of concealment which has the effect of reducing the incidence of enacted stigma. Paradoxically, felt stigma was more disruptive of people's lives and well-being than was enacted stigma, which was in fact rarely experienced.

Rectal cancer

If in the nineteenth century tuberculosis stood out as the disease arousing the most dread and repulsion, cancer is its twentieth-century equivalent. Sontag (1977) has argued that it is likely to occupy this role until its aetiology is clarified and its treatments as effective as those of tuberculosis. Rectal cancer accounts for 10% of cancer diagnoses. Two-thirds of those with rectal cancer are left with a permanent colostomy following amputation of the anus and rectum. A colostomy is an incontinent, artificial anus which, with no sphincter to control it, can release faeces and flatus unpredictably, generally into a plastic bag attached to the abdomen. Macdonald (1988) has examined patients' perceptions of what amounts to a family of stigmas: 'the shame, taboos and fears associated with mutilation of the body, with faecal incontinence, with seeing and handling faeces, and with cancer'.

MacDonald found that 49% of her sample reported 'some stigma' and 16% 'severe stigma'; these proportions rose to 54% and 26%, respectively, for those with a colostomy. Most felt as if they had been assaulted and were unclean. Like those with epilepsy, many opted for concealment as a first-choice strategy, felt stigma once more being the motivating factor. They were ashamed by noise and odours from the stoma and filled with self-disgust at the need to handle bags of faeces and to clean faeces from their bodies. They feared exposure because they thought others would be embarrassed or offended and drift away. Some practiced 'withdrawal' rather than confront the potential hazards of 'passing as normal'. Many of those in situations where they were discredited rather than discreditable adopted a strategy of 'covering': they took all possible steps to reduce the salience of their stigma for others, to render it unobtrusive (Goffman, 1963). A third had never shown the colostomy to their spouses, and more than four-fifths had never shown it to anyone outside the hospital. MacDonald concludes that, although most people in her study learned to accommodate their stomas fairly well, 'a large fraction' suffered impaired quality of life because of their experiences of the stigma of cancer and colostomy.

AIDS, STIGMA AND HEALTH POLICY AND PRACTICE

Throughout its brief history, AIDS has been both medicalized as 'disease' and moralized as 'stigma'. Weeks (1989) elaborates on this theme by tracing three distinct phases in social responses to AIDS thus far; these are described below.

The dawning crisis (1981–82)

It was not until the summer of 1981 that the health problems increasingly being experienced in the gay community, and leading to much debate therein, became 'an embryonic public issue' in the USA, with physicians and the press beginning to take note. Exploratory attempts were made to understand the nature of the disease known initially as 'the gay cancer', then GRID (gay-related immune deficiency). (The acronym AIDS was finally accepted in 1982.) *Risk categories* outside the gay community were soon identified: heroin users, haemophiliacs and, most controversially, Haitians. The Federal Administration, however, remained largely inactive, partly because it was intent on public expenditure cuts at the time, and partly because AIDS seemed to be confined to marginal and, with the possible exception of haemophiliacs, 'politically and morally embarrassing' groups.

Moral panic (1982–85)

From about 1982 a moral panic set in, with a rapid escalation of media and public hysteria. This was the period of the New Right and Moral Majority onslaught in the USA, and of stories of the 'gay plague' in the tabloid press. Around the same time, 1983–84, HIV was identified and named, opening up new opportunities for medical engagement. In addition, the communities most affected, notably the gay community, began to organize for self-help, for example through Gay Men's Health Crisis in New York and the Terrence Higgins Trust in London. The identification of the virus and progress in understanding modes of transmission shifted attention from risk categories to *risk activities*.

Crisis management (1985–present)

The present phase commenced in 1985, when it was recognized that AIDS as a disease constituted a global threat, and to heterosexual as well as to gay or socially marginal communities. Governments in the USA and Britain, mobilized by the perceived threat to 'the general population', began to commit resources, especially to prevention. It is ironic that in so doing they drew on the experience and expertise of the gay self-help groups. The self-help groups themselves became more professional as public funds became available to them and as demands on their services increased. An uneasy alliance was formed between the self-help groups and the medical profession.

Weeks' brief history and current debates highlight a number of important issues concerning the role of physicians. First, not only was AIDS — uniquely combining sex, drugs, death and contagion — itself highly stigmatizing, but it was initially discerned in an already markedly stigmatized population, that of gay men. For several years political and popular homophobia meant that both effective research and health interventions were delayed, and that specialist physicians came under some pressure to sanction or facilitate punitive action against 'guilty' HIV/AIDS carriers — like gay and bisexual men and, later, injecting drug users — if not against 'innocent' carriers — like haemophiliacs and babies of infected mothers. Fortunately such pressure, and the guilty/innocent dichotomy underlying it, has been largely resisted by the British medical profession: the evidence of history is that the punitive medical policing of socially marginalized groups, quite apart from infringing civil rights, is counter-productive in that it leads to further marginalization and losses of contact and capacity to influence through health education or 'user-friendly' services.

There is some indication that, although the great majority of AIDS cases at the end of the 1980s involved gay or bisexual men and injecting drug users, analysis of known cases of HIV infection in Britain suggests increased spread into the heterosexual population. Whether or not this turns out to be true, a second issue is the certain involvement of an increasing number of general, as opposed to specialist, physicians in the care of HIV/AIDS patients. This will constitute a considerable challenge to the primary-care sector. Although general practitioners have become better informed about AIDS, there is evidence of lack of commitment to health education about AIDS and of wide divergencies of attitude towards the provision of counselling and treatment and over the issue of confidentiality. In one national study, 70% of general practitioners reported that they found it difficult to discuss the sexual practices of gay men during consultations. Nearly half of the same sample said they would not knowingly accept anybody injecting drugs onto their practice list (Rhodes et al. 1989). It is not surprising, perhaps, that many people with HIV or AIDS are reluctant to consult their general practitioners, either uncertain of the reaction, in fear of a negative one, or anxious about confidentiality (King 1988).

STIGMA AND PHYSICIAN–PATIENT ENCOUNTERS

Whether patients have epilepsy, rectal cancer, HIV/AIDS or any other stigmatizing condition, the quality of the care they receive is a major concern. The enhanced salience of medical audit will be important here. But quality of care encompasses more than biomedical thoroughness, and numerous studies have documented patient unhappiness at physicians' preoccupation with diagnosis and management and apparent lack of interest in psychological and social aspects of care. Scambler (1989) has noted that the accusation that physicians, especially hospital specialists, lack the time, training or motivation to elicit and address patients' own perspectives on their epilepsy is a common one. He goes on to distinguish analytically between three dimensions to patient's perspectives:

1. *felt stigma* — a sense of shame and apprehension at meeting with discrimination;
2. *rationalization* — a deep need to make sense of what is happening, to restore cognitive order; and
3. *action strategy* — a need to develop modes of coping across a diversity of roles and situations.

Research suggests that physicians tend to be interested in those aspects of patient rationalization that promise to facilitate diagnosis or management, but not in the process *per se*. Neither felt stigma nor action strategy tend to be on the medical agenda for consultations, and are typically handled inexpertly and cursorily if raised by patients.

The point has often been made that patients' perspectives need to be respected and explored in their own right. Physicians do not merely need to inform and advise, but also to listen. To do this effectively, particularly in relation to stigmatizing conditions, requires what Schneider and Conrad (1983) have termed 'co-participation in care'. Scambler (1990) has argued that physicians need to provide a competent and up-to-date technical service covering the investigation, diagnosis and management of epilepsy — at optimum cost — and to engage in health education oriented to demythologizing and destigmatizing epilepsy in the community. As far as physician–patient encounters are concerned, he advocates:

1. acceptance of the principle of *co-participation in care*, which involves coming to terms with 'patient autonomy', or the patient as decision-maker;
2. acceptance also of an *open agenda* in physician–patient encounters;
3. an *holistic* rather than exclusively biomedical orientation to care, with the emphasis on informing, advising and helping 'persons in context' rather than merely managing disease; and
4. the development of *counselling skills* to complement technical skills, which presupposes both an awareness of the impact of epilepsy on quality of life and learned expertise in advising on coping strategies.

The literature suggests that these prescriptions are pertinent to a wide range of chronic and stigmatizing illnesses, and to surgical procedures such as mastectomy and colostomy which have stigmatizing results.

REFERENCES

Davis, F. (1964) Deviance disavowal: the management of strained interaction by the visibly handicapped. In: *The Other Side*, ed. H. Becker. Glencoe, IL: Free Press.

Freidson, E. (1970) *Profession of Medicine*. New York: Dodds, Mead & Co.

Gerhardt, U. (1987) Parsons, role theory and health interaction. In: *Sociological Theory and Medical Sociology*, ed. G. Scambler. London: Tavistock.

Giddens, A. (1989) *Sociology*. Oxford: Polity Press.

Goffman, E. (1963) *Stigma: Notes on the Management of Spoiled Identity*. New York: Prentice-Hall.

Gove, W. (1970) Societal reaction as an explanation of mental illness: an evaluation. *Am. soc. Rev.*, **35**, 873–884.

Higgins, P. (1980) *Outsiders in a Hearing World: A Sociology of Deafness*. Beverley Hills, CA: Sage Publications.

King, M. (1988) AIDS and the general practitioner: views of patients with HIV and AIDS. *Br. med. J.*, **297**, 182–184.

Lemert, E. (1967) *Human Deviance, Social Problems and Social Control*. New York: Prentice-Hall.

MacDonald, L. (1988) The experience of stigma: living with rectal cancer. In: *Living with Chronic Illness: the Experience of Patients and their Families*, ed. R. Anderson & M. Bury. London: Allen & Unwin.

Parsons, T. (1951) *The Social System*. London: Routledge & Kegan Paul.

Rhodes, T., Gallagher, M., Foy, C., Philips, P. & Bond, J. (1989) Prevention in practice: obstacles and opportunities. *AIDS Care*, **1**, 257–267.

Scambler, G. (1989) *Epilepsy*. London: Tavistock.

Scambler, G. (1990) Social factors and quality of life and quality of care in epilepsy. In: *Quality of Life and Quality of Care in Epilepsy*, ed. D. Chadwick. London: Royal Society of Medicine.

Scambler, G. & Hopkins, A. (1986) Being epileptic: coming to terms with stigma. *Soc. Hlth Illness*, **8**, 26–43.

Scheff, T. (1966) *Being Mentally Ill*. Chicago, IL: Aldine.

Schneider, J. & Conrad, P. (1983) *Having Epilepsy: the Experience and Control of Illness*. Philadelphia: Temple University Press.

Scott, R. (1969) *The Making of Blind Men*. New York: Russell Sage Foundation.

Sontag, S. (1977) *Illness as Metaphor*. New York: Allen Lane.

Weeks, J. (1989) AIDS: the intellectual agenda. In: *AIDS: Social Representations, Social Practices*, ed. P. Aggleton, G. Hart & P. Davies. London: The Falmer Press.

PART V

Organization of health services

PART IV

Organization of health services

14

Origins and development of the National Health Service

Nicholas Mays

There is a wide range of arrangements for the organization and financing of health care in different countries. Each health-care system is the product of the social, economic, demographic and technological context and the political philosophy of the country. All exhibit their own balance of advantages and limitations when judged on criteria such as equity, efficiency, accessibility, acceptability and relevance to needs (see Chapter 20).

The British National Health Service (NHS) is perhaps the best known example of a *health-service* solution to the financing and allocation of health care in which the vast majority of health care is financed from general taxation and provided through a publicly planned system. The goal of the NHS is to make health care available to all the population through an arrangement in which there is universal access to a general practitioner (GP) through whom nearly all referrals for specialist and hospital care are made.

The history of health care in Britain in the last 150 years mirrors the trend in all advanced western countries towards greater government involvement in health care in response to calls for better access to and coordination of services (Thane 1982). Until very recently in Britain this meant increasing state funding *and* state provision of services. However, following the major reforms of the NHS introduced in 1991, the role of the state as a direct provider of health care may be reduced for the first time, even though health care continues to be primarily publicly financed.

HEALTH CARE IN BRITAIN BEFORE THE NATIONAL HEALTH SERVICE

Health-care provision in Britain in the nineteenth and early twentieth century comprised a number of disparate elements: GP services; the voluntary hospitals; municipal hospitals; and local authority public health measures and related services.

General practitioners

In the nineteenth century, hospitals were primarily used by the poor. They remained dangerous places until the very end of the century when developments in anaesthesia and antiseptic surgery improved their success rate. For those of the population who could afford it, fee-for-service consultation with a qualified practitioner, either in his surgery or at home, was the main means of obtaining medical care. Gradually, a variety of insurance schemes were also developed, organized by Friendly Societies (non-profit-making mutual-benefit organizations) and trade unions, which enabled other groups, mainly skilled workers, to use GPs. Increasing numbers of GPs participated in these schemes, particularly in poorer areas where private fees alone did not provide an adequate income. The GP was paid by capitation, receiving an annual sum for each patient enrolled on his list by the insurer. By providing the GP with a modest but reasonably secure income, the Friendly Societies and trade unions put themselves in a strong position to specify standards of care, such as home visiting, and to limit the clinical freedom of the GP in order to control costs on behalf of their working-class subscribers.

By the end of the nineteenth century, only about half the working class was covered by these schemes of contributory insurance. The poor physical condition of recruits for the Boer War (1899–1901), one-third of whom were judged unfit to serve, alarmed military planners in the government at a time of international tension. Industrialists were anxious to see a healthier and, therefore, more productive male work-force. The early twentieth century was also a period of considerable social unrest with working-class uprisings in Germany and an attempted revolution in Russia in 1905. In Britain, the Labour Party, based on the new mass trade unions and the widening of the franchise in 1885, had gained seats in Parliament. Britain's rulers were actively seeking ways of halting the spread of socialist ideas. The German government had already sought to diffuse the revolutionary potential of disaffected sections of the working class by social reforms designed to improve living standards and quality of life. In 1883, for example, Germany's Chancellor, Bismarck, had introduced a system of state-run social insurance covering sickness, accidents at work and old age and invalidity pensions to reduce social unrest. Influenced in part by Germany, Britain introduced old age pensions in 1908 and in 1911, Lloyd George, the Chancellor of the Exchequer, introduced a National Health Insurance (NHI) scheme in the face of medical opposition. The profession feared state control of their work and lower pay. Neither fear was justified in the event.

The scheme, covering manual workers between 16 and 65 years of age whose earnings were below the threshold for payment of income tax, provided funds for sickness, accident and disability benefits in cash, and access to GP services free of charge. Hospital and specialist care were not included. It excluded the self-employed, agricultural workers, many unemployed people and nearly all non-manual workers. Crucially, it excluded all dependants of the insured person, mainly women and children, who had either to pay directly for care or make their own insurance arrangements. Contributions to the NHI fund were made by the employer, the employee and the Treasury. Entitlement to benefits and GP services was limited to the level of past contributions, so that in cases of chronic illness and unemployment workers could find themselves without cover. Like the earlier Friendly Society schemes, the participating GPs had a list or 'panel' of insured workers and were paid a capitation fee for each, rather than a salary. The NHI scheme was administered in a fragmentary way through the existing Friendly Societies and commercial insurance companies, each of which exercised considerable discretion in deciding the level and entitlement to benefits.

The NHI improved the remuneration of GPs because it provided additional public funds to subsidize the treatment of many more poorer patients while continuing to allow 'panel' doctors to work for other insurers and in fee-for-service private practice. This strengthened the financial position of the GPs, which enabled them to resist the Friendly Societies' previous control over their clinical activities. However, it meant that GPs in poorer areas (usually industrial areas and in the north), though better off than before 1911, were paid far less and had far larger lists than those in more affluent areas such as the Home Counties, where private practice was more profitable.

By 1939, approximately 40% of the working population had coverage for GP services through the NHI scheme and about two-thirds of GPs were involved in 'panel' work (Carpenter 1984).

Hospital services

Hospital care was available from two separate sources: the voluntary hospitals and the municipal or local authority hospitals.

The Voluntary Hospitals

There were 1100 voluntary hospitals with 90 000 beds in Britain before World War II. They were charitable foundations and treated 36% of all hospital patients in 1938 (Abel-Smith 1964: 385). They ranged from GP cottage hospitals, financed by local subscription, to the large, prestigious teaching hospitals which were chartered institutions, established as far back as the Middle Ages in some cases, and supported by extensive endowments. The teaching hospitals concentrated on acute medicine and surgery and undertook most of the training of doctors and nurses. Their consultants offered their services at the hospital without payment so that the hospital could provide free care to patients who could not afford private treatment. In return, they were relatively free to choose to treat the complex and 'interesting' cases. Consultants' incomes were derived from private practice undertaken outside the hospital. GPs, and those doctors who worked for Friendly Societies or the municipal hospitals, were largely prevented from admitting and treating their own patients in the voluntary hospitals. In return, consultants agreed only to accept patients when they were referred to them by GPs.

After World I, inflation reduced the real value of the income from bequests and donations to the voluntary hospitals. Medical science and technology were becoming increasingly complex and expensive. As a result, the voluntary hospitals found themselves with mounting financial problems. They responded by trading on their reputations to raise money from the public — as well as by means-testing and charging the growing numbers of more affluent patients who were now using their services — as the effectiveness of hospital care increased. Hospitals set up their own contributory pre-payment schemes for those who had some money but could not afford to pay a lump sum when they used services. Another source of income was to undertake work on contract to local authorities, some of which were extending their provision of hospital care in the 1930s. By 1937, at least one-third of the voluntary hospitals were virtually bankrupt (Political and Economic Planning 1937). The government had given them some money to reduce their deficits but had refused to take over responsibility for their finances.

Despite the pre-payment schemes, many middle-class people found that hospital acute care between the two World Wars was very expensive since the charges they paid had to finance the care of lower-income patients who were still entitled to free services. However, poor patients brought no income to the voluntary hospital and so there was an incentive for the hospital to neglect them, passing responsibility for their care to the municipal hospitals. Both poor and affluent people became dissatisfied with this state of affairs.

Municipal (Local Authority) Hospitals

The nineteenth-century system known as the Poor Law provided public assistance to the very poorest people and the unemployed. The system distinguished between the 'undeserving poor' whose poverty was presumed to be the result of indolence and fecklessness, and the 'deserving poor' made paupers by old age, mental infirmity or sickness. Provision for the first group was the bare minimum available in the workhouse where conditions were deliberately harsher than those facing the poorest people in work according to the principle of 'less eligibility'. This was to encourage the recipients to find employment and leave. The second group, essentially the sick and elderly poor, were supposed to be treated better in separate infirmaries which were often attached to the workhouses.

In 1929 the Poor Law hospitals were taken over by the local authority health departments headed by the Medical Officer of Health (MOH). They continued to provide mainly chronic care for those unable to obtain treatment in the voluntary hospitals or by private means. By 1939 there were 400 000 beds in public hospitals run by the local authorities: 200 000 in 'asylums' serving the mentally ill and mentally handicapped, and 200 000 in a range of tuberculosis sanatoria, isolation hospitals for infectious diseases and former Poor Law infirmaries.

The local authority hospitals tended to be less well equipped than the voluntary hospitals, although standards in the local authority hospitals rose appreciably during the 1930s. They were generally regarded as of lower status because of the taint of their Poor Law origins. The local authorities paid doctors relatively poorly and attempted to control their work which antagonized the profession. There were big differences in the extent to which local authorities attempted to develop a modern public hospital system in their areas, with some simply perpetuating Poor Law standards. Indeed, the economic depression of the 1930s meant that many local authorities lacked the money to invest in hospitals. Although the two hospital movements were, in a loose sense, complementary, there was little liaison or coordination between them.

Public health and community health services

The earliest and most significant aspect of state involvement to protect the population's health in the nineteenth century comprised the public health legislation enacted between 1848 and 1875. This led to major improvements in water supplies and sewerage and, ultimately, the control of infectious diseases, which made a far greater impact on the general standard of health than anything undertaken in the field of curative medicine up to that time (see Chapter 1). By the end of the nineteenth century, each local authority was required by law to have a MOH who was responsible for environmental health, control of infectious diseases, certification of causes of death and a range of preventive services. By the 1930s, the MOH, who was the predecessor of the public health physician in today's NHS, headed a health department in every local authority, with responsibility for maternity services, child health and welfare (health visiting in modern terminology), the school medical service and a range of services provided particularly to the elderly in their own homes (e.g. district nursing).

An overview of health care in Britain before World War II

Despite a reasonably effective pattern of public health and preventive health services, a series of reports between the two World Wars, both official and unofficial, identified major deficiencies in the other health services:

1. financial barriers to the use of health services remained since NHI was not available to more than half the population and did not cover dependants;
2. NHI did not include hospital care;
3. specialists, GPs and hospital beds were unevenly distributed across the country;
4. there were wide variations in standards in all services;
5. there were mounting financial problems, especially in the voluntary hospitals, and shortages of equipment and skilled staff; and
6. the local authority services, the voluntary hospitals and the GP services were uncoordinated.

ESTABLISHING A NATIONAL HEALTH SERVICE

By the late 1930s there was growing support for the idea that everybody should have the right to good quality health care, but how this should be accomplished was a matter of hot dispute. Decisions would have to be made about, for example, the funding, administration and payment of doctors in any new system: whether services should be funded from general taxation or by extending NHI; whether hospitals should be administered by *ad hoc* bodies or by the existing local authorities; whether doctors should become salaried employees of the state or remain independent contractors.

The experience of World War II showed how the state could intervene positively in many areas of national life; it also generated demands for a better post-war society. Key factors in relation to the development of health services after World War II were the Emergency Medical Service and the Beveridge Report of 1942. The necessity for a national, universally available health-care system was a central plank in Beveridge's famous blueprint for post-war reconstruction, which proposed a 'welfare state' to combat the five 'giants' barring the road to progress: 'want, disease, ignorance, squalor and idleness' (Beveridge Report 1942). In 1939, a state-run centrally organized Emergency Medical Service (EMS), funded by the Treasury, was set up to deal with civilian and military casualties. It was free; it took over two-thirds of the hospitals; it established a national blood-transfusion service and coordinated ambulance services; and it showed that a NHS was feasible. Working in the EMS, leading members of the medical profession also saw for themselves the weaknesses in the existing services, particularly the poor conditions outside the leading teaching hospitals.

It was not possible to establish a NHS without securing the cooperation of the medical profession. Between 1942 and 1948 there was continuous negotiation about almost every aspect of the finance, organization and control of a new unified service between the government and key interest groups, particularly the representatives of the medical profession (Eckstein 1958). The GPs resisted a salaried service to preserve professional autonomy. The hospital specialists refused the proposal for local authority control. The British Medical Association (BMA) fought, unsuccessfully, for the extension of NHI and was suspicious about the pay implications of a NHS. The system which finally emerged was the profuct of skillful compromises by the Labour Minister of Health after 1945, Aneurin Bevan, and reflected these concerns to a considerable degree, although it was never formally agreed by the BMA.

The main concessions to the profession in the 1946 NHS Act were:

1. GPs remained independent contractors but most were made better off by the NHS;
2. hospital consultants were paid for the hospital work they had previously done for nothing;
3. consultants were allowed to work part-time in the NHS on good salaries and keep their private practices;
4. beds for private patients ('pay beds') were permitted in NHS hospitals;

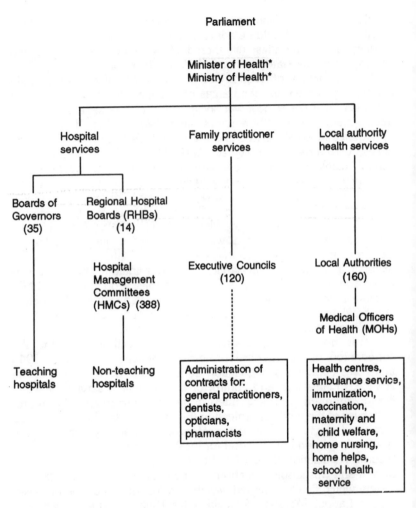

*Secretary of State for Social Services and Department of Health and Social Security (DHSS), respectively, from 1968

——— Direct managerial authority
----- Administrative responsibility

Figure 1. The structure of the NHS in England and Wales, 1948–74.

5. a system of distinction (merit) awards controlled by the profession was established for hospital consultants but not GPs;
6. doctors were to play a major role in deciding policy at all levels; and

7. hospitals were not to be controlled by local authorities.

From the outset, therefore, despite its apparent radicalism, the NHS represented a compromise between principles of traditional medical authority and rational public administration (Klein 1989).

THE NHS IN 1948

The new NHS was open to the whole population solely on the basis of health-care need, free at the point of use and mainly funded from the general tax revenues of central government. The aim was to secure equality of access throughout the country and provide a comprehensive range of modern services accessible by referral from a GP except in emergencies.

The NHS which began in 1948 nationalized the existing pattern of services. Thus the NHS inherited many of the strengths and weaknesses of the previous arrangements including the historical divisions between general practice, local authority health services and the teaching hospitals and inequalities in the geographical distribution of hospital beds, staff and equipment.

The structure in England and Wales was *tripartite* (see Fig. 1) since the administration was shared between three statutory authorities:

1. the 14 Regional Hospital Boards (RHBs), appointed by the Minister of Health, were responsible for the Hospital Management Committees (HMCs) which ran the former local authority hospitals;
2. the local authorities ran preventive and community health services under the MOH; and
3. the Executive Councils dealt with the GPs, dentists, opticians and pharmacists.

The teaching hospitals continued to have elite status. Their Boards of Governors were outside the RHB structure and had direct access to the Ministry of Health. Thus, the administration of the NHS fell far short of the ideal of full integration. Similar but separate structures existed in Scotland and Northern Ireland. In terms of overall control, finance and access, the system had changed markedly. The assumption was that a 'free' NHS would particularly benefit the working class. In practice, because many working-class people had had access to subsidized or free health care before World War II, the NHS, paradoxically, did as much to remove the financial barriers facing middle-class patients as those facing working-class patients.

THE NHS, 1948–74

The NHS was immediately very popular with the public and rapidly proved financially attractive to the vast majority of medical practitioners. However, two main sources of discontent marked the first 25 years: the level of expenditure and the organization of the service.

The level of expenditure

The original expenditure estimates drawn up by the architects of the new Service were relatively modest and assumed that spending would rapidly stabilize. The planners had reckoned without the popularity of the NHS, rising public expectations, inflation and post-war developments in technology and drugs; all of these drove up the cost of the Service. By 1953, expenditure had reached such an unexpectedly high level that the Minister of Health ordered an enquiry into the cost of the NHS (Ministry of Health 1956). Instead of profligacy, the Guillebaud committee could find no evidence of inappropriate treatment and noted that health-care spending had actually declined as a percentage of the national income. Most of the increase in spending was due to price inflation and necessary pay awards. The committee recommended an *increase* in spending to remedy the chronic lack of investment in NHS buildings. In a belated response, the government announced a Hospital Plan for England and Wales in 1962 with the objective of ensuring that a modern district general hospital (DGH) was made available for each population of approximately 250 000 people (Ministry of Health 1962).

The demand for health care continued to rise in the 1960s fed by professional and public aspirations. The period 1960–74 was marked by a steady expansion in spending in real terms and in the volume of services provided through the NHS. By the mid-1970s, when the growth in resources began to slow down, the NHS was having to face up to the dilemmas imposed by the requirement, which faces all health systems, to reconcile seemingly infinite demand for care with inevitably finite resources (see Chapter 19). One possible solution was to get more from the existing level of resources through a more efficient organization.

Towards an integrated service

By the 1960s it had become apparent that the NHS not only had a curative role, but that it also had growing numbers of chronically ill and disabled people to *care* for who could be looked after best outside hospitals. This emphasis on developing 'community care' (see Chapter 16) highlighted the importance of an *integrated* pattern of acute (curative), caring and rehabilitative services for client groups (e.g. the elderly) whose needs crossed administrative divisions. The difficulties encountered in providing continuity of service for groups like the elderly highlighted the lack of linkage between the three arms of the NHS (see Fig. 1). By the late 1960s, there was consensus on the need to reform the structure of the NHS to provide better coordination and a more efficient, planned allocation of resources.

REFORM BY REORGANIZATION, 1974–82

The NHS reorganization of 1974

After lengthy consultation and analysis, the NHS was reorganized in 1974 (see Fig. 2). The NHS remained accountable to Parliament through a cabinet minister (the Secretary of State for Social Services). Below the Department of Health and Social Security (DHSS), established in 1968, were 14 Regional Health Authorities (RHAs) in England. Their main function was to allocate finance, plan major projects and monitor the activities of 90 Area Health Authorities (AHAs). The new AHAs had responsibility for both the hospitals and the community health services formerly managed by the local authorities. An AHA could be divided into between one and five operational districts depending on population size. A similar reorganization took place in Wales, Scotland and Northern Ireland.

At each level of administration, management was undertaken by a multidisciplinary team comprising an administrator, an accountant, a senior nurse, a public health physician (now employed by the health authority), a consultant and a GP. Decisions could only be taken when there was a consensus in favour among the members of the team ('consensus management'). This system was deliberately devised to incorporate the main professional groups in the decision-making process. In each district, there was a Community Health Council (CHC), independent of the health authority, to act as the public's 'watch-dog' and to represent the views of patients and the public to the professionals. The CHC was given rights of access to information from district managers and to premises and had to be consulted on major service developments. The GPs remained independent contractors outside the new structure. The Executive Councils were replaced by Family Practitioner Committees (FPCs) which administered the contracts of family practitioners in much the same way as before. Neither the AHAs nor the FPCs had any

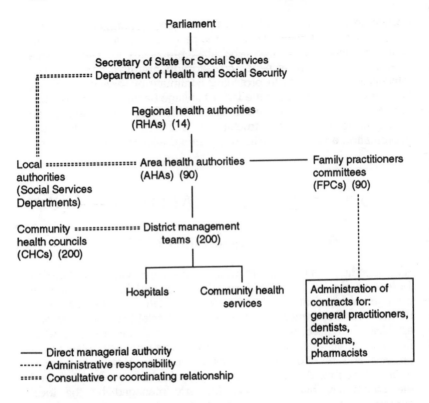

Figure 2. The structure of the NHS, 1974–82.

significant influence over how the GPs behaved.

The reorganization was designed to facilitate the implementation of an ambitious cyclical process of short- and long-term rational planning and priority setting by region, area and district which began in 1976. This was accompanied by the introduction of the Resource Allocation Working Party (RAWP) formula to redistribute finance fairly between different parts of the country on the basis of the size and needs of the population.

Further reorganization, 1982

The 1974 reorganization went some way to unifying the NHS and improving the opportunities for coordination with local authority social services. It failed, however, to solve the problem of how to reconcile effectively the role of central government in setting policy, overseeing expenditure and monitoring performance, with the requirement for local, delegated authority and freedom to implement policy at area and district levels. The new structure was criticized for having too many tiers of administration, an over-elaborate planning system, too many consultative committees of doctors, nurses and other health workers, and consensus management which was said to lead to slow and ineffective decision-making.

In 1982, the government simplified the structure by abolishing the 90 areas and handing their powers to the districts, thus making them health authorities in their own right so that power might be devolved to the lowest feasible level in the NHS. The professional advisory machinery was also slimmed down. Each of the DHAs had a chairman appointed by the Secretary of State and 16 members: four appointed by the local authority and the remainder by the RHA, including a nurse, a GP, a consultant and a medical school nominee.

MANAGERIAL REFORM, 1982–87

From 1979 to 1983 the government had encouraged those at local level in the NHS to take decisions in the light of local circumstances. However, this posed the problem of how to ensure that local managers were using resources efficiently and in line with central policy. There was also a pressing need from the government's perspective to find ways of preventing health authorities overspending their budgets.

Where previous enquiries had concentrated on the *structure of the NHS,* a small team of private-sector managers, led by Roy Griffiths of Sainsburys, was asked in 1983 to undertake an inquiry into its *management* practices. Griffiths found a lack of individual responsibility and accountability among the senior officers in the consensus teams for the attainment of objectives. He concluded that the NHS needed a stronger, clearer management system (DHSS 1983). At every level in the NHS the consensus teams were replaced by a single general manager with the power to take executive decisions over the resources under his or her control. Within the DHSS, two bodies were created: a Health Services Supervisory Board to make strategic decisions about objectives, and an NHS Management Board to direct operations in the NHS.

By establishing a hierarchy of general managers on fixed-term contracts and paid according to their performance, the Griffiths reforms enabled the centre to exercise greater control over activity at all levels, increased the powers of managers and reduced the influence of health authority members, particularly those from local authorities. Full-time managers began gradually to introduce more controls over the way traditionally autonomous clinicians used the resources available to them. For example, clinicians are now increasingly responsible and accountable for delivering an agreed workload efficiently within a set budget through systems of 'resource management'.

Overall, far greater emphasis was placed on considerations of efficiency and obtaining greater 'value-for-money' than ever before. The traditional, professional viewpoint that medical services could and should not be susceptible to measurement, external evaluation and control was increasingly challenged. For example, the NHS Management Board instituted annual reviews of each DHA by its RHA to ensure that resources had been spent effectively and in line with objectives; set up a system of quantitative performance indicators (PIs) to measure and compare the activity and costs of each district and unit; established a limited list of drugs of proven effectiveness which GPs were allowed to prescribe on the NHS; instituted competitive tendering for support services (e.g. catering, cleaning, portering and security) involving the private sector; implemented new cost–benefit methods for assessing building schemes; and brought in strict DHA cash limits linked to compulsory 'cost improvement programmes' to generate savings for new services.

THE NHS REVIEW, 1988

Despite the emphasis on greater efficiency in the later 1980s, the NHS continued to face the, by now familiar, problem of reconciling increasing demand for its services, generated by an ageing population and new technology, with the available funds. From 1982, health authorities were allocated a sum of cash at the beginning of each year with no allowance for unforeseen price increases during the year. Despite the fact that more than ever was being spent in real terms and more patients were being treated, by the autumn of 1987 the NHS had entered a particularly severe financial crisis. Many DHAs were having to use their cash reserves, delaying payment of bills, closing wards and cancelling non-emergency admissions to stay within budget while meeting the extra costs of national pay awards. Waiting lists, which had always been a cause of public concern, shot into the headlines. Professional and public pressure for more money for the NHS grew. In January 1988, the Prime Minister, Margaret Thatcher, announced a wide-ranging review of the NHS, the results of which were to be published within a year.

An avalanche of analysis and blueprints for reform were submitted to the review team. The review team was forcibly reminded that the *advantages* of the existing arrangements included the ability to control the level of expenditure (the lack of such control was a problem in most western countries) and the system of GPs, which allowed many problems to be dealt with inexpensively without recourse to costly hospital care. These led to a comparatively low level of spending by international standards (6% of the gross domestic product (GDP)), for which the whole population was given equitable access to a comprehensive range of high-quality services, regardless of the ability to pay, and with low administrative costs.

However, the NHS was perceived to have *weaknesses*, often relating directly to its strengths. Evidence was brought forward to show that the NHS was chronically under-funded and that this was reflected in the lack of repair of buildings, waiting lists for elective procedures, the poor quality of care in specialities such as mental handicap and low pay. The most influential economic critique was that the NHS was badly flawed because there were no incentives for health-care providers to be efficient (Enthoven 1985). Studies which demonstrated big variations in patterns of clinical activity (e.g. referral rates to hospital (Andersen & Mooney 1990)) were said to prove that resources were not being used as well as they could be (see Chapter 19). Furthermore, there was no incentive for a hard-working hospital to become more efficient and treat more patients, since the hospital budget would remain the same (the 'efficiency trap').

There was also criticism of the limited extent of patient choice and the insensitivity of managers to consumer views in the NHS. These were blamed on the near-monopoly position of the NHS in the health-care market, which had allowed a paternalistic, professionally dominated and inflexible system to develop. The NHS was also criticized for perpetuating the divisions between primary care, community care and hospital care, which hampered the effective delivery of services.

Options for reform

The options for reform fell essentially into two categories: options concerned with *finance* and options concerned with the *organization* or delivery of health care. The main alternative to finance from general taxation was some form of social insurance (see Chapter 20) or, alternatively, an ear-marked 'health tax'. An extreme free-market option was to introduce a basic system of public health care for the poor with private health insurance for the remainder of the population. There was, however, little support for any radical change in the financing of the NHS. General taxation was judged to be the cheapest and fairest way to raise money.

The debate about organizational change reflected the influence of

American ideas, especially economist Alain Enthoven's proposal in 1985 for an 'internal market' within the NHS as a remedy to the lack of explicit incentives to efficiency in the monolithic NHS (Enthoven 1985). The basic idea behind the 'internal market' was that it was possible to separate the role of districts as *purchasers* of health care from their role as *providers*. Under this arrangement, the DHAs would concentrate on planning and purchasing services for their resident populations but would be free to obtain these services from any NHS unit. Units (e.g. individual hospitals) would concentrate on providing the best quality of care at the least cost, and in competition with other units. It was argued that competition within a tax-funded NHS would improve efficiency. A number of variations on this proposal were put forward during the review (Butler & Pirie 1988; Goldsmith & Willetts 1988), including the idea of using the GP practice as the key purchaser and abolishing DHAs (Maynard et al. 1986). All the proposals for change were accompanied by measures to strengthen the accountability of doctors to health authorities and steps to manage clinical activity more effectively.

THE GOVERNMENT WHITE PAPER 'WORKING FOR PATIENTS', 1989

For a review initiated by a radical Conservative administration and in response to a *funding* crisis, the NHS White Paper of 1989 (Secretaries of State 1989) was notable, firstly for the things which it did *not* change and, secondly, for the fact that the main changes concerned the *means of delivery* of health care and not the sources or level of finance (Klein 1989). It also said nothing about the balance of priorities in the NHS (e.g. the level of spending on prevention and public health relative to curative services).

The NHS was to continue to be financed mainly from taxation, to be available to all regardless of income, and to be predominantly free at the point of use. The level of funding would remain a political decision by the government of the day. The only proposal on finance was the introduction of tax relief on private health insurance premiums for the over-60s.

There were four main sets of proposals brought forward in *Working for Patients* (Secretaries of State, 1989) and in a new contract for GPs covering: the provider market, professional accountability, management hierarchy and general practice.

The provider market: the main proposal for change was the introduction of what is now referred to as a 'provider market' in the NHS, based on the separation of the roles of purchaser and provider along the lines suggested by Enthoven (1985). DHAs would be financed according to the needs of their residents by a variant of the former RAWP formula. They would be free to purchase services from public-, private- or voluntary-sector providers, including their own directly managed units, or 'NHS trusts'. Major acute hospitals and other units were encouraged to apply for NHS trust status which would given them freedom from DHA control. Providers such as hospitals would be funded on their ability to win contracts to undertake an agreed amount of work for a DHA. The theoretical incentive for providers, therefore, was to minimize costs and maximize quality in order to stay in business. At the same time, GP practices with more than 9000 patients were encouraged to become 'GP fund holders' and to take control of their own budgets for the non-emergency hospital care of the patients on their lists. The idea was that the fund-holding practice would act as an informed agent on behalf of its patients and place contracts for services such as routine diagnostic investigations and elective surgery with those providers who were offering a good standard of service at a reasonable price.

Figure 3 sets out the main elements in the 'provider market' intended to create conditions for 'managed competition' in the NHS. The aim is to bring the supposed benefits of competition between suppliers, together with business management, to the NHS without jeopardizing its basic principles.

Professional accountability: a second group of proposals aimed to make doctors more accountable to managers for their performance. Medical audit (that is, the systematic analysis of the quality of clinical care) was to be compulsory in hospitals and general practice. Hospital consultants were to have job descriptions which explicitly set out their clinical time commitments in the NHS. General managers were to be involved in the appointment of new consultants and in the allocation of merit awards.

Management hierarchy: a third group of proposals extended the Griffiths' management reforms by removing the remaining local authority and professional representatives from health authorities. The authorities were slimmed down to 10 members and were to become managerial bodies akin to the boards of directors of private companies. Senior managers became members of the new health authorities in their own right. The central NHS Supervisory Board and the NHS Management Board were transformed into a NHS Policy Board, chaired by the Secretary of State for Health, to set overall objectives, and a NHS Management Executive in England with a Chief Executive, to run the NHS, including family practitioner services (Fig. 4). Chief executives were also appointed to run the NHS in Wales, Scotland and Northern Ireland through separate management structures.

General practice: the final main set of proposals concerned general

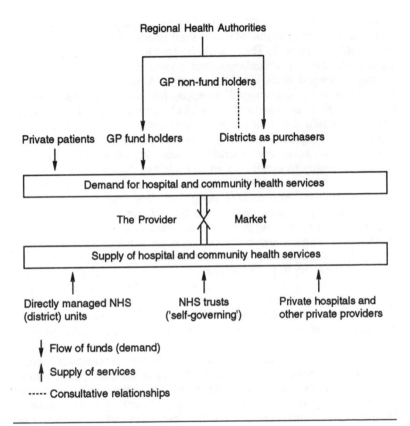

Figure 3. The provider market for NHS services from April 1991. (Source: Robinson (1989).)

practice and aimed to encourage more preventive activities such as screening by GPs, more patient choice between GPs, a degree of competition between practices for patients and greater cost-effectiveness. A new GP contract was introduced in 1990 which enables GPs to advertise their services and requires them in any event to provide more information about their services to the public. A higher proportion of GP remuneration will come from capitation (from 46% to 60% on average) in order to encourage GPs to be more responsive to patients' needs. Other elements in the pay of GPs are now linked to the attainment of activity targets set by the government (e.g. achieving specified rates of take-up for cervical cytology). It has also been made easier for patients to change GP. All GPs have been given an official indication of the amount they should be spending on drugs to exert downward pressure on their expenditure. High prescribing GPs will be given advice on how to reduce costs without denying patients the drugs they need. Family Practitioner Committees (FPCs) have been retitled Family Health Services Authorities (FHSAs) and have been given greater powers to audit and monitor the work and spending of family practitioners.

Despite a concerted campaign of opposition from the BMA and the other NHS trade unions, the proposals in *Working for Patients* (Secretaries for State, 1989) became law in the *NHS and Community Care Act* (1990) and have been rapidly implemented. The main elements of the 'provider market' began operation in April 1991, although full-blooded competition is unlikely for some time. The 1990 Act and the new GP contract define a package of significant and challenging — but previously unpiloted — changes, while leaving largely intact the fundamental principles of the NHS. It will take several years before the consequences of the combination of provider competition in a publicly funded service and tighter managerial control begin to be known. Meanwhile, the NHS faces a period of turbulence and uncertainty.

Overview of the Conservative reforms, 1991

The reformed NHS will retain its original 1946 principles for the foreseeable future. It will continue to be tax funded, available on the basis of need, largely free at the point of use and equally accessible throughout the country. The one breach of the equitable basis of the NHS concerns the new public subsidy to private health insurance for the elderly. The longstanding divisions between general practice, community care and hospital services are also retained in the new system (see Fig. 4). The radicalism of the solution is confined to the arrangements for *delivery* of services in the shape of 'provider markets' in which the state retains its role as *funder*, but services will gradually come to be provided by a variety of private, voluntary and public suppliers operating in competition with one another (see Fig. 3). This approach can be seen as the logical extension of the earlier policy of compelling DHAs to contract out their support services (see above).

It is too early to say how the new arrangements will work in practice. It has been suggested that as long as the bulk of finance comes from public sources and secures access to health care for all, the question of who owns and runs competing health-care facilities is secondary (Ham et al. 1990). In economic theory, competition is supposed to increase efficiency by giving consumers choice and, therefore, power. Yet the market created by *Working for Patients* will not be an ordinary market (Le Grand 1990). For example, patients will themselves often be unable to choose the services they receive. In practice, the GP fund-holder or the DHA will be making the expert

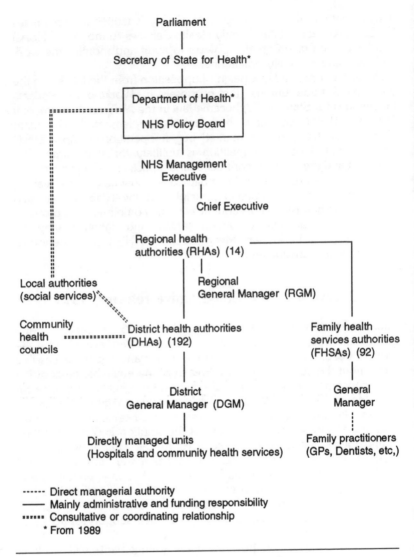

Figure 4. The structure of the NHS in England from April 1991.

purchasing decisions *on their behalf*, and will do so through a series of service agreements with particular hospitals. The arrangements also leave the purchasers with the problem of assessing the quality of rival providers in terms of the effectiveness of their services (see Chapter 18). A competitive contract system in health care cannot be guaranteed to produce high standards automatically. Routine data on effectiveness and resource use are required, but these are rudimentary in the NHS at present. There also remains the risk that the elderly and the chronically sick, who are less vocal in demanding services and difficult and expensive to treat, will be ignored or excluded.

These problems all point to the need for careful monitoring and regulation of the new 'provider market' by the Department of Health and the RHAs if it is to deliver an acceptable balance between the conflicting objectives of the NHS in the 1990s: for example, between equity and efficiency; between patient demand and expenditure control; and between consumer responsiveness and professional judgements of need. There will need to be routine assessment of the costs, quality, effectiveness and appropriateness of the services purchased by Districts and by GP fund-holders (King's Fund Institute 1989). As Rudolf Klein has observed: 'the more the public sector withdraws from the production of services, the greater becomes its responsibility for regulating what is produced by others. In short, the new "pluralism" [the range of potential providers] or whatever we may choose to call it, will give additional impetus to the transformation of the Welfare State into the Regulatory State' (Klein 1989: 242–243).

The NHS still remains one of the most ambitious publicly funded health systems in the world. Other western European countries are experimenting with similar combinations of market-style and regulatory measures to tackle the universal problems of health-care provision (see Chapter 19). A future British government with a different ideological slant might arrive at a different judgement about the optimum balance of market-driven versus planned services, but would be unlikely to ignore completely the changes made in the NHS in the decade since 1979, and the desirability of combining the best elements from competitive and bureaucratic systems while minimizing their drawbacks.

REFERENCES

Abel-Smith, B. (1964) *The Hospitals 1800–1948*. London: Heinemann.

Andersen, T.F. & Mooney, G. (eds) (1990) *The Challenges of Medical Practice Variations*. London: Macmillan.

Beveridge Report (1942) *Inter-departmental Committee on Social Insurance and Allied Services, Cmnd. 6404*. London: HMSO.

Butler, E. & Pirie, M. (1988) *Health Management Units*. London: Adam Smith Institute.

Carpenter, G. (1984) National Health Insurance: a case study in the use of private non-profit making organisations in the provision of welfare benefits. *Publ. Admin.*, **62**, 71–89.

Department of Health and Social Security (1983) *NHS Management Inquiry: Report* (Chairman: Mr R. Griffiths). London: DHSS.

Eckstein, H. (1958) *The English Health Service.* Cambridge, MA: Harvard University Press.

Enthoven, A.C. (1985) *Reflections on the Management of the National Health Service.* London: Nuffield Provincial Hospitals Trust.

Goldsmith, M. & Willetts, D. (1988) *Managed Health Care: a New System for a Better Health Service.* London: Centre for Policy Studies.

Ham, C., Robinson, R. & Benzeval, M. (1990) *Health Check: Health Care Reforms in an International Context.* London: King's Fund Institute.

King's Fund Institute (1989) *Managed Competition: a New Approach to Health Care in Britain. Briefing Paper No. 9.* London: King's Fund Institute.

Klein, R. (1989) *The Politics of the National Health Service,* 2nd edition. London: Longman.

Le Grand, J. (1990) *Quasi-markets and Social Policy. Studies in Decentralisation and Quasi-markets No. 1.* Bristol: School for Advanced Urban Studies.

Maynard, A., Marinker, M. & Gray, D.P. (1986) The doctor, the patient and their contract. III. Alternative contracts: are they viable? *Br. med. J.,* **292,** 1438–1440.

Ministry of Health (1956) *Report of the Committee of Enquiry into the Cost of the National Health Service* (Chairman: Mr C. Guillebaud), *Cmnd. 9962.* London: HMSO.

Ministry of Health (1962) *A Hospital Plan for England and Wales, Cmnd 1604.* London: HMSO.

Political and Economic Planning (1937) *Report on the British Health Services.* London: PEP.

Robinson, R. (1989) New health care marker. *Br. med. J.* **298,** 437–439.

Secretaries of State for Health, Wales, Northern Ireland and Scotland (1989) *Working for Patients, Cmnd 555.* London: HMSO.

Thane, P. (1982) *The Foundations of the Welfare State.* London: Longman.

15

Health Professions

David Blane

Medical care in contemporary Britain is provided by a work-force much of which is organized into a number of different professions. Hospital doctors, for example, work alongside nurses, physiotherapists, radiographers, speech therapists and medical laboratory scientific officers, while general practitioners integrate their work with pharmacists, health visitors, community nurses and social workers. Relations between these professions are sometimes strained. The members of one profession, for example, may feel that the members of another insufficiently understand their general approach to their work, or fail to behave towards them without the respect which they think is their due. Given the large number of professions which work within health care, there is considerable potential for such inter-professional conflict.

Better relations between professions can hopefully be fostered by an understanding of the nature of professions and the history of their development. At first sight the far from exhaustive list of professions which have already been mentioned share a commitment to the welfare of their patients and clients and a prohibition against exploiting their dependency. This professional attitude to those in their care is part of each profession's code of ethics, but a code of ethics is only one of the characteristics of a profession. The general characteristics of a profession as a form of occupational organization is considered in this chapter. The chapter then continues by examining the medical and nursing and other health professions in more detail and ends by considering some of the effects on health care of a professionalized work-force.

PROFESSIONS

Although medical care contains many professions, it by no means has a monopoly of them. Lawyers, accountants, teachers, priests, surveyors and civil engineers are examples of non-medical professions (Carr-Saunders & Wilson 1933). Attempts to identify what all these professions have in common, and what distinguishes them from other occupations, have produced a list of core features or defining characteristics (Friedson 1970). Firstly, professions tend to be found in the highly skilled sector of the labour market. They possess a body of *specialized knowledge* to which they add by research and which is passed on to trainees in institutions controlled by the profession, usually in a university setting. Secondly, they have a *monopoly* of their field of work which depends on both State registration and, because the state rarely makes unqualified practice illegal, also on agreement by the State and other large employers to employ only those who are duly registered. Thirdly, professions have considerable *autonomy* in organizing, defining the nature of, and developing their work; a freedom from outside control which is defended on the grounds that only a member of the same profession is competent to assess a professional's work. Fourthly, professions espouse a *code of ethics* which prohibits the exploitation of clients and regulates intra-professional relations. In addition, one could consider a further characteristic, namely *status*; professions are middle-class occupations whose members are assigned to social classes I or II on the Registrar General's classification.

Professional socialization

The above characteristics ensure that professions are among the more privileged occupations in the labour market. The nature of their work involves intellectual challenge and interest, their monopoly ensures a measure of job security, their autonomy gives relative freedom from supervision, their code of ethics encourages the satisfaction of aiding others, and their status provides respect and, in some cases, relative affluence. Not surprisingly, therefore, there are many applicants for professional training and professions can be selective about the trainees they choose to admit. This selection is the first stage of professional socialization, which is the process by which members of the lay population are turned into members of a particular profession. Professional socialization involves more than simply the acquisition of relevant knowledge; it also involves the transfer of what are considered appropriate attitudes and behaviour towards clients, colleagues and fellow workers, although it tends to be only the knowledge which is formally examined. Professional training is, by definition, lengthy and takes place in institutions which are controlled by the profession and somewhat isolated from the rest of higher education. This setting promotes effective socialization and gives considerable power to the senior members of a profession to mould new members in their own image. Professions are, therefore, slow to change and tend to be the focus of their members' self-identity and loyalty.

The process of professional socialization can be illustrated by studies of medical and nursing education. One study of a medical school, which relied heavily on interviews with the staff, stressed the distinction between the formal and the informal curriculum. The formal curriculum consisted of the knowledge considered necessary for a doctor, while the informal curriculum involved the attitudes, beliefs and behaviour considered appropriate. A student's success in the former was monitored through regular examinations, while their performance in the latter respect was noted, rather than being formally examined, and used to make decisions whenever there was sufficient room for such discretion (Merton et al. 1957). Another study of medical education, which relied on participant observation among the students, drew attention to some of the unintended consequences of this process. Students as they went through medical school increasingly substituted means (passing examinations) for ends (helping sick people) and learned to divide patients into 'good examination material' and 'crocks' (Becker et al. 1961). In other words, the students' initial idealism about the practice of medicine was replaced by a concern with the day-to-day details of getting through medical school, even when this led them to behave in ways which their earlier idealism would have condemned. Whether this was intended or not, the students were being taught to see the disease rather than the patient and to put medical interests before patients' needs.

A study of nursing education found a similar process at work when students were interviewed during both ward and formal academic segments of their training. The student nurses tended to divide their ward work into 'real nursing' and 'just basic nursing care'. The latter, which was the less highly prized, involved serving the basic needs of helpless patients. 'Real nursing' in contrast was more technical, involving drips and drugs, and responsible in the sense that a mistake could harm a patient. 'Real nursing' was emphasized in the formal academic part of their training and to some extent overlapped with the work of doctors. 'Just basic nursing care' received little formal attention and was often performed interchangably with untrained nursing auxiliaries (Melia 1987). Such studies illustrate the ability of a profession to instil into trainees its values and assumptions about what is desirable in its work (e.g. 'good examination material' and 'real nursing') and what can be downgraded (e.g. 'crocks' and 'just basic nursing care'). Professionalization refers to the process by which an occupation achieves such powers.

PROFESSIONALIZATION

The comparative approach which has been used so far in this chapter is useful because it identifies those characteristics which professions share and which distinguish them from other occupations. One limitation of this approach, however, is its inability to inform us about the origins of these characteristics and the order in which they were obtained. The comparative approach might suggest, for example, that society gave medical practitioners their status and power in recognition of their proven ability to save lives and promote health. In order to test such ideas an historical approach is used in the next section which deals firstly with the medical profession and then with the nursing profession.

The historical approach quickly dispenses with the idea that medical practitioners were the passive recipients of their professional powers. These powers were not given by a grateful society; rather they were achieved piecemeal by doctors applying pressure to a series of social institutions. The Voluntary Hospitals of the early nineteenth century, for example, were financed by local subscribers who received in exchange the right to nominate patients to a certain number of hospital beds. The honorary physicians and surgeons who gave their services to these hospitals, which were the only hospitals at the time, had no control over which patients were admitted. The subscribers tended to use their right to admit patients as a way of caring for their elderly relatives and dependants. The physicians and surgeons, however, were interested in patients whom they could use as teaching material, an activity from which they did derive income, and during the course of the nineteenth century they slowly wrested control of admissions policy from the lay subscribers. This measure of professional autonomy was firstly achieved by persuading the subscribers on humanitarian grounds that accidents and, later, emergencies could be admitted by medical staff without a subscriber's authority. The physicians and surgeons also obtained the subscribers' agreement to a policy of excluding certain categories of patients. The number of excluded categories increased as the century progressed and came to include all infectious diseases, terminal illnesses, pregnancy, children, all psychiatric conditions, mental handicap, epilepsy and the elderly. As a result of a prolonged diplomatic campaign, therefore, the physicians and surgeons obtained sufficient control over admissions policy to ensure that the patients in the voluntary hospitals reflected their interests rather than those of the subscribers (Abel-Smith 1964).

The campaign which achieved professional monopoly was almost as prolonged as that which gained autonomy in relation to hospital admissions policy. By the early nineteenth century a third type of medical practitioner, the apothecary-surgeon or 'general practitioner', was rising in importance to join the physicians and the surgeons. These three types of medical practitioners were united into a single occupational group, called doctors, by the 1858 Medical Act which established the General Medical Council. This reform of the professional licensing system was neither forced upon medical practitioners nor easily conceded to them. The 1858 act was preceded by 16 unsuccessful Parliamentary bills which failed to become law, partly because of disagreements among their medical supporters but also because Parliament was sceptical about whether medical practitioners could be trusted with this professional mono-poly (Peterson 1978). The legislation which was finally enacted did not give medical practitioners the legal monopoly for which they had long campaigned; the General Medical Council was empowered to keep a register of suitably trained practitioners, but unqualified practice was not made illegal. Nevertheless, registration became the basis of the profession's monopoly because an increasing number of employment opportunities were limited to those who were registered. In particular, Poor Law and Friendly Society appointments (of which more later) were restricted to General Medical Council registrants, who also increasingly became the chosen medical practitioners of the growing middle class. The profession's monopoly, therefore, was neither given nor was it complete; rather a sustained campaign by medical practitioners partially succeeded in enlisting the support of the state, and this was subsequently reinforced by the employment practices of local government, voluntary institutions and those private consumers who could afford their services.

Qualified medical practice before 1858 had always been vulnerable to competition from the unqualified who charged lower fees. This was inhibited by the 1858 act, which thus strengthened the doctors' market position, a development which was further enhanced when the output of qualified practitioners lagged behind the growth in the proportion of the population able to afford professional care (Waddington 1984). This relative shortage of doctors enabled them to press for further professional powers. The British Army, for example, had refused to grant full officer status to its doctors, who resented the automatic precedence of all combatant officers over them and such slights to their officer status as not being saluted by barrack sentries, having to be dismounted on parade and having to make private arrangements for the grooming of their horses. In 1896 the British

Medical Association responded to these longstanding grievances by securing the agreement of medical school deans to actively discourage their students from applying for army posts. As a result of this boycott the army quickly resolved these grievances to the doctors' satisfaction (Cantlie 1973).

At the same time as the doctors were organizing to raise their status within the British Army, they were also engaged in 'the battle of the clubs' for increased autonomy over their working-class patients. These 'clubs', Friendly Societies and, later, some trade union branches, were organizations of, predominantly, working men which offered insurance protection against sickness and death. In order to prevent abuse of the sickness benefit, they hired doctors to certify incapacity for work (see Chapter 13) and these duties were gradually extended to include the full range of general practitioner care. By the end of the nineteenth century, Friendly Societies covered more than 4 million members of the working class and employed at least 50% of general practitioners on a full or part-time basis. Each 'club' tended to employ only one doctor who was responsible to the club's committee and whom all the club's members had to consult. The doctors generally disliked supervision by their collective patients, in the form of the club's elected committee, and they particularly disliked the right of dissatisfied patients to complain to the committee, thus risking their employment and the loss of all their patients, not just the aggrieved party. They organized a boycott similar to the one which had recently been successful against the British Army, but lack of solidarity in their ranks frustrated this attempt to increase their autonomy. The balance of power between the doctors and the 'clubs' of their working-class patients was only altered in the doctors' favour by the 1911 National Health Insurance Act. This act 'nationalized' many of the functions of the Friendly Societies and placed their administration in the hands of local health committees which contained strong medical representation. This degree of medical control was only conceded to doctors in response to persuasive lobbying and the British Medical Association's threat of non-cooperation with the new scheme; the original bill had left control of medical benefit with the Friendly Societies (Honigsbaum 1979). The 1911 act thus freed general practitioners from any immediate control by these patients, an extension of their autonomy which was not given to doctors but was achieved by them through influencing the state.

Two additional points need to be made about these four episodes in the professionalization of medicine. Firstly, success in each case was accompanied by an increase in income. Achieving control of hospital admissions policy allowed physicians and surgeons to select cases for teaching their fee-paying students and for investigating the type of diseases most likely to be seen in fee-paying patients. Achieving registration in 1858 removed much low priced competition and gave relative scarcity value to qualified practitioners. The achievement of full officer status in the British Army in 1898 was accompanied by increased remuneration, and the increase in autonomy which resulted from the 1911 act was accompanied by a 75% increase in the capitation fee and full reimbursement of the cost of all medicines and drugs. Secondly, and more importantly perhaps, the acquisition of these professional powers occurred before doctors had the means to alter the course of most diseases to any significant extent (see Chapter 1). Doctors, of course, already had a body of specialized knowledge, but it rarely achieved great success when applied. The development of more effective knowledge came later; it was produced by a health care system over which doctors had already achieved considerable professional control, and it involved an increasingly elaborate division of labour within, particularly, the hospital sector of this system.

Nursing and paramedical staff

Until recently, most general practitioners worked on their own, often with their wives acting as receptionist, chaperone and filing clerk. Only since the mid-1960s has a form of primary care developed in which general practitioners are supported by practice nurses and clerical staff and integrate their work with health visitors, midwives and specialist community nurses (Jefferys & Sachs 1983). The development of a similarly complex division of labour started at a much earlier date in hospitals. In the early voluntary hospitals, medical practitioners, most often apothecary-surgeons, performed much of the skilled care of patients, for example distributing medicines, dressing wounds and monitoring the patient's state. Their only assistants were domestic servants who received no more training than other domestic servants and who performed normal domestic duties in exchange for little more than their own subsistance (Davies 1980). From the middle of the nineteenth century this division of labour began to change under the influence of reformers such as Fry and Nightingale who established a grade of trained nurses and schools of nursing in which to train them. These trained nurses were inserted into the division of labour between the doctors and the nurse-domestics, and they increasingly undertook much of the work at the ward level which had formerly been performed by the apothecary-surgeons. The combination of training and skilled work formed the basis of the professionalization of nursing, a process which continued with the formation of a national professional body, the College of Nursing, in 1916 and state registration in 1918 (Abel-Smith 1960). The new occupation of trained nursing thus adopted a similar form of organization to that which was proving advantageous to medical practitioners.

In contrast to the experience of doctors, however, the professionalization of nursing achieved relatively small increases in autonomy and remuneration. Low pay remains endemic and, although the chain of command lies within the profession, the content of nurses' work is still largely determined from outside (i.e. by doctors). The professionalization of nursing, therefore, demonstrates that those characteristics of a profession which were listed earlier do not necessarily go together, and that the advantages of professionalization do not inevitably follow the adoption of its organizational form (Dingwall et al 1988). Several explanations have been offered for this comparative failure. One stresses nursing's lack of a distinctive body of specialized knowledge and its dependence on medicine in this respect. Another points to the relatively weak monopoly which has been achieved, which allows the shortage of registered nurses to be met by the recruitment of less qualified enrolled nurses and nursing auxiliaries rather than by an improvement in the position of the fully qualified. Finally, it has been suggested that the professionalization of medicine succeeded because it was the first profession to develop within the nineteenth century's rapidly expanding health-care sector, and that the subsequent professionalization of other occupations within this sector was limited by medicine's already established dominance. The former two types of explanation underlie the efforts particularly of those who are based in the schools of nursing to encourage research and university degree courses, and hence the development of a distinctive body of knowledge. The latter type of explanation fits better with the behaviour of those who value their profession as a source of training and qualifications, but who turn to trade unions in order to achieve the benefits which professionalization promised but seems unable to deliver. Both strategies, however, are likely to face similar problems. As a largely female work-force confronting a predominantly male medical profession and administrative civil service, nurses may be met by assumptions of superiority and the belief that women do not need to be paid a 'family wage'. In addition, nursing staff are the largest group employed within medical care (see Table 1). For the employers, conceding to nurses the salary levels and control over resources which are the norm in other professions will have far greater cost implications than those which were involved in the professionalization of doctors.

Since the mid-nineteenth century, many other occupations within the health-care sector have shared nursing's experience of professionalization. Ophthalmic opticians, health visitors, midwives, medical laboratory scientific officers, pharmacists, physiotherapists, radiographers and chiropodists, for example, have all sought to develop their knowledge base, extend control over their work situation and

——— **Table 1** ———
Number of staff working in the different grades in the NHS (England 1987).

Hospitals	
Nursing staff	337 052
Ancillary	114 498
Administrative and clerical	110 700
Professional and technical	77 394
Medical staff	38 018
Midwives	19 261
Works and maintenance	18 363
Ambulance staff	15 973
Primary care	
Residential care staff*	88 243
Home helps*	59 510
District and specialist nurses and health visitors	37 131
Day-care staff*	27 162
General medical practitioners	27 023
Social workers*	27 016
General dental practitioners	14 765
Ophthalmic opticians	5 213

Source: Department of Health (1989: Table 3.1).
* Employed by local authorities, but involved in primary care.

obtain state registration. These developments, however, have been negotiated within a division of labour already dominated by the medical profession and, while they have redrawn the boundaries between these occupations, they have not equalized all the parties involved. It seems important, therefore, to distinguish between those professions which develop within an already established division of labour and those which are agents of the division of labour itself. Occupations such as social work and clinical psychology are exceptions to this general rule, in the sense that they possess a knowledge base which owes little to medicine and which is distinctively their own. They work along side medicine but are not part of its division of labour, and they can thus claim professional equality with it. In practice, however, the medical profession proves to be resistant to this claim; social workers, for example, have obtained an employment base in the local authorities' rather than the health-care sector in order to maintain their professional autonomy in relation to doctors (Stacey 1988).

The four episodes in the professionalization of medicine, together with the brief consideration of this process within other health-care occupations, suggest certain generalizations. Firstly, the professional characteristics which have been identified by means of the comparative approach are not obtained *en bloc* by occupation; rather they are obtained piecemeal in a variety of specific historical situations. Secondly, these characteristics are not given to an occupation; they are fought for and won by its members, often only after a protracted struggle. Thirdly, knowledge plays a complex role in this process. The claim to a body of specialized knowledge and the establishment of training institutions to pass on this knowledge would seem to be preconditions for professionalization. It does not appear to be necessary, however, for this knowledge to be effective and, in the case of medicine at least, therapeutic effectiveness was a consequence rather than a precondition of professionalization. Fourthly, the acquisition of status and income which accompanies professionalization means that it involves a form of occupational upward social mobility which is in contrast to the more usual movement of individuals between social classes. Finally, professional powers are achieved by an occupation through negotiations with the relevant powers-that-be. In the case of medicine these were the state and institutional employers, while in the cases of the other professional occupations within health care the powers-that-be included the already established medical profession. In the latter cases, therefore, there was less room for occupational improvement through professionalization and trade unionism has subsequently developed as part of a combined occupational strategy.

EFFECTS OF PROFESSIONS

The nature and effects of professions have recently become issues within the policy debate about the provision of health care. The rising cost of medical care has raised a fear among those who finance this sector that these costs will grow exponentially. The growing involvement of large industrial and financial corporations in hospital construction, instrument manufacture, pharmaceutical production and medical insurance introduces powerful new vested interests into the provision of medical care. Lastly, rising rates of litigation against doctors and protests, such as that by the women's movement against high rates of induced labour, suggest that patients are becoming less deferential. It is thus possible to see the medical profession's autonomy increasingly limited by managerial attempts to control costs, by capital's attempts to ensure profitability and by patients' attempts to shape their own medical care. These changes can be clearly seen in the USA (Light & Levine 1988), where managerial attempts to control costs seem to be having the most immediate impact. Similar developments are discernible in Britain and, in this context, it is useful to attempt a balance sheet of the effects of professionalization.

From the point of view of consumers of health services, professions have the great advantage of guaranteeing the qualifications, and thereby hopefully the knowledge, of those who are registered. The General Medical Council register, for example, was established because 'it is expedient that persons requiring medical aid should be enabled to distinguish qualified from unqualified practitioners' (General Medical Council 1980). The ability to make this distinction is equally useful to both individual patients and employers such as health authorities. Similarly advantageous is a profession's code of ethics, which constrains exploitative behaviour on the part of the professional and provides some redress if this nevertheless occurs. Any assessment of professions, however, needs to balance these advantages against other less desirable effects.

Team work

Modern health care involves the work of many different occupations, among whom doctors form a small minority and nurses are the largest group (see Table 1). The way in which their work is integrated is, therefore, of considerable importance to patient care. Two models of integration can be seen. One type, which involves a decision-maker who gives instructions that are carried out by the other participants, is appropriate in an emergency situation such as cardiac arrest. In other situations, however, this hierarchical model can be counter-productive because it inhibits the upward flow of information and ideas about patients whose health is changing more slowly. In these situations the model of a team is more appropriate in which, although there may be a final decision-maker, decisions are only made after an open and equal discussion between the participants involved. The earlier sections of this chapter have indicated that the professionalization of health care has tended to lock integration into the hierarchical model. This historical legacy is in conflict with the growing predominance of chronic diseases for whose care the team model is more appropriate. The logic of many doctors' work therefore drives them to try to create a team approach in a situation where each participant's primary loyalty is to their own profession and relations between these participants reflect the established inter-professional hierarchy. Success in this endeavour tends to depend more on the personal characteristics of those involved than on institutional arrangements, and such teams are always vulnerable to disintegration, with their members drawing back into their traditional professional roles and inter-professional relationships (Beales 1978). Although this problem affects most parts of health care, it is particularly important in relation to the community-care programme which depends upon coordination of health services and the personal social services provided by local authorities (see Chapter 16). As has already been mentioned, social workers have maintained their professional autonomy in relation to doctors by obtaining separate employment in local authorities rather than the health service. The success of the community care programme, therefore, depends in part on doctors and social workers reconciling their different approaches and establishing a *modus vivendi* which respects the autonomy of both professions.

Communication with patients

A second, less desirable, consequence of a professionalized work-force in health care is the gap it creates between the professionals and their patients, a gap which is probably widest in the case of doctors. A number of elements contribute to this gap (see Chapter 4), and some of these are related to professional status. There tends to be a large difference in medical knowledge, although the size of this gap can easily be exaggerated and, at the very least, is probably quite small in the case of the half-million health workers who are also patients. Secondly, there is a difference in control over resources, with the doctor being the patient's sole point of access to desired goods such as prescribed medication, sickness benefit and medical care. Finally, there is usually a difference in social class, and often in gender, with most doctors being middle-class men and the largest group of patients being working-class women. These differences in knowledge, control over resources, social class and gender combine to produce a marked inequality in power between doctor and patient, which is likely to interfere with effective communication between them. In some clinical situations this inequality can probably be justified in terms of facilitating prompt emergency treatment, although even in these cases the patient's informed consent is required and this presupposes effective communication. In general, however, patients prefer a consultation style which has been described as 'mutual participation', in which the doctor listens to the patient, encourages the patient's questions and answers them comprehensibly. This more equal relationship between doctor and patient is also clinically appropriate in many situations, particularly those which involve the management of chronic diseases. Good clinical practice, therefore, often requires doctors to learn subtle communication skills in order to overcome impediments to effective communication which themselves are derived in part from doctors' own collective actions towards professionalization.

Medical priorities

Control over priorities within health care is a third aspect of professionalization which needs to be considered. It is widely acknowledged that the so-called 'cinderella services' provide relatively poor care to certain categories of patients such as the mentally and physically handicapped, the terminally ill, those with chronic psychiatric conditions and the elderly infirm. It is possible to account for the low priority accorded to these patients in terms of the values of the wider economic system, in the sense that they offer little prospect of being useful parts of the work-force. This explanation, however, ignores the history of the professionalization of medicine in which, as has already been described, the physicians' and surgeons' eventually successful struggle to control hospital-admissions policy resulted in the exclusion of precisely those categories of patients which are now confined to the cinderella services. There would appear to be a coincidence of interests, therefore, between the economic system, which values productive workers, and the medical profession which values acute diseases offering the prospect of successful treatment. The profession's interest in acute diseases is based on their traditional employment as curers of the sick, but their professional autonomy over health care allows this interest to shape the whole of the health-care system. A second example of this power can be seen in the relative importance which the health-care system gives to diagnosis and treatment compared with the study of the causes of disease and their prevention.

Alternative medicine

A final questionable aspect of professionalization concerns its monopoly and consequent power to marginalize rival forms of therapeutic practice. As has been described, the 1858 Medical Act effectively discriminated against unqualified practitioners; some of these were undoubtedly opportunistic quacks, but among their number were also practitioners of other therapeutic traditions. These alternative forms of medical treatment continue to be denigrated by most members of the established medical profession, and treatment by their practitioners has been excluded from the state-financed health-care system. Psychoanalysis and osteopathy are examples of such excluded forms of therapy, as are Vedic and Chinese medicine, to which many recent immigrants from these cultures remain committed. Homeopathy is one partial exception to this general rule. Possibly because of the Royal Family's support for this form of therapy, the National Health Service contains one homeopathic hospital. The professionalization of medicine thus allowed its practitioners' hostility towards alternative therapies to be translated into the marginalization and exclusion of their rivals. In some instances the counter-productive nature of this reflex is, in retrospect, accepted even by the medical profession; for example, the profession's slow acceptance of the germ theory of disease was probably due to Pasteur's position outside the profession as an agricultural biochemist.

CONCLUSIONS

The health care available to patients has been profoundly influenced by the struggles of its providers to increase their authority, status and income. The success of medicine in this respect encouraged other occupations within health care to emulate their strategy, producing a highly professionalized work-force. Patients have benefitted from this process in terms of the competence and ethical behaviour of those who care for them, but they may suffer as the result of other effects such as poor team-work, poor communication between themselves and professionals, priorities which reflect professional interests rather than their needs and limitations on the range of treatments available to them.

These disadvantages of professionalization may also handicap conscientious professionals in the performance of their work as, for example, when they struggle to integrate the work of a multi-professional team in order to provide effective care, when they coax patients to overcome their diffidence in order to obtain a full account of what is wrong with them, or when they attempt to deal with the financial problems consequent on a patient's need for psychoanalysis. Such problems are endemic in the present organization of health care and, in the absence of fundamental change, individual professionals have little choice but to learn new skills in order to overcome them. In the longer term, however, individual solutions rarely form a satisfactory response to structural problems. The earlier sections of this chapter described how the contemporary structure of health care has its roots in the nineteenth century when its development was part of, and took place in the context of, rapid and profound change in the wider society. On this basis at least it can be suggested that any major change in health care will depend upon a similar period of wider social change.

REFERENCES

Abel-Smith, B. (1960) *A History of the Nursing Profession*. London: Heinemann.

Abel-Smith, B. (1964) *The Hospitals 1800–1948*. London: Heinemann.

Beales, J. (1978) *Sick Health Centres and How to Make Them Better*. Tunbridge Wells: Pitman Medical.

Becker, H., Greer, B., Hughes, E. & Strauss, A. (1961) *Boys in White*. Chicago, IL: University of Chicago Press.

Cantlie, N. (1973) *A History of the Army Medical Department*, Vol. 2. London: Churchill Livingstone.

Carr-Saunders, A.M. & Wilson, P.A. (1933) *The Professions*. Oxford: Clarendon Press.

Davies, C. (1980) *Rewriting Nursing History*. London: Croom Helm.

Department of Health (1989) *Health and Personal Social Services Statistics for England*. London: HMSO.

Dingwall, R., Rafferty, A.M. & Webster, C. (1988) *An Introduction to the Social History of Nursing*. London: Routledge.

Freidson, E. (1970) *Profession of Medicine*. New York: Dodds, Mead & Co.

General Medical Council (1980) *Constitution and Functions*. London: GMC.

Honigsbaum, F. (1979) *The Division in British Medicine*. London: Kegan Page.

Jeffreys, M. & Sachs, H. (1983) *Rethinking General Practice*. London: Tavistock.

Light, D. & Levine, S. (1988) The changing character of the medical profession: a theoretical overview. *Millbank Q.*, **6**, 10–32.

Melia, K. (1987) *Learning and Working*. London: Tavistock.

Merton, R.K., Reader, K. & Kendall, P.L. (1957) *The Student-Physician*. Cambridge, MA: Harvard University Press.

Peterson, M.J. (1978) *The Medical Profession in Mid-Victorian London*. San Francisco, CA: University of California Press.

Stacey, M. (1988) *The Sociology of Health and Healing*. London: Unwin Hyman.

Waddington, I. (1984) *The Medical Profession in the Industrial Revolution*. London: Gill and McMillan.

16

Community Care

Nicholas Mays

Community care has been the goal of government policy in the UK since the late 1950s for the care of the elderly, the chronically ill, the mentally handicapped and other dependent groups. While it has been acknowledged that there will always be a core of people who require long-term institutional care because of their frailty or social circumstances (DHSS 1981a), for the vast majority community care has been seen as a solution to the many problems associated with long-term care in institutions (Open University Health and Disease Team 1985) (see Chapter 6). An important element in the durability of the policy and in its appeal to successive governments lies in the fact that it appears self-evidently good and humane. Yet, on closer inspection, the meaning and objectives of a policy of community care are surrounded by considerable confusion and ambiguity.

In a very broad sense, the term community care is attractive because it sums up our aspirations towards a society in which close-knit, supportive social relations exist to support dependent people, but, as Jones and colleagues have pointed out, in practice community care can mean very different things to different people:

> To the politician it is a useful piece of rhetoric; to the sociologist it is a stick to beat institutional care with; to the civil servant it is a cheap alternative to institutional care which can be passed to the local authorities for action or inaction; to the visionary it is a dream of the new society in which people really do care; to social services departments it is a nightmare of heightened public expectations and inadequate resources to meet them. We are only just beginning to find out what it means to the old, the chronic sick and the handicapped. (Jones et al. 1978)

This chapter considers the origins and justification for community-care policies, the development of such policies since the 1950s, and the extent to which their objectives have been achieved. It continues by looking at the main obstacles to the implementation of community-care policies, before studying informal care by lay people which remains the basis for the care of most dependent people in our society. The chapter ends with a description of recent attempts by the Government to reform the finance and organization of community care.

WHAT IS COMMUNITY CARE?

It is helpful to start by attempting to define what is meant by community care. Unfortunately, as the above quotation from Jones et al. makes plain, there is no single definition of the term. For some people community care is no more than residential care outside a major institution. For others it includes enabling dependent people to participate as fully as possible in normal life. There is an important distinction between the use of the term as a *prescription* for how people *should* meet the health and social needs of dependent people, and as a *description* of a set of services which *are* currently provided. As a description of services, the term community care is generally used today to refer to those health and social services which provide professional and quasi-professional help as an alternative to large-scale residential or institutional care. However, when used prescriptively, the emphasis in official statements of community-care policy has altered over time. In the 1950s, 1960s and early 1970s, government policy statements implied that community care consisted mainly of formal domiciliary services provided primarily by staff employed by local authorities. By the mid-1970s the term had expanded, confusingly, to include other services such as day hospitals, hostels and residential homes. Whatever the precise definition, the emphasis in this period was on formal care in the community. After 1979, when the Conservative Party was elected to office, public services were still discussed, but there was a far greater emphasis in policy documents on an ideal of care by the community; that is, care by family, relatives, neighbours and friends and by voluntary organizations (DHSS 1981b).

THE JUSTIFICATION FOR COMMUNITY CARE

The policy of community care and the desire to reduce the use of institutions and enable vulnerable groups to live an ordinary life has been sustained since the 1950s, firstly, by a belief that community care (however defined) is better than the alternative. This view was prompted and underpinned by a number of influential research studies carried out in the UK and the USA in the 1950s and 1960s, which showed the failure of a variety of institutional settings to meet the emotional, social or physical needs of their inmates and, in some cases, actively to worsen residents' disabilities. In Britain, Townsend (1962) concluded that residential homes for the elderly should be replaced by a different form of help and support which would enable residents to maintain their dignity and independence. In the USA, Goffman (1961) argued that long-stay hospitals for the mentally ill bore many of the characteristics of 'total institutions', in which inmates were separated from the rest of society and managed according to depersonalizing 'batch processes' which, over time, led to a reorganized conception of self subordinate to the requirements of the institution. This debilitating process has been referred to as 'institutionalization', sometimes resulting in 'institutional neurosis' (Barton 1959), and was regarded as incompatible with any possibility of rehabilitation and return to ordinary life (see Chapter 6).

Secondly, the critique of institutional care was stimulated in the UK in the late 1960s and early 1970s by a series of scandals in which cruelty and negligence by staff, together with poor living conditions and unstimulating care regimes, were revealed at a number of long-stay hospitals. A third factor, favouring a policy of community care specifically for the mentally ill, was the development of new psychotropic drugs which could help control some of the more severe symptoms of mental illness and which facilitated the care of patients outside custodial settings. From the point of view of the government, community care offered additional attractions since the long-stay hospitals periodically suffered difficulties in recruiting nursing staff and were mainly Victorian institutions which were beginning to require major programmes of maintenance and modernization. The belief that community care might be not only better but also cheaper than institutional care, although far from proven, has attracted successive governments anxious to limit public expenditure.

THE DEVELOPMENT OF COMMUNITY CARE POLICY

The policy of achieving care within community settings began with the mentally ill during the 1950s. The 1959 Mental Health Act set course towards a comprehensive community care service for people with mental illness, with hospital care reserved for acute episodes and a small number of severe cases. The 1962 Hospital Plan proposed a massive programme of closures of Victorian psychiatric hospitals with the aim of halving the number of beds by 1975 and locating acute psychiatry in the district general hospital (Ministry of Health 1962).

During the 1960s, community care principles were gradually extended to other dependent groups. In the 1970s a series of official policy documents stressed the development of local community-based alternatives to institutional care, better domiciliary services and the importance of joint planning between the local authority and the local health services to meet the needs of the elderly, the physically handicapped, the mentally ill and the mentally handicapped. Specific targets were set by central government, for example, to reduce the number of hospital beds, to build up small-scale hostels and to train facilities in the community and increase domiciliary services.

Progress towards community care

How successful were the succession of official documents and plans in shifting the balance of care from large-scale, institutional provision towards the range of provision labelled community care?

In 1986, the Audit Commission, an independent body set up by an Act of Parliament to assess the efficiency and effectiveness of local authority and national health services, investigated the extent to which there had been a change in the balance of care, and most notably, replacement of institutional care by community care in the previous 15 years. The Commission concluded that progress had been limited (Audit Commission 1986). For example, domiciliary services for the elderly were struggling to keep up with the increasing proportion of the very elderly. There had been a decrease in reliance on long-stay hospital care for the elderly, but this had been more than offset by a rapid, unplanned increase in private residential care funded out of social security board-and-lodging payments. There had been very limited progress towards the targets of provision outside hospital for the mentally ill and of day care for the mentally handicapped (now generally known as 'people with learning difficulties'):

> The result is poor value for money. Too many people are cared for in settings costing over £200 a week when they would receive a more appropriate care in the community at a total cost to public funds of £100–£130 a week. Conversely, people in the community may not be getting the support they need' (Audit Commission 1986: 3).

The Commission argued that more flexible, cost-effective alternatives to institutional provision were under-developed. There was
some research evidence from experiments to support this view,
showing that even very frail elderly people could be maintained at
home with carefully organized domiciliary support at lower cost than
for residential care (Challis & Davies 1986).

The continued dominance of institutional care in the spectrum of
formal, professionally provided services for dependent people,
despite 30 years of community care policies, was vividly shown in a
study of six districts in England in the late 1980s. When spending on
acute health services and general practice was excluded from the
calculation, as much as 73% of the remaining health and social
services expenditure by the Health Service and the local authorities
was still devoted to institutional care of one kind or another (Gray et
al. 1988). There was also considerable variation between the districts
in how much was spent on community care, which appeared to be
unrelated to the needs of the locality. Furthermore, there is no
evidence that areas which spend little on institutional care spend
more on community care or vice versa (Hudson 1987).

PROBLEMS IN IMPLEMENTING COMMUNITY CARE

How can we explain the gap between policy statements and the
reality of what has been provided? There have been two main types
of obstacle to community care implementation: a lack of resources,
and managerial difficulties. The Audit Commission (1986) identified
the following problems in more detail:

1. a mismatch between the resources made available and the
   aims of policy;
2. a lack of 'bridging' finance to enable a simultaneous run-down
   of institutions and development of community care;
3. the perverse incentive towards institutional care created by the
   availability without limit of social security board-and-lodging
   payments, while local authority domiciliary care was strictly
   cash-limited;
4. organizational fragmentation and confusion between the National
   Health Service (NHS), the local authority social services and
   housing departments and the social security system in their
   responsibility for community care; and
5. inadequate arrangements for training staff to work in community care settings.

The policy of attempting to close old, long-stay, mental hospitals exemplifies many of these financial and managerial problems. It has proved very difficult to close hospitals and transfer resources and personnel into community care without additional finance in the form of 'bridging' loans. This is because resources cannot be released, except in a small way, from hospitals until all the patients have been transferred to alternative care; and, in turn, the discharge of patients cannot occur until resources are available for community care.

The intention was that many of the consequences of closing long-stay institutions in the NHS would be met by the local authorities, which were expected to provide community care alternatives to hospitalization. This required close cooperation between the local authority and the local health authority in the form of joint planning and, ultimately, a substantial transfer of resources from the NHS to the local authorities. In practice, health authorities have proved reluctant to pass funds to the local authorities. This reluctance has been exacerbated by differences in working style, priorities, organization and systems of accountability between doctors, nurses, social workers, occupational therapists, housing managers, home-help organizers and all the other staff involved in caring for dependent groups in the NHS and in local authorities.

In the case of closing mental hospitals, there has also been powerful resistance from sections of the medical and nursing professions to government policy for a variety of reasons: least laudably, out of professional self-interest and an unwillingness to surrender power to local authority staff; and more appropriately, perhaps, from a genuine belief in the continuing need for places of 'asylum' or refuge for chronically ill people and a fear that adequate community care support would not be forthcoming, leaving vulnerable people to fend for themselves in a harsh environment. More and more of the prison population and of the homeless on the streets of the big cities are former patients of long-stay hospitals. The anxieties of psychiatrists are reinforced by evidence that society as a whole is at best ambivalent, and at worst hostile, to the idea of the mentally ill living outside hospitals. There have been a series of cases in which the fear and stigma attached to mental illness have united the community in campaigns to exclude former mental patients from participation in ordinary patterns of living.

INFORMAL CARE

The preoccupation of public policy towards dependent groups with getting people out of hospitals risks obscuring the fact that the vast majority have always lived outside institutions, cared for informally at home, usually by family, relatives or friends (see Chapter 11).

The scale of informal care

The 1985 General Household Survey revealed that 14% of people over 16 years of age 'were looking after, or providing some regular service for, someone who was sick, elderly or handicapped' (Green 1988). When applied to the population of Britain, this suggests a total of about 6 million carers, of whom 1.4 million were providing at least 20 hours care per week either to someone living with them or in another household (Parker 1990). It was estimated that this volume of care would have cost between £15 billion and £24 billion a year in 1988 if it had been provided by the state (Green 1988). This dwarfs the contribution to community care from formal health and social services.

Eighty per cent of informal carers help with tasks such as cooking, shopping and gardening; 45% provide nursing care and physical help; and 50% offer help with personal care such as washing, dressing and toileting. Women carers are more likely to be involved with intimate tasks and physical help than are male carers (see Chapter 9).

Who provides informal care?

'Care is socially divided between the state and the family and between family members. In practice "community care" is overwhelmingly care by kin, and especially female kin, not the community' (Walker 1982: 23). Care by the community tends to be based primarily on kinship obligations between the immediate family (e.g. daughters caring for fathers and mothers), with a limited contribution from 'moral communities' such as churches and ethnic groups (Abrams 1980). Care from neighbours is relatively rare. The chances of being a carer are not only increased for women, they also increase with age. It is not uncommon for an elderly person to be responsible for the care of someone far older than themselves.

The relationship between formal and informal care

Only a relatively small amount of help is received by informal carers from the statutory agencies, although it can be crucial in assisting a carer to cope. For example, the General Household Survey (Green 1988) shows that two-thirds of carers who look after a dependent

----------- **Table 1** -----------
Effect on the immediate family of caring for a mentally ill
adult at home.

Aspect of family life	% of families	
	Some disturbance	Severe disturbance
Health of closest relatives		
Mental	40	20
Physical	28	—
Bringing up children	24	10
Domestic routine	13	16
Income	14	9
Employment (other than the mentally ill person)	17	6

Source: Sainsbury and Grad de Alarcon (1974).

person in the same household receive no regular visits from any
formal services. State policies for allocating formal services tend to
hinge on the assumption that it is natural for family members, which
means in practice women, to provide care for others. The notion of
'natural' family care assumes that the dependent person lives with or
near their family and that the family is itself stable and has an able-
bodied woman at home supported financially by a husband at work.
This applies to only 15% of contemporary families. State interference
in 'natural' caring has thus been regarded as potentially harmful and,
as a result, providing support for carers has not been a priority of
policy. Indeed, services are frequently withheld on the grounds that a
dependent person has help from relatives. For example, an elderly
person living alone or living with a spouse is much more likely to
receive the services of a home help or meals-on-wheels regardless of
the degree of dependency than if they live with other family members
(Parker 1990). This approach to rationing formal care is liable to
penalize women who take on primary responsibility for unpaid caring
rather than complementing what informal carers can offer.

The costs of caring

Official community care policy has tended to ignore the financial and
social costs to families of caring. As a consequence, informal care can
appear very cheap. However, it has become apparent that the true
costs are disproportionately borne by informal carers themselves. For
example, combining paid employment with informal caring responsibilities in the absence of financial or practical recognition by the
state of the costs of caring, can impose great financial, physical and

psychological strains on carers and also on their immediate families (see Table 1). Forty-two per cent of lay carers who care for at least 20 hours per week also have a paid job (Henwood 1990). The relatively private, and therefore invisible, daily grind of physical and emotional caring has now been vividly documented in a number of studies (e.g. Nissel & Bonnerjea 1982; Finch & Groves 1983; Parker 1990). Future community care policies should be framed to take these hidden costs into account.

Trends in informal care

In the future, there will be larger numbers of people living in the community who need care and support, but there may well be fewer people available to provide it. A combination of smaller families, a decline in the proportion of single women, who comprised the traditional recruits to care giving in the population, increased female participation in the labour market and greater geographical mobility, will all limit the extent to which families can care for their dependent members without formal help from outside. The tensions between paid work and unpaid caring, for women particularly, are likely to intensify because of a reduction in the number of younger entrants to the labour market and a rising demand for women's labour.

RECENT INITIATIVES IN COMMUNITY CARE POLICY

The Audit Commission's critical investigation of community care proposed that there should be a strategic review of the available options for the finance and organization of community-care services. Ideally, according to the commission, there should be a single budget for the care of each dependent group managed by a single agency.

The Griffiths review of community care (1987–88)

In 1987 the government appointed Sir Roy Griffiths, the Deputy Chairman of the Sainsbury supermarket chain and, at that time, the government's chief adviser on health service management, to report on ways of making more effective use of the public funds available for community care. Griffiths concluded that the respective roles of health authorities and local authority social services departments had to be clarified to avoid confusion and overlap and each should be made accountable for particular care groups and services (Griffiths 1988). To this end, he recommended that the local authorities should be given the primary responsibility for community care, to act as the 'designers, organisers and purchasers' of 'packages' of services tailored to the needs of individuals, rather than directly providing all services themselves according to the views of their experts. Local authorities would be obliged to stimulate a 'mixed economy' of care by encouraging private and voluntary providers to tender for local authority services. Access to private residential homes would be controlled by the local authority to avoid unnecessary or inappropriate placement subsidized by social security payments. Overall, the Griffiths proposals meant a transfer of funds from central to local government and from health and social security to social services.

The Government White Paper *Caring for People* (1989)

The Conservative Government's response to the Griffiths report published in November 1989 took the form of a White Paper entitled *Caring for People* which defined the tasks of community care as 'providing the right level of intervention and support to enable people to achieve maximum independence and control over their own lives' (Secretaries of State for Health, Social Security, Wales and Scotland 1989). There were three main elements in the White Paper proposals:

1. The care element in the social security board-and-lodging payments to residents of private homes was to be transferred from social security to the local authorities, where it would form part of an overall budget to meet the costs of care in relation to need, irrespective of whether an individual was living at home or in a residential setting.
2. The local authorities were to become the lead agency in community care and appoint 'case managers' whose job was to assess the needs of individual clients, design appropriate packages of care for them, ensure that services were delivered and monitor their quality. Local authorities were to make the maximum use possible of the voluntary and commercial (private) sectors of care by contracting out provision to produce a cost-effective 'mixed market' for services.
3. A specific grant was to be paid to NHS Regional Health Authorities (RHAs), subject to central approval of a care plan, to enable them to discharge mental patients to new community-care facilities run by local authorities. There were to be no earmarked community care grants for other client groups.

An assessment of *Caring for People*

The proposals in *Caring for People* which formed part of the 1990 NHS and Community Care Act (see Chapter 14 for discussion of the other changes brought about by this act), fall far short of achieving a single, integrated budget for community care managed by a single agency responsible for 'case management'. There will still be separate budgets for each of the elements in community care (e.g. housing and social services). There has even been a delay in the one element of financial integration — the transfer of money from social security board-and-lodging payments to the local authorities — despite the fact that it was a principal objective of the reforms. 'Case managers' will, therefore, remain reliant on the goodwill of staff in other organizations to ensure coordinated service provision for clients whose needs cross agency boundaries. Doubts also remain about the level of funding which local authorities will have for community care. Patients risk being discharged before community support has been built up (House of Commons Social Services Select Committee 1990). Furthermore, local authorities will need to develop rigorous systems of quality assurance if contracting out to the commercial and voluntary sectors is to produce high-quality services (Walker 1989).

CONCLUSIONS

The partially reformed formal care system in Britain continues to be dominated by institutional provision, but based on the assumption that the bulk of caring for vulnerable people will continue to be provided mainly by female kin with little help from the state. Rather than acting to share care between formal and informal carers in order to avoid putting an excessive burden on informal carers, the formal system is still funded and organized to intervene only when informal caring relationships have broken down. It is becoming increasingly doubtful whether this approach can be sustained in the future. Demographic trends and women's increasing participation in the paid economy are combining to increase the need for care, while reducing the supply of informal carers. This is likely to lead to growing pressures on lay people to care, but there is also a greater awareness of the financial and emotional costs to carers. In this situation the state will have to find ways of 'caring for the carers', particularly to ensure that they do not suffer financially or in their employment. To do this, formal care will need to be far more closely dovetailed with the pattern of informal care, rather than operating as an entirely separate system. One possibility for the future which might be attractive to some carers, would be to categorize caring for a frail or disabled relative as a proper job attracting a full or part-time salary from the state.

They do have an attendance attendance.

REFERENCES

Abrams, P. (1980) Social change, social networks and neighbourhood care. *Socl Wk Serv.*, **22**, 12–23.

Audit Commission (1986) *Making a Reality of Community Care.* London: HMSO.

Barton, R. (1959) *Institutional Neurosis.* Bristol: Wright.

Challis, L. & Davies, B. (1986) *Case Management in Community Care.* Aldershot: Gower.

Department of Health and Social Security (1981a) *Care in Action: a Handbook of Priorities for the Health and Personal Social Services in England.* London: HMSO.

Department of Health and Social Security (1981b) *Growing Older.* London: HMSO.

Finch, J. & Groves, D. (eds) (1983) *A Labour of Love: Women, Work and Caring.* London: Routledge & Kegan Paul.

Goffman, E. (1961) *Asylums.* New York: Anchor Books.

Gray, A., Whelan, A. & Normand, C. (1988) *Care in the Community: a Study of Services and Costs in Six Districts.* York: Centre for Health Economics, University of York.

Green, H. (1988) *General Household Survey 1985: Informal Carers.* London: HMSO.

Griffiths, R. (1988) *Community Care: Agenda for Action.* A report to the Secretary of State for Social Services. London: HMSO.

Henwood, M. (1990) *Community Care and Elderly People: Policy, Practice and Research Review.* London: Family Policy Studies Centre.

House of Commons Social Services Select Committee (1990) *Community Care: Services for People with Mental Handicap and Mental Illness,* Eleventh Report Session 1989–90. London: HMSO.

Hudson, R. (1987) Steering a course through the myths of community care. *Hlth Serv. J.*, **28 May** (Suppl.).

Jones, K., Brown, J. & Bradshaw, J. (1978) *Issues in Social Policy.* London: Routledge & Kegan Paul.

Ministry of Health (1962) *A Hospital Plan for England and Wales. Cmnd. 1604.* London: HMSO.

Nissel, M. & Bonnerjea, L. (1982) *Family Care of the Handicapped Elderly: Who Pays?* London: Policy Studies Institute.

Open University Health and Disease Team (1985) *Caring for Health: Dilemmas and Prospects.* Milton Keynes: Open University Press.

Parker, G. (1990) *With due care and attention: a review of research on informal care. Occasional Paper No. 2,* 2nd edition. London: Family Policy Studies Centre.

Sainsbury, P. & Grad de Alarcon, J. (1974) The cost of community care and the burden on the family of treating the mentally ill at home. In: *Impairment, Disability and Handicap,* ed. D. Lees & S. Shaw. London: Heinemann.

Secretaries of State for Health, Social Security, Wales and Scotland (1989) *Caring for*

People: Community Care in the Next Decade and Beyond. Cmnd 849. London: HMSO.

Townsend, P. (1962) *The Last Refuge.* London: Routledge & Kegan Paul.

Walker, A. (1982) The meaning and social division of community care. In: *Community Care: the Family, the State and Social Policy,* ed. A. Walker, pp.13–39. Oxford: Basil Blackwell/Martin Robertson.

Walker, A. (1989) Community care. In: *The New Politics of Welfare: an Agenda for the 1990s?,* ed. M. McCarthy, pp.203–224. London: Macmillan.

17

Prevention and Health Promotion

David Locker

By the middle of the twentieth century, health-care systems had become major institutions within industrialized nations. The scientific discoveries and therapeutic successes of modern medicine, which began in the 1930s and accelerated in the following decades, were accompanied by a significant expansion in health-care facilities and a massive increase in the number of health professionals and other workers responsible for the delivery of health care. Government policies at this time were concerned with increasing the *provision* of health services and ensuring that the population had *access* to them.

The belief underlying initiatives such as the National Health Service (NHS) in Britain, and universal public health insurance in Canada, was that better access to health care led to better health. When the NHS was founded it was anticipated that health-care costs would rise initially but then fall as the population became healthier and less in need of medical care. This did not happen: the post-World War II period has been one in which health-care costs have risen systematically, both in absolute terms and as a proportion of gross national product (see Chapter 19).

This belief in the effectiveness of health services, characteristic of the immediate post-World War II period, has been tempered by a growing scepticism and awareness that increases in spending on health care now have a limited impact on the health of the population. Increased inputs in the form of financial and other resources are no longer matched by increased outputs such as improvements in life expectancy. This can be illustrated by examining the performance of the NHS since its inception in the late 1940s to the early 1970s. During this time, expenditure rose by more than 60%, hospital medical and nursing staff more than doubled and the number of prescriptions issued rose by more than 40%. The impact of these increases in the allocation of resources on mortality rates was rather small. Between 1948 and 1970, life expectancy for new-born males rose by 2.4 years, for males aged 25 by 0.8 years, and for males aged 45 by 0.4 years. In the USA, massive increases in spending on health care also failed to bring about continuing improvements in health.

CRITICAL APPRAISALS OF THE HEALTH-CARE SYSTEM

During the 1970s a number of critical appraisals of modern health-care systems began to appear (see Chapter 18). These addressed this input–output problem.

The *scientific critique* is usually associated with Cochrane (1972). He examined the effectiveness and efficiency of medical practice and concluded that many therapies commonly employed were used because they were traditional or established practices, not because there was any scientific evidence to support their efficacy. He advocated the use of randomized controlled trials and analyses of cost-effectiveness to ensure that therapies did more good than harm to the patient and produced good outcomes at the lowest cost.

A more fundamental appraisal is to be found in the *ecological critique*. This explains the input–output problem in terms of the nature of medical practice and the distribution of resources in medical care. That is, modern medicine is based on high technology, hospital-based provision and has, as its main focus, the cure rather than the prevention of disease (Davies 1979).

McKeown (1979), extrapolating from his anlaysis of the social and environmental factors that affect health (see Chapter 1), suggested that curative, high-technology medicine is too limited in scope to bring about further improvements in the health of modern populations. This is because the major health problems of industrialized societies are chronic, degenerative diseases which cannot be cured. However, most can be prevented by environmental change or changes in life-style. McKeown advocated a shift in health-care resources from curative medicine to the prevention of disease and the care of those with chronic disabling conditions. In arguing that more attention be paid to prevention, McKeown was convinced that the most productive approach was to bring about changes in personal behaviour, since he believes these to be more significant than the environment in influencing health.

THE SCOPE FOR PREVENTION

Some impression of the potential impact of prevention can be gained from a brief overview of the major causes of mortality and morbidity in modern populations. These are cardiovascular disease, cancer, motor-vehicle accidents, alcohol-related problems, suicide, respiratory disorders, congenital and genetic disorders and sexually transmitted disease, including acquired immunodeficiency syndrome (AIDS). The majority of these are associated with one or more risk factors which can be modified to prevent disease, disability and death.

Cardiovascular disease (CVD) has been in decline since the 1970s but still ranks as the leading cause of death in most industrialized societies. Its underlying cause is atherosclerosis and contributory factors include: smoking, high blood pressure, obesity, lack of physical exercise, high levels of dietary fat, blood cholesterol levels and genetic factors. The majority of these factors are amenable to change through preventive health practices. Although controversy surrounds some of the preventive approaches related to CVD, there is no doubt that its incidence could be reduced by dietary and other changes.

Cancers tend to be the second leading cause of death and, although the aetiology of most cancers is unknown, many are related to smoking, diet and exposure to carcinogens in the occupational environment. The close relationship between smoking and lung cancer is well documented. Approximately one-third of men and more than one-quarter of women are regular smokers. While rates are declining among men, they are increasing among women, so that female deaths from lung cancer are rising rapidly. Clearly, a reduction in the prevalence of smoking would be reflected in significant decreases in the incidence of this form of cancer. Smoking is also a major factor in respiratory diseases such as chronic bronchitis and emphysema, although environmental problems such as air pollution have also been linked to rates of respiratory illness.

Various diseases and/or health problems are associated with alcohol consumption, including cirrhosis, suicide and motor-vehicle and other accidents. It has been estimated that 2% of all deaths are directly attributable to alcohol, with 10% of deaths being alcohol related. Deaths from cirrhosis have increased over the past four decades and alcoholism is also one of the main reasons for admission to mental hospitals. Alcohol consumption has increased since the post-World War II period, one factor influencing levels of consumption being price — when expressed as a proportion of average weekly salary, the price of alcohol has fallen by 80% over this period.

The same principle applies to the other diseases listed above. Once the many risk factors associated with a disease are known, attempts can be made to reduce or eliminate one or more factor to bring about a corresponding reduction in the social and economic burden of illness. The overall fall in sexually transmitted diseases among homosexual men has been brought about through changes in sexual practices in the face of AIDS. This is testimony to what can be achieved by means of appropriate preventive interventions.

Primary, secondary and tertiary prevention

Traditional approaches to prevention are based on clinical interventions at three levels: primary, secondary and tertiary prevention. Primary prevention is the most basic and seeks to prevent the onset of disease. Immunization to confer immunity on an individual is a good example of this. Secondary prevention consists of the early detection and treatment of disease or states likely to lead to disease. Screening by a clinician for diseases such as human immunodeficiency virus (HIV) infection, tuberculosis or cervical cancer, or screening for major risk factors such as high blood pressure and cholesterol levels, are examples of secondary prevention. The objective of tertiary prevention is to minimize the disability and handicap from a disease state that cannot be cured or leaves the individual with some loss of function.

Screening can be defined as the active early diagnosis of risk factors for disease as a prelude to intervention. It can take one of many forms. *Mass screening*, such as programmes for breast and cervical cancer, involves large numbers of people who are offered the service and participate on a voluntary basis. Some screening procedures are *routine*, such as the screening of the newborn for various congenital abnormalities. Screening also occurs as part of the *normal course of medical care*, where a patient presenting with one condition or complaint is screened for another. In some instances screening may be *selective* and directed towards high-risk groups. *Multiphasic* screening involves tests for numerous diseases and/or risk factors at one time.

Screening has a certain logic; it can reduce morbidity and save lives by identifying and treating individuals at the earliest possible stage in the disease process. Nevertheless, a number of criticisms have been directed at screening programmes. A major criticism is that, with a few exceptions, they may be of little benefit. Many studies

of the outcomes of multiphasic screening, or screening for coronary
heart disease, have shown disappointing results, with no differences
in the morbidity and mortality experience of screened and non-
screened control groups (Stoate 1989). However, we are also
beginning to recognize that screening has psychological and other
costs which must be weighed against any benefits obtained (Marteau
1989).

A number of studies of people who have participated in screening
programmes have shown that screening can have negative psychological and behavioural outcomes. Revealing previously undiagnosed
hypertension resulted in more absenteeism from work, lower self-
esteem and disruptions in marital relationships (Haynes et al. 1978;
Mossey 1981). Bloom and Monterossa (1981) undertook a study of
people who were initially diagnosed as hypertensive but subsequently given a clean bill of health following further testing. They
found that such people reported more depression and a lower state
of general health than a control group — evidence of the lasting
effect of this initial labelling. Even a negative result may have
untoward consequences. The 'certificate-of-health effect' noted by
Tijmstra and Bieleman (1987) may reinforce unhealthy life-styles and
foster the impression that the individual is not vulnerable to this
disease.

These problems point to the significance of counselling prior to and
following screening procedures. In some areas, testing for HIV
infection is not undertaken until the individual has had such
counselling.

New directions in prevention

During the mid-1970s, a number of governments published policy
documents which gave official recognition to the emerging debate
about the most effective strategy for maintaining and improving
health. The Lalonde Report was released by the Canadian Government in 1974 and is now considered a turning point and landmark in
the development of a new approach to public health (Lalonde 1974).
This report was based on the *health field concept,* which emphasized
the significance of four elements in health: human biology, the
environment, life-style and health-care organization. As has already
been noted, since World War II major efforts to improve health have
focussed on the formal health-care system and on treating illness
already manifest. Yet the pattern of diseases affecting modern
populations clearly indicates that the potential for further improvements in health lies with the other three elements.

In 1976 the British Government issued a similar document,
Prevention and Health: Everybody's Business (DHSS 1976), in which

the prevention of the major health problems affecting the British population emerged as a key strategy in improving health. This document identified the causes of these health problems and outlined a response. The diseases of modern populations are 'related less to man's outside environment than to his own personal behaviour; what might be termed our lifestyle' (DHSS 1976: 17). Consequently, 'much of the responsibility for ensuring his own good health lies with the individual' (DHSS 1976: 95). The responsibility of governments and health professionals 'is limited to ensuring that the public have access to such knowledge as is available about the importance of personal habits to health and, at the very least, no obstacles are placed in the way of those who decide to act on that knowledge' (DHSS 1976: 62).

The implication of this particular view of health is that prevention can be achieved simply by the provision of information to the population about the risks to health posed by aspects of our life-style, like smoking, drinking and an inadequate diet. Although at one point in the document it is acknowledged that the government's role is a broader one, involving fiscal and legal controls on the manufacture and sale of health-damaging commodities, the solution to the problem is largely reduced to one of health education.

Naidoo (1986) has criticized the philosophy of individualism underlying the approach described in *Prevention and Health*. This sees health as a matter of individual responsibility and free choice. It assumes that many of the behaviours damaging to health are freely chosen and can be avoided once the individual is informed of their negative effects. Providing this information is the responsibility of governments and health-care professionals, but the responsibility for change lies with the individual. Within the framework of a philosophy which values free choice, education, rather than coercion by legal or fiscal means, is the preferred approach to the prevention of disease.

One potentially damaging outcome of an emphasis on individual responsibility is its ready translation into 'victim blaming' and the attribution of guilt (Allison 1982). A second negative consequence of this approach to prevention is its failure to acknowledge the extent to which health is linked to social, economic and environmental conditions which lie outside the control of the individual (see Chapter 8). The individual is relatively powerless to act against a health-damaging environment produced by a society which frequently values profit and economic expansion above health.

McKinlay (1974) addresses the significance of the social and political environment in his analysis of the political economy of health. According to McKinlay, the efforts of the health-care system can be called 'downstream activities', devoted as they are to the rescue of the sick. However, this type of activity cannot influence the level of health of a population when various interest groups and large-scale profit-oriented corporations are operating 'up-stream', constantly adding to the pool of those in need of rescue. Problems such as lung cancer, heart disease, obesity, alcohol abuse and road-traffic accidents can be linked to organizations such as the food and tobacco industries, who spend billions of dollars promoting unhealthy life-styles. The battle between these 'manufacturers of illness' and health educators is an unequal one. The tobacco industry, for example, commands massive resources and has access to sophisticated techniques of persuasion in maintaining and promoting smoking as a desirable activity. McKinlay believes they are effective because they tie at-risk behaviours such as smoking to dominant cultural themes and images. Consequently, it is inaccurate to talk of freedom of choice when considering such behaviours. Individual choice is shaped and limited by environmental factors and commercial interests which profit from unhealthy life-styles. Because free choice does not operate in these situations, McKinlay advocates legislation to curb the activities of the manufacturers of illness.

McKinlay's approach to improving the health of the population is usually referred to as a 'structural' approach. This seeks to improve health by means of strategies to modify the social, political and economic environment in which we live. Such changes only come about as the result of action by governments and communities. From this perspective, part of the task of health educators is to teach individuals and communities to recognize health-damaging aspects of home, workplace and community and to foster community action to deal with them.

HEALTH PROMOTION

Health promotion is often called the 'new public health', a reference to the public-health movement of the nineteenth century which, through sanitary reform, brought about a significant decline in deaths from infectious disease. It has been defined as 'the process of enabling people to increase control over and to improve their health' (World Health Organization 1984). It employs both individualist and structuralist approaches to ensure that health choices are easy choices. Health promotion has its roots in a socio-ecological conception of health which emphasizes the inextricable links between individuals and the environment in which they live. From this perspective, health is broadly conceived as:

> the extent to which an individual or group is able, on the one hand, to realise aspirations and satisfy needs, and, on the other

hand, to change or cope with the environment. Health is seen therefore as a resource for everyday life, not the objective of living; it is a positive concept emphasising social and personal resources as well as physical capacities (World Health Organization 1984).

Consequently, health promotion consists of a comprehensive set of strategies which go beyond health education and life-style change:

Health promotion policy combines diverse but complementary approaches including legislation, fiscal measures, taxation and organizational change. It is coordinated action which leads to health, income and social policies that foster greater equity. Joint action contributes to safer goods and services, healthier public services and cleaner, more enjoyable environments (World Health Organization 1984).

The joint action referred to above involves governments, health and other social and economic sectors, voluntary organizations, local authorities, industry and the media. It entails the creation of physical environments conducive to health and social and political environments within which people can take action to improve their own health and support each other in managing personal and community health problems.

From this perspective, responsibility for health does not lie with the individual. Individuals can do much to maintain or improve their own health, but only if they are presented with meaningful opportunities for doing so. It is through the collaborative efforts of all sectors of society that such opportunities can be realized and maximized.

Health-promotion principles

One of the clearest statements of health-promotion principles is to be found in a discussion document released by the European Office of the World Health Organization (WHO) in 1984 (World Health Organization 1984). It identified five important issues in relation to the development of policies and programmes in health promotion:

1. health promotion involves the population as a whole in the context of their everyday lives, rather than focusing on people who are sick or at risk for specific diseases;
2. health promotion is directed towards action on the determinants or causes of health;
3. health promotion combines diverse methods or approaches;
4. health promotion aims at effective and concrete public participation; and
5. although health promotion is not a medical service, health

professionals have an important role in terms of health education and advocacy.

The document also identified five general areas for the development of health promotion activity.

1. The central focus of health promotion is *access to health*. This means eliminating inequalities in health and ensuring equal opportunities to improve health.
2. The improvement of health depends on an *environment conducive to health,* especially at work and in the home.
3. Health promotion involves the *strengthening of social networks and supports*. This is based on the recognition of the importance of social relationships as significant resources in health.
4. The promotion of *life-styles conducive to health* means developing positive health behaviours and effective coping strategies.
5. Since information and education are prerequisites for informed choices, health promotion should aim to *increase knowledge and disseminate information related to health*.

Later documents, produced by the WHO and national governments, described additional concepts and principles central to health-promotion efforts. For example, a discussion paper issued by the National Department of Health and Welfare in Canada identified three health challenges not currently addressed by the health-care system, along with three mechanisms and three strategies for health promotion (Health and Welfare Canada 1986). The health challenges were: reducing income inequities in health; reducing the burden of preventable illness; and increasing people's capacity to cope with emotional stress, chronic disease and disability. The mechanisms central to health promotion were: self-care, or the actions that individuals take to enhance their own health; mutual aid, or the actions that people take to support each other; and healthy environments, or the creation of living conditions which reinforce rather than damage health. The implementation of these mechanisms is dependent upon three strategies: healthy public policy, community action and comprehensive public health services.

The Ottawa Charter for Health Promotion (WHO 1986) emphasized the major role to be played by healthy public policy and community action in health promotion. Healthy public policy means that health should be a central issue for all planners and policy-makers, irrespective of the social or political sector in which they work. All public policy needs to be structured in ways which have positive rather than negative consequences for health. The political obstacles to the adoption of healthy policies in sectors such as agriculture and nutrition, taxation, energy, transportation and housing should be identified and removed. The aim here is to ensure that social and economic development is in tune with the overall goal of health for all. Because this nearly always involves conflicts between different interests in society, the health professions, along with voluntary groups, must mediate between these interest groups and campaign for the pursuit of health. In adopting such a role, health professionals are a key part of a process which seeks to strengthen and complement the existing health-care system.

Health-promotion efforts cannot be left solely to governments and formal organizations but should emerge out of communities themselves; community action is an important component of health promotion. Communities can take responsibility for identifying their own health needs, the setting of priorities and the identification of strategies for improving health. In order to do this, they need access to information and other resources for effective decision-making. Here, the role of the health professional is to enable communities to take control of health issues by collaborating in the identification of health needs and solutions to community health problems. Government actions to address these problems is more likely to be realized if communities are organized and able to lobby effectively on their own behalf. In a sense, a healthy community is one which has control over the many factors having a bearing on health.

These concepts clearly indicate that the new public health requires a fundamental shift in the distribution of power and resources in society. This highlights the essentially social and political nature of health and takes us a long way from the notion of individual responsibility which underlies traditional approaches to disease prevention.

Health promotion in action

The health-promotion approach is readily illustrated using motor-vehicle accidents as an example. These are a leading cause of death in young people and, as a result, account for the largest proportion of potential-years-of-life lost.

Motor-vehicle accidents, like any other health problem, can usefully be analysed using the health field concept. The main causes of such accidents are the attitudes of and risk-taking by drivers, the design of cars and roads, and the availability of trauma services, with the first being by far the most important (Shah 1990). Consequently, life-styles, environment and health-care organization are aspects of the problem needing attention, with human biology being of little or no significance. Motor-vehicle accidents, which fall into the life-style category, can be further differentiated into those that are the result of carelessness, speeding, failure to use seat belts and impaired driving.

Actions to reduce such accidents have largely concentrated on legislation designed to modify these life-style factors. Many countries have adopted legislation to control speeding, enforce the wearing of seat-belts and deal with the impaired driver. Young drivers, who are responsible for a high proportion of motor-vehicle accidents, are being singled out for attention. Less effort has been directed towards increasing the safety of cars or changing driver attitudes through controls on advertising, which currently promote counter-productive images of cars and driving. Consumer groups have a role to play in addressing both these issues.

Criticisms of the health-promotion approach

Health promotion is not without its critics. Some have noted that attempts to implement the health-promotion approach at the national level have not gone much beyond attempts to change individual life-styles by health education or legislation. Attempts to control the 'manufacturers of illness', or to deal effectively with health-related issues such as poverty, housing and the environment, have been much less evident. However, a number of national and local governments have begun to move against the tobacco industry in a much more systematic way. Far more stringent curbs are being placed on the advertising of tobacco products, the size of health warnings on cigarette packets has been increased, and legislation prohibiting smoking in public places, especially the workplace, is becoming common. Such legislation protects non-smokers from the harmful effects of secondary smoking and supports smokers in their attempts to quit. This is, perhaps, one of the more concrete examples of helping to make healthy choices easy choices.

A more fundamental critique has been offered by those who are concerned about 'healthism' that is, making health the central cultural value governing individual action and social relationships (see Chapter 12). Becker (1986), for example, cautions against the tyranny of health promotion, in which all aspects of our lives become prescribed in the name of health. This should alert us to the fact that health promotion does not entirely escape the moral dilemmas involved in balancing personal and public responsibility for health.

REFERENCES

Allison, K. (1982) Health education: self-responsibility versus blaming the victim. *Hlth Educ.*, **20**, 11–13.

Becker, M. (1986) The tyranny of health promotion. *Publ. Hlth Rev.,* **14,** 15–25.

Bloom, J. & Monterossa, S. (1981) Hypertension labelling and sense of well-being. *Am. J. Publ. Hlth,* **71,** 1228–1232.

Cochrane, A. (1972) *Effectiveness and Efficiency: Random Reflections on the Health Service.* London: The Nuffield Provincial Hospitals Trust.

Davies, C. (1979) Hospital centred health care: policies and politics in the NHS. In: *Prospects for the National Health,* ed. P. Atkinson & A. Murcott. Beckenham: Croom Helm.

Department of Health and Social Security (1976) *Prevention and Health: Everybody's Business.* London: HMSO.

Haynes, R., Sackett, D., Taylor, D., Gibson, E. & Johnson, A. (1978) Changes in absenteeism and psychosocial function due to hypertension screening and therapy among working men. *New Engl. J. Med.,* **299,** 741–744.

Health and Welfare Canada (1986) *Achieving Health for All: A Framework for Health Promotion.* Ottawa: Minister of Supply and Services.

Lalonde, M. (1974) *A New Perspective on the Health of Canadians.* Ottawa: Minister of Supply and Services, Canada.

Marteau, T. (1989) Psychological costs of screening. *Br. med. J.,* **299,** 527.

McKeown, T. (1979) *The Role of Medicine: Dream, Mirage or Nemesis?* Oxford: Blackwell Scientific Publications.

McKinlay, J. (1974) A case for refocussing upstream: the political economy of ill-health. In: *Applying Behavioral Science to Cardiovascular Risk. Proceedings of the American Heart Foundation Conference, Seattle.*

Mossey, J. (1981) Psychosocial consequences of labelling in hypertension. *Clin. Invest. Med.,* **4,** 201–207.

Naidoo, J. (1986) Limits to individualism. In: *The Politics of Health Education,* ed. S. Rodmell & A. Watt. London: Routledge & Kegan Paul.

Shah, C. (1990) *Public Health and Preventive Medicine in Canada.* Toronto: University of Toronto Press.

Stoate, H. (1989) Can health screening damage your health: *J. R. Coll. gen. Pract.,* **39,** 193–195.

Tijmstra, T. & Bieleman, B. (1987) The psychological impact of mass screening for cardiovascular risk factors. *Family Practnr.,* **4,** 287–290.

World Health Organization (1984) *Health Promotion: A Discussion Document on the Concept and Principles.* Copenhagen: Regional Office for Europe.

World Health Organization (1986) *Ottawa Charter for Health Promotion.* Ottawa: Health and Welfare Canada, Canadian Public Health Association.

18

Measuring health outcomes

Ray M. Fitzpatrick

In the course of the twentieth century, health problems in the industrialized societies have steadily shifted from the infectious diseases to chronic and degenerative diseases. Health services are now expected to have an impact on a diverse range of health problems that variously involve what we may term the 'five Ds': death, disease, disability, discomfort and dissatisfaction. The health services that have emerged to respond to such demands are of unprecedented size, diversity and complexity. Perhaps the greatest challenge now facing health services is to assess their impact upon health problems. Especially now that public funds are an essential component of financial support for health care, governments of all political persuasions have begun to require evidence of the effectiveness of health services. At the same time, the health professions are also beginning to look more closely at the impact that their treatments and interventions may have. The common focus of such concerns is upon assessing the *outcomes* of health care, i.e. the impact upon patients and populations of health services.

In this chapter I examine some of the different ways of conceptualizing and measuring health outcomes and some of the lessons to be gained from such evidence. I am concerned with the evaluation of health services. It is customary to distinguish between three different components of health-care evaluation. Firstly we may be concerned with the *structure* of services. This involves focusing upon such matters as the numbers, distributions and qualifications of doctors, nurses and other health professionals. A second focus of evaluation is upon the *processes* of health care. We would now be concerned with the therapeutic, diagnostic and other activities performed by health professionals for patients. Only with the third and most important focus in evaluation — *outcomes* — do we finally consider the ultimate results achieved for patients by health services.

MORTALITY

Our first measure of outcome is important for a number of reasons. Most obviously it is a central concern of clinicians and society to prevent deaths. From the perspective of measurement it is relatively simple to define compared with most other dimensions of health status. Moreover, particularly in industrialized societies, national recording systems have virtually complete information about deaths, something that cannot be said for most other measures of outcome.

Mortality rates may be used for a number of purposes. Thus they indicate inequalities in health status between different parts of England and Wales. The highest standardized mortality ratios (SMRs) consistently occur in the northern Regional Health Authorities and the lowest in the south and west. We have seen elsewhere the use of SMRs to examine inequalities between social and ethnic groups (see Chapter 8). Mortality rates can also be used to examine improvements over time. In England and Wales, life expectancy — a summary measure of the mortality rates prevailing at any time — has increased for females from 42 years in 1841 to 78 years in the 1980s. Most of this improvement has occurred because of reductions in infant mortality; life expectancy at later ages has not improved so markedly. A woman of 65 in 1841 could expect to live another 12 years. This figure had only increased to 17 years in the 1980s. Nevertheless, mortality rates can be used to show significant progress in some areas in the recent past. Thus, amongst young men, there has been a dramatic 44% reduction in lung cancer in the period 1975–87, a change almost entirely due to reductions in smoking and the tar content of cigarettes (Doll 1990). Over the same period, mortality rates due to some other cancers, such as Hodgkin's disease, leukaemia and cancer of the testis, have declined markedly due to medical interventions such as radiotherapy and chemotherapy. This is persuasive evidence that counter-balances the more pessimistic analyses of progress against cancer.

Infant mortality tends to be used as a particularly sensitive measure of the overall health of a country. Variations between countries in infant mortality are considered to be a reflection of social and economic conditions generally as well as the quality of maternity and neonatal care.

Avoidable mortality

One important approach to mortality statistics is to focus on deaths from certain conditions considered amenable to health-service intervention. Maternal and infant mortality may be used as indicators of the quality of obstetric and infant care. This approach has been extended to other causes of death where variations in death rates may indicate limitations of health-care provision, particularly if deaths below particular ages are the focus of attention. For example, cervical cancer is regarded as in principle avoidable by a combination of screening and early treatment by surgery or radiotherapy. Similarly preventive immunization or drug therapy for established cases is highly effective against tuberculosis, so that most mortality is in principle avoidable. Hypertensive disease can be detected by screening and ought to be amenable to dietary and smoking advice together with drug management. A study in Finland showed that over the period 1969–81 death rates for causes amenable to medical intervention declined by two-thirds for individuals aged 64 years or less (Poikolainen & Eskola 1986).

One problem of interpretation is that many of the causes of death considered amenable to medical intervention are also influenced by social and environmental factors. However, if mortality rates are calculated for health authorities on a range of such causes of death, statistically controlling for social and environmental factors, considerable variation in scores for different areas of England and Wales are obtained (Charlton et al. 1983). Furthermore, the amount of variation is greater than could have occurred by chance. Areas with particularly poor scores included Walsall, Bolton and Sandwell; whereas the most favourable scores were obtained in Sheffield, Oxfordshire and north Tyneside. Subsequent analyses have shown that, whilst death rates for all avoidable causes of death except asthma declined over a 5-year period, the relative positions of different health authorities on a 'league table' of avoidable deaths stayed fairly stable (Charlton et al. 1986). The purpose of such analyses is to use mortality as an indicator of the quality of medical care. Such information is intended to pinpoint areas with high death rates that might require further investigation. The approach has been criticized for not properly controlling all the social factors that might influence mortality rates, and for not actually demonstrating a relationship between health-service resources and the mortality indices selected. Moreover, at local level the absolute numbers of such deaths is quite small and extreme caution is needed in drawing inferences about the quality of medical care.

Medicaid —otes
Medicare - elorer

Hospital deaths

Deaths may nevertheless be an important alarm signal in health care and, as information systems become more effective and public concern over issues of quality increases, it can be expected that increasing attention will be given to hospital mortality data. A great deal of controversy followed the publication in the USA of the death rates for different hospitals of public sector (Medicare) patients. For example, mortality in a 30-day period following admission for pneumonia varied from 0% to 60% between different hospitals. It was argued that such evidence pointed to serious potential deficiencies in the quality of care of certain hospitals about which the public had a right to know. On the other hand, technical objections may be raised regarding the quality of mortality data and incautious interpretations regarding their significance. In particular, account needs to be taken of the variation in the severity and complexity of illness of patients admitted to different hospitals. Moreover, for many hospital admissions, such as end-stage cancer, death may be the inevitable and accepted outcome and other criteria, such as the dignity of care, would be the most appropriate measure of quality (Kahn et al. 1988). Again, as with avoidable mortality, there is a practical problem that deaths for particular hospital units are mercifully too infrequent an event to rely on for purposes of assessing outcomes and quality of care.

HEALTH STATUS AND QUALITY OF LIFE

For many health problems treated by health services, not only is death an uncommon and inappropriate measure of outcome but also, more importantly, the primary purpose of treatment is to improve patient's functioning and well-being. Consider, for example, drug treatment for rheumatoid arthritis, epilepsy or migraine, hospice care of the terminally ill, or surgery for ulcerative colitis. In all such instances we are concerned with the broad, pervasive effects that health problems have on the patient in terms of pain, disability, anxiety, depression, social isolation, embarrassment, or difficulties in carrying on daily life. From the patient's perspective, health care is largely judged in terms of impact on these broader aspects of personal well-being. In recent years outcome measures have emerged in an attempt to capture such aspects of patients' experiences. Frequently termed quality-of-life measures, they may often also be referred to as health-status instruments.

An early attempt to assess quality of life in patients systematically

Karnosky
Peformeric
Index

─────── **Table 1** ───────

The Karnofsky Performance Index.

Description	Scale (%)
Normal, no complaints	100
Able to carry on normal activities; minor signs or symptoms of disease	90
Normal activity with effort	80
Cares for self. Unable to carry on normal activity or to do active work	70
Requires occasional assistance but able to care for most of his needs	60
Requires considerable assistance and frequent medical care	50
Disabled; requires special care and assistance	40
Severely disabled; hospitalization indicated although death not imminent	30
Very sick. Hospitalization necessary. Active supportive treatment necessary	20
Moribund	10
Dead	0

Source: Fallowfield (1990).

was The Karnofsky Performance Index (Karnofsky & Burchenal 1949) (Table 1). The scale was designed particularly for use in the field of cancer and involves the clinician making a simple rating of the patient. It is still one of the more frequently used 'quality-of-life' scales. The scale has a number of limitations, however, as a measure of outcome. Firstly, Fallowfield (1990) points out the fallacy behind the use of a unidimensional scale. Such a scale requires the assumption that a bed-bound person must have a quite poor score even if, for example, he or she is well adjusted to illness, receives full social support and sees life as fulfilling. Conversely, someone ambulant but otherwise depressed, isolated, with low self-esteem and anxious about health status would, nevertheless, receive a favourable score. In other words, instruments such as the Karnofsky Performance Index do not allow for the multi-dimensional nature of quality of life. It is not surprising, therefore, that the index is deficient in a basic requirement for such instruments in that it is not reliable; different raters disagree in applying the scale to patients. As serious a deficiency is that clinicians disagree with patients' self ratings on the scale. Such problems have underlined the need for instruments that patients may, whenever possible, complete themselves.

Health-status instruments

A number of instruments (variously termed 'health-status' — or 'quality-of-life' — instruments) have therefore emerged, designed to be used as questionnaires for self completion. An instrument quite widely used in the UK is the Nottingham Health Profile (NHP) (Hunt & McEwen 1980). The NHP contains 38 simple statements (such as 'I sleep badly at night' or 'I am in pain when I walk') to which the respondent gives 'yes' or 'no' answers. The items fall into one of six scales addressing different aspects of subjective health: physical mobility, pain, sleep, energy, social isolation and emotional reactions. Each item has a weighted score obtained from panels of judges who have rated the relative severity of different statements. Subjects completing the questionnaire thus get a score for each of the six scales determined by the proportion of items to which they give positive answers. The designers of the instrument have made considerable effort to establish that the instrument is reliable (i.e. produces consistent responses if completed on different occasions not too far apart), and is able to distinguish individuals with different types and severity of health problem. The NHP has now been used to examine the impact on individuals' subjective health of a number of different health-care interventions, ranging from heart transplants, intensive care and elective surgery, through trials for anti-inflammatory drugs and hospital management of diabetes and rheumatoid arthritis.

Instruments such as the NHP are ambitious in that they are intended to assess the impact on the patient's well-being and quality of life of a wide range of different health problems. Often we want to assess the patient's perspective with an instrument more specifically designed to be sensitive to one particular disease. One very typical and quite successful instrument of this kind is the Arthritis Impact Measurement Scale (AIMS) which, by means of simple questions, assesses the impact of rheumatic disease on patient well-being in areas such as mobility, dexterity, household activities, pain and depression. The instrument has been shown to be sensitive to improvements in patients within just 4 weeks of treatment with non-steroidal anti-inflammatory drugs (Anderson et al. 1989). In a chronic disease, such as rheumatoid arthritis, where improvements to the patient's condition may be quite subtle and undramatic, such instruments have a vital role to play in improving our understanding of outcomes, especially in view of evidence in rheumatology that they may be no less reliable and accurate than conventional laboratory and radiological measures and often provide the clinician with more meaningful information on the impact of treatment (Deyo 1988).

Adverse consequences of health care

Many medical treatments have harmful side-effects. This may be the case in, for example, cancer therapies which are designed to prolong life but which may have a variety of adverse effects at the same time. Cytotoxic chemotherapies may produce nausea, vomiting, hair loss and tiredness, as well as mood effects such as depression. In some cases the costs to the patient from treatments may outweigh benefits to be gained in terms of longevity. Quality-of-life measures allow us to give some quantitative expression to such adverse effects. Thus Croog et al. (1986) used a battery of quality-of-life measures to assess the impact of three alternative drugs for controlling hypertension. They measured general well-being, physical symptoms, sexual function, work performance, emotional state, cognitive function (e.g. memory), social participation and life satisfaction. Whilst achieving similar levels of blood pressure control, one drug stood out from the other two as having less harmful effects on quality of life. They found that some of the harmful side-effects of drugs produced broadly equivalent effects on quality of life to those found by individuals who have just lost their jobs. Another study showed harmful effects on quality of life of transdermal glyceral trinitrate compared with placebo treatment for angina (Fletcher et al. 1988). Possibly because of increased headaches, the active treatment group were less able to maintain social contacts with friends and family. Broadly based measures of quality of life make it possible to detect and assess harmful effects that might occur in any of a wide range of aspects of patients' lives.

Attaching values to health

All health-care systems have to make choices between different health-care interventions; resources are not available to fund and provide all of the treatments that, in principle, are available. This requires extremely difficult choices to be made between interventions for very different health problems, let us say between coronary bypass surgery, renal transplants, lipid screening and day hospitals for psychiatric patients. One of the many problems complicating such choices is that there is no single numerical scale in terms of which to measure the diverse states of health and illness treated by different health-care programmes. Utility measurement is an approach which can be used to produce numerical values on a scale between 0 and 1 for all possible health states by assessing their relative value to individuals. In principle, it then becomes possible to assess in a standard way the improvements to health that may result from otherwise widely differing medical interventions.

A number of techniques have been developed to elicit how desirable individuals regard one health state compared with another. One such technique is the so-called standard gamble technique (Torrance 1986). At the heart of this approach, a subject is asked to

——— **Table 2** ———
Valuation matrix of different health states.*

| | Distress rating | | | |
Disability rating	No distress	Mild	Moderate	Severe
No disability	1.000	0.995	0.990	0.967
Slight social disability	0.990	0.986	0.973	0.932
Severe social disability and/or slight physical impairment	0.980	0.972	0.956	0.912
Physical ability severely limited (e.g. light housework only)	0.964	0.956	0.942	0.870
Unable to take paid employment or education, largely housebound	0.946	0.935	0.900	0.700
Confined to chair or wheelchair	0.875	0.845	0.680	0.000
Confined to bed	0.677	0.564	0.000	-1.486
Unconscious	-1.078	NA	NA	NA

Source: Drummond (1989).
* Healthy=1.0, dead=0.0. NA, not applicable.

choose between a particular state of ill health on the one hand and a gamble on the other hand. The gamble involves a hypothetical treatment which can cure the individual of the state of ill health, but with a particular probability of death from the treatment. For states of ill health perceived by the subject to be very undesirable one would expect the individual to prefer the gamble even with quite high probabilities of death. This probability is experimentally varied to reveal how ready the individual is to take the gamble rather than choose (hypothetically) to carry on living in the particular state of ill health being investigated. Data can be gathered from a sample of experimental subjects in such a way as to produce numerical values for a range of health states.

An alternative method (magnitude estimation) is to ask subjects to state how much worse they regard each of a number of ill-health states relative to one standard health state. One research group (Rosser & Kind 1978) asked subjects to rate the relative undesirability of 29 different states of illness produced by a matrix formed from combinations of two dimensions, varying degrees of *distress* and *disability*. The resulting relative values or 'utilities' of different health states are shown in Table 2. It is worth noting that some health states were rated as worse than 'dead' by judges. The research group found that values attached to different health states were reliable in the sense that individuals' responses were consistent over time.

―――――― **Table 3** ――――――
'League table' of costs and QALYs for selected health-care
interventions (1983–84 prices).*

Intervention	Present value of extra cost per QALY gained (£)
GP advice to stop smoking	170
Pacemaker implantation for heart block	700
Hip replacement	750
CABG for severe angina LMD	1040
GP control of total serum cholesterol	1700
CABG for severe angina with 2VD	2280
Kidney transplantation (cadaver)	3000
Breast cancer screening	3500
Heart transplantation	5000
CABG for mild angina 2VD	12600
Hospital haemodialysis	14000

Source: Drummond (1989).
* CABG, coronary artery bypass graft; LMD, left main disease; 2VD, two vessel disease; GP, general practitioner.

QUALITY-ADJUSTED LIFE-YEARS

Some health economists have argued that the values attached to different states of health and illness by methods such as those outlined above can be combined with survival data on years lived as a result of medical treatments to produce a generic output measure, the 'quality-adjusted life-year' (QALY) (Williams 1985). This standard, unitary means of expressing the benefits of medical treatments permits comparisons across treatments. Typically, information on QALYs has been combined with information about the costs of different treatment programmes (cost–utility analysis) and comparisons between programmes expressed in terms of costs per QALY gained, as in Table 3. It is argued that health authorities, faced with a scarcity of resources to meet all health problems need to maximize their use of resources. The methodology of QALYs identifies treatments that maximize the use of resources by obtaining the greatest gain in terms of health for a unit of resource. From Table 3 one might infer that general practitioners giving advice to stop smoking is a dramatically more effective use of resources than, say, hospital haemodialysis. Such information appears to provide a more explicit and more rational basis for making decisions about the allocation of resources.

Controversies surrounding QALYs

The approach outlined above has generated intense debate. In the first place there are at least six distinct methods that have been developed to assess individuals' valuations of health, of which 'standard gamble' and 'magnitude estimation' are two (Froberg & Kane 1989). It is argued that different methods of obtaining valuations of health produce only moderate agreement; others point to the evidence that health can mean different things to people of different backgrounds, although the evidence to date suggests that current experience of illness has a greater influence than social or cultural background in influencing how people judge health states (Frober & Kane 1989). Doctors appear to rate states of ill health as less desirable than do patients (Rosser & Kind 1978). Furthermore, it is suggested that judging the relative undesirability of different health states is an inherently unnatural task and that we have little idea of how judgements made in an experimental situation correspond to 'real-life' evaluations.

Other criticisms point to the strange trade-offs that this methodology produces. Is a gain of 1 year of completely healthy life really equivalent to 10 years of life with a health utility of 0.1? Such trade-offs generate ethical unease about making complex moral choices from unthinking use of numerical formulae. To some this approach may all too easily be used to provide apparently scientific justification for cut-backs in the provision of health services. Above all, it is argued that QALYs systematically disadvantage particular social groups such as the elderly or the terminally ill, the treatment of whom inevitably involves high cost per QALY gained.

To all such objections advocates of the QALYs approach have a simple and compelling response. Decisions about resource allocation are an unavoidable and daily reality in all health-care systems, whether made by individual clinicians or at the level of health planning for different patient groups in the population as a whole. It is acknowledged that there are insufficient data at present for evidence such as that given in Table 3 to be anything other than tentative approximations to be examined by more extensive research. QALYs nevertheless offer an explicit approach to questions of value that should force decision-makers to examine the tacit judgements behind current resource allocations and at the very least require a debate about alternative methods to the QALY. At present QALYs are far from being a practical aid to decision-making about health care, not least because, quite apart from the paucity of research on the more controversial subject of individuals' health values and utilities, we have so little of the more basic data required to assess the impact of treatments upon survival, disability and distress!

PATIENT SATISFACTION

The patient's perspective

One source of evidence about the outcomes of health care that has, until recently, been all too frequently neglected is the patient's view. This neglect was partly due to the widespread assumption that the patient is insufficiently well informed to comment on his or her health care. Undoubtedly there is also a tendency in many large bureaucratic organizations such as the National Health Service (NHS) to pursue internally generated routines and objectives without seeking external evidence of their reception by users. It should be clear that a primary objective of any health-care system is to provide services in a manner that is acceptable to the patient. The Griffiths NHS Management Inquiry was highly critical of the NHS's failure to act on this principle by systematically obtaining consumer feedback about the quality of services (DHSS 1983). Since that report, most health authorities have made much more effort to conduct such surveys.

There is also ample evidence from social scientific research to indicate how important the issue of patient satisfaction is. Patients who are dissatisfied with their health care are more likely not to follow the medical advice or regimen that they receive. In a sample of patients attending a neurological clinic for chronic headache, those who when interviewed after their consultations were more dissatisfied with the consultation were significantly less likely to take the medication that had been prescribed for them (Fitzpatrick & Hopkins 1981). Similar results have been obtained between satisfaction and compliance in hypertension and paediatric clinics, and in general practice. Dissatisfied patients may be less likely to reattend for further treatment (Roghmann et al. 1979). Satisfaction may also be an indication of how successful a treatment has been (Fitzpatrick et al. 1987).

A common distinction made in relation to health care is that between the technical and interpersonal aspects of care. Technical aspects of care refer to the technical competence with which treatment is provided. Interpersonal aspects focus on how doctors, nurses and other health professionals treat the patient — in other words, the degree of personal care and concern shown. Patient satisfaction is a particularly important indicator of interpersonal aspects of care. Thus, in a study of mothers attending a paediatric clinic with their children, the medical consultations were tape-recorded and analysed and mothers independently interviewed by researchers after the consultation to assess satisfaction (Korsch et al. 1968). Satisfaction was higher when the doctor displayed a friendly manner to the mother. Satisfaction was also positively related to directly questioning mothers early in the consultation as to the main worries and concerns that had prompted the consultation. In a similarly designed study of general medical clinics in which analyses of tape-recorded consultations could be related to subsequent patient satisfaction, those patients who were given encouragement by the doctor to explain their medical problem in their own terms were significantly more satisfied than patients who reported their symptoms in response to more structured doctor-focused questioning (Stiles et al. 1979).

One of the more important of interpersonal skills in health care is giving information. Failures in this area are one of the most important sources of patient dissatisfaction. It can also be shown experimentally that efforts to improve the communication of information are appreciated by patients. Ley (1982) reported a study in which medical inpatients were allocated to one of three different patterns of communication. A 'placebo' group experienced the normal and routine pattern of communication from doctors. A 'control' group received in addition one visit from a junior doctor who discussed general matters not specifically related to the patient's admission. In the 'experimental' group the junior doctor, in the one visit to the patient, made a point of giving an explanation to the patient of the treatments and procedures he or she was receiving. All three groups subsequently completed questionnaires and the 'experimental' group produced significantly higher satisfaction scores.

Methods of assessing patient satisfaction

There are a number of alternative ways of obtaining patients' views about health care with differing advantages and disadvantages. The most common method is to use a self-completed questionnaire in which the respondent selects from various fixed response categories. Among the advantages of such an approach are that it is simple to administer and analyse and is relatively inexpensive. The disadvantage is that the investigator imposes his or her priorities on the patient by selecting the issues included in the questionnaire and the range of possible answers. So, an alternative method is to interview patients in such a way that their own concerns are given as much scope to emerge as possible. The obvious problem with sensitively conducted

——— **Table 4** ———
Dissatisfaction with regard to aspects of the NHS.

Out-patients	(%)	In-patients	(%)
Information about progress	37	Woken too early	43
Time waiting for hospital transport	28	Information about progress	31
		Food	21
Waiting for first appointment	21	Waiting for admission	20
Length of time at hospital	19	Washing and bathing facilities	19
Adequacy of waiting room	18		
Length of wait to see doctor	16	Toilet facilities	15

Source: OPCS (1978).

interviews is that they require well-trained interviewers and are relatively expensive to conduct. A general problem with all methods is that patients of different backgrounds tend to differ in readiness to express critical comments about health services. Younger patients, those with poorer health status and individuals with higher levels of education are more likely to express dissatisfaction.

Surveys in the NHS

In order to aid its deliberations, the Royal Commission on the NHS commissioned a survey of a sample of patients who had recently experienced either in-patient or out-patient treatment. The results of the national survey carried out by the Office of Population Censuses and Surveys are likely to be very similar to those that are obtained in local surveys of a particular hospital or district (OPCS 1978).

As can be seen from Table 4, much of the dissatisfaction could be traced to problems of having to wait for out-patient appointments or hospital admission and to the length of time waiting to see a doctor. Other complaints focused upon amenities such as food and washing facilities in wards and the waiting room in out-patient clinics. A particularly large number in both patient groups were dissatisfied with information. It might be noted that absent from either group is any complaint about medical treatment or the benefits obtained from medical care. This largely reflects the decision of the investigators here, as in other studies, to focus on matters such as amenities and not to ask questions about patients' views on medical care. Investigators appear to have avoided this subject, either because of limited faith in patients' competence to judge the benefits of treatment, or because this subject is perceived as a purely clinical matter to be assessed solely by professional criteria. As a result we

know far less than we should about patients' perceptions of the value
of medical care.

OUTCOMES AND THE
EVALUATION OF SERVICES

Evaluation and the medical profession

One of the features that may distinguish a profession from other kinds
of occupations is that it retains a very high level of control in assessing
the value and quality of the product it provides to the public (see
Chapter 15). The medical profession has historically exercised this
control by means of a number of methods such as monitoring the
content and standards of the training provided for new or established
members of the profession, or by penalizing individual doctors who
fail to uphold required professional standards. In Britain the General
Medical Council was established after lengthy negotiations between
the state and the newly emerging medical profession in the middle of
the nineteenth century as one of the main institutions to ensure
satisfactory performance by doctors. However, health care has now
become so complex and costly that traditional methods of upholding
professional standards are no longer sufficient. Moreover, society has
profoundly changed since the nineteenth century. The state is now
intimately involved in health care through funding medical services
with public money. It seeks evidence that such funds are well spent.
In the USA, in addition to the Federal Government's concern about
public-health-care spending, industry has become concerned about
the value of medical services because so much is paid for from
employers' insurance contributions. In other words, powerful forces
such as government and business are seeking clearer evidence of the
value of health care. In addition, the consumer has also become
more knowledgeable, more demanding and more sceptical in dealing
with health professionals.

The medical profession has not only faced external pressures to
evaluate its activities. From within, epidemiologists such as Cochrane
(1972) have argued that insufficient attention has been given to the
scientific appraisal of the impact upon health of medical interventions. The response of the medical profession to such pressures has
been to take more seriously its responsibility to examine and monitor
the quality and value of its services, in particular by practising *medical
audit*. Medical audit has been defined as 'looking at what we are
doing with the aim of making improvements in patient care and use
of resources' (Difford 1990). It is conventional to distinguish between

audit of *process*, in which the focus is the evaluation of medical activities (normally against agreed standards), and audit of *outcome* in which the question concerns the impact of activities upon illness. The latter is, as this chapter establishes, more difficult, so that most audit has been concerned with examining process, by methods such as reviewing samples of case notes, analysing hospital statistical data or comparing local use of procedures such as X-rays against published expert advice (McKee et al. 1989).

However, audit is still not widely practiced. This has been interpreted by some as evidence of complacency or indeed defensiveness on the part of a profession anxious not to expose its limitations (Wilding 1982). The White Paper *Working for Patients* insists that all doctors in the NHS should take part in audit, and urges that hospital units only be allowed to train junior doctors if adequate audit is in operation (Secretaries of State for Health, Wales, Northern Ireland and Scotland 1989). It does not, however, specify what constitutes adequate audit and leaves much of the detail to professional peer control. Thus it may be that other sections of the White Paper will provide greater incentives to impose explicit audit of outcomes. District Health Authorities, as part of their contract to purchase health care from hospitals, will be obliged to ensure the quality of the care provided for the local population. With these statutory obligations it will be very hard for both authorities and hospitals to avoid examining the impact of treatments on outcomes such as mortality, quality of life and patient satisfaction.

Evaluation and the future of health care

There are at least three different views we can take of the impact that measurement of outcomes may have upon health care. For many observers the evaluation of outcomes will be a fundamental turning point in the history of medicine, allowing for explicit, rational, scientific answers to all of the problems arising from current uncertainties as to the value of medical treatments. As is examined in Chapter 19, outcomes research must address the enormous variations in the rates at which many medical and surgical treatments are performed, even amongst populations with similar levels of medical need. The hope is that all parties — the doctor, the patient and the purchaser — will have access to clearer information as to the likely results of investigations and treatments, and will, therefore, be able to make more informed decisions about health care. A second position about future developments in this area is to adopt a more cautious stance and to argue that at present the advocates of outcomes measurement are expressing something of an article of faith. Despite enormous advances in computers and information systems, we are a very long way from the kinds of integrated systems that can monitor the longer term impact of medical interventions in populations, and the kinds of practical and valid measures of outcome that can be used on a large scale are only just now beginning to be developed and examined. To understand the outcomes of most procedures, long-term studies integrating hospital and community data, to an extent that is not yet feasible outside of very special research contexts, will be required.

There is also a third, longer term view of these developments. Analysts of both British and American health care (Ham 1981) have suggested that two distinct interest groups have tried to shape the future of health care. One group — the 'professional monopolizers' — have sought to defend the traditional privileges and practices of the medical profession, particularly the clinical autonomy of the doctor. A second group — 'the corporate rationalizers' — emphasize the many irrationalities and inefficiencies that bedevil health-care systems when traditional professional autonomy is left unchecked by planning and evaluation. According to such analyses there has for a very long time been a stalemate in health policy between these two conflicting philosophies, and the present debate over outcomes is unlikely to result in decisive shifts. According to this view, for the foreseeable future health services will defy precise measurement of their value because of the inherent uncertainties and complexities of medical practice. Whatever the future direction of medical care, the assessment of outcomes will remain a central concern of health services.

REFERENCES

Anderson, J., Firschein, H. & Meenan, R. (1989) Sensitivity of a health status measure to short term clinical changes in arthritis. *Arthr. Rheum.,* **32,** 844–850.

Charlton, J., Hartley, R., Silver, R. & Holland, W. (1983) Geographical variation in mortality from conditions amenable to medical interventions in England and Wales. *Lancet,* **i,** 691–696.

Charlton, J., Lakhani, A. & Aristidou, M. (1986) How have 'avoidable death' indices for England and Wales changed? 1974–78 compared with 1979–83. *Comm. Med.,* **8,** 304–314

Cochrane, A. (1972) *Effectiveness and Efficiency.* London: Nuffield Provincial Hospitals Trust.

Croog, S., Levine, S., Testa, M. et al. (1986) The effects of antihypertensive therapy on the quality of life. *N. Engl. J. Med.,* **314,** 1657–1664.

Department of Health and Social Security (1983) *NHS Management Inquiry.* London: HMSO.

Deyo, R. (1988) Measuring the quality of life of patients with rheumatoid arthritis. In: *Quality of Life: Assessment and Applications,* ed. S. Walker & R. Rosser. Lancaster: MTP Press.

Difford, F. (1990) Defining essential data for audit in general practice. *Br. med. J.*, **300**, 92–94.

Doll, R. (1990) Are we winning the fight against cancer? An epidemiological assessment. *Europ. J. Cancer*, **26**, 500–508.

Drummond, M. (1989) Output measurement for resource allocation decisions in health care. *Oxford Rev. Econ. Pol.*, **5**, 59–74.

Fallowfield, L. (1990) *The Quality of Life: The Missing Measurement in Health Care.* London: Souvenir Press.

Fitzpatrick, R. & Hopkins, A. (1981) Patients' satisfaction with communication in neurological outpatient clinics. *J. psychosom. Res.*, **25**, 329–334.

Fitzpatrick, R., Bury, M., Frank, A. & Donnelly, T. (1987) Problems in the assessment of outcome in a back pain clinic. *Int. Disabil. Stud.*, **9**, 161–165.

Fletcher, A., McLoone, P. & Bulpitt, C. (1988) Quality of life on angina therapy: a randomised controlled trial of transdermal glyceral trinitrate against placebo. *Lancet*, **ii**, 4–9.

Froberg, D. & Kane, R. (1989) Methodology for measuring health-state preferences — III: Population and context effects. *J. clin. Epidem.*, **42**, 585–592.

Ham, C. (1981) *Policy Making in the National Health Service.* London: McMillan.

Hunt, S. & McEwen, J. (1980) The development of a subjective health indicator. *Sociol. Hlth. Illness*, **2**, 231–246.

Kahn, K., Brook, R., Draper, D., Keeler, E., Rubenstein, L., Rogers, W. & Kosecoff, J. (1988) Interpreting hospital mortality data: how can we proceed? *J. Am. med. Assoc.*, **260**, 3625–3628.

Karnofsky, D. & Burchenal, J. (1949) The clinical evaluation of chemotherapeutic agents in cancer. In: *Evaluation of Chemotherapeutic Agents. Symposium at New York Academy of Medicine, New York*, ed. C. Macleod, pp. 191–205. New York: Columbia University Press.

Korsch, B., Goszzi, E. & Francis, V. (1968) Gaps in doctor patient communications: 1. Doctor patient interaction and patient satisfaction. *Paediatrics*, **32**, 855–871.

Ley, P. (1982) Satisfaction, compliance and communication. *Br. J. clin. Psychol*, **21**, 241–254.

McKee, C., Lauglo, M. & Lessof, L. (1989) Medical audit: a review. *J. R. Soc. Med.*, **82**, 474–478.

Office of Population Censuses and Surveys (1978) *Royal Commission on the National Health Service: Patients Attitudes to the Hospital Service.* London: HMSO.

Poikolainen, K. & Eskola, J. (1986) The effect of health services on mortality: decline in death rates from amenable and non-amenable causes in Finland 1969–81. *Lancet*, **i**, 199–202.

Roghmann, K., Hengst, A. & Zastowny, T. (1979) Satisfaction with medical care: its measurement and relation to utilisation. *Med. Care*, **17**, 461–477.

Rosser, R. & Kind, P. (1978) A scale of valuations of states of illness: is there a social consensus? *Int. J. Epidem.*, **7**, 347–358.

Secretaries of State for Health, Wales, Northern Ireland and Scotland (1989) *Working for Patients. Cmd 555.* London: HMSO.

Stiles, W., Putnam, S., Wolf, M. & James, S. (1979) interaction exchange structure and patient satisfaction with medical interviews. *Med. Care*, **17**, 667–679.

Torrance, G. (1986) Measurement of health state utilities for economic appraisal: a review. *J. Hlth Econ.*, **5**, 1–30.

Wilding, P. (1982) *Professional Power and Social Welfare.* London: Routledge & Kegan Paul.

Williams, A. (1985) Economics of coronary bypass grafting. *Br. med. J.*, **291**, 326–329.

19

Organizing and funding health care

Ray M. Fitzpatrick

In the twentieth century health care has developed from a collection of small-scale and low-cost services to a complex, labour-intensive and diverse industry. In modern industrialized societies a large and generally growing proportion of resources is now devoted to health care. As the size and scope of this industry have expanded, so too have individuals' rights and expectations with regard to health. Governments have thus become increasingly committed to making health services available to their citizens. The very scale of modern health care has prompted governments of all political persuasions to raise fundamental questions. How effective are health services? How efficient are they in delivering health care? Ultimately, the common theme of such questions concerns the value of modern health care. The answers are often sought by looking for lessons from alternative systems of health care. The most striking feature of modern health care is the diversity of funding and organization in different countries. This chapter describes the different types of health-care systems that have emerged in industrialized societies and the ways they shape the practice of medicine, and then examines the strengths and weaknesses of different systems.

TYPES OF HEALTH-CARE SYSTEMS

A basic requirement for any product or service such as health care is that some method is needed to permit consumers to obtain the product from the producer. The simplest method to understand is the *market*, wherein the consumer directly purchases the product from the producer at a price agreed between the two parties at the time of the transaction. This is the basic principle behind many transactions in modern industrial societies, and indeed, until quite recently, was the dominant means of providing and obtaining health services. However, health services have tended to evolve away from basic market transactions in two respects. Firstly, potential consumers of health services have increasingly preferred to take out insurance to cover possible costs of health care, rather than face unpredictable and often expensive costs incurred at the time of illness. Secondly, an additional party has mediated between the producer and consumer of health care to provide resources necessary for the provision of health care. This 'third party', very often the government but also employers, trade unions, sick funds, insurance societies and charities, has tended to become increasingly influential in the way services are provided. The more that third parties provide funds directly to the producers (hospitals, doctors and the pharmaceutical industry) to allow them to provide care to those entitled to services, either because of citizenship or an adequate record of insurance contributions, the further the system has evolved away from market mechanisms.

All health-care systems can be understood in terms of the different ways in which transactions occur between these three key parties. In particular, systems differ in the extent to which market versus third-party mechanisms, particularly public provision, dominate transactions and, more specifically, in the ways that individuals obtain insurance against health-care costs. Field (1973) has introduced a simple typology that distinguishes four major alternative systems of health care.

1. The *pluralistic* health system. A wide variety of co-existing schemes (voluntary insurance, compulsory insurance for the elderly and fee for service) provide funds for health services. Health-care facilities are owned by a diverse array of institutions (non-profit-making and for-profit organizations, federal state and municipal government). The USA is the best example, and its health care has sometimes been described as a 'non-system' because of the diversity of competing institutions involved. It most closely resembles the properties of a competitive market for health-care services.

2. The *health insurance* system. Resources for health care are gathered by a third party in the form of compulsory insurance contributions from individuals and their employers. The third party reimburses the hospital and the doctor. The third party may be federal and provincial government (Canada) or non-

   profit-making sick funds (Holland and Germany). In Germany
   there are some 1200 funds and membership tends to be
   determined by geography or employment. Similiar arrangements are found in Holland which has 45 sick funds.
3. The *health service* system. A system in which most facilities are
   owned by the state, and doctors, although independent, receive
   most of their income from the state. The British National Health
   Service (NHS) is a prime example, in which resources for health
   care are largely gathered from general taxation. A small
   independent private health-care system co-exists with the NHS.
4. The *socialized* health system. All health-care facilities are owned
   by the state and most health-care personnel are salaried state
   employees. The Eastern European countries and the USSR
   currently have health-care systems of this type, although
   changes are likely in the 1990s.

Payment mechanisms

In addition to the wide variety of organizational arrangements that
have emerged in different western countries, there are also major
differences in the methods of paying doctors which can also exert
considerable influence on the nature of medical care. We can
distinguish three major types of method, although in most health-care
systems a mixture of the methods can co-exist and, often, individual
doctors may be paid by more than one method.

Fee-for-service involves the patient paying the doctor a fee for each
separate item or element of care for which the doctor wishes to
charge. In its simplest and historically earliest form, this involves direct
patient payments at the time of use. This is still one of the most
important methods of paying for health bills in the USA, involving
28% of all personal health expenditure. Insurance systems have
emerged in most western countries that reduce or eliminate the need
for direct patient payments. However, very often the medical
profession has insisted on retaining fee-for-service as their method of
payment, with the fees being reclaimed from federal and provincial
government (Canada), from the patient's private insurer (USA), or
from sick funds (Germany).

Capitation reimburses the doctor by paying a fixed, usually annual,
sum for each patient under his or her care. It is most naturally a
method employed in primary care where the doctor has a continuous
list or 'panel' of patients for whom he or she is responsible. Britain
and Holland are two of the main examples.

Salary is the last method and involves an employer paying the
doctor an annual income in return for his or her services. It is the
method for paying hospital doctors in Britain, Sweden and Germany.

Unfortunately, there is no perfect method of paying doctors. Each method is known to have certain potentially harmful effects on the provision of health care. The most serious and most clearly documented problems are those associated with fee-for-service. It encourages doctors to perform those procedures specifically rewarded by fees, which in most systems tend to be technical investigations and more interventionist treatments. To put it bluntly, many fee-for-service systems do not recognize talking to the patient as a distinct item of service! Fee-for-service requires more mechanisms than other methods of payment to control potentially wasteful treatments or investigations. Another problem that tends to occur in countries where doctors are paid by fee-for-service is that doctors tend to be poorly geographically distributed, as economic incentives encourage concentrations in more affluent areas. Capitation provides more financial incentives that encourage doctors into under-doctored areas. Amongst its main limitations are that it does not provide financial rewards for good quality care (as income is unrelated to quality or amount of activity) and may encourage doctors to refer on difficult medical problems. Salaried payment is also not without problems. In principle it requires the doctor to be more concerned about pleasing his or her superiors or employers, who determine rewards and promotions, and less concerned with pleasing the patient. Generally the medical profession has been quite conservative, preferring to keep to the particular system of payment historically established in each country. However, an overall trend can be detected for more doctors to be paid on a salaried basis, typically as employees of an organization.

Health expenditure in different countries

Western countries vary not only in how they organize and fund health services, but also, most dramatically, in the amount of funds devoted to health care. Comparisons of levels of expenditure are not easy because of problems of what is included and excluded in the category of health care in different countries, and also because of unstable exchange rates for countries' currencies. Nevertheless, the most recent figures produced on a systematic standardized basis show differences in levels of expenditure between countries that have remained fairly stable over time (Table 1). It is clear that there are considerable differences between countries that might all be regarded as similarly advanced industrial societies, whether expressed as absolute amounts of expenditure or as proportions of the gross domestic product (GDP) used as the most reliable measure of countries' overall wealth. The table shows that, for example, the USA

——— **Table 1** ———

The per capita expenditure on health, the percentage of wealth
(GDP) spent on health and the various mortality rates for
selected countries.*

Country	Per capita expenditure on health (US$)	Proportion of GDP (%)	GDP (US$)	Life expectancy at birth (years)		Infant mortality (% live births)	Perinatal mortality (% live and still births)
				Male	Female		
USA	2051	11.2	18 338	71.5	78.3	1.00	1.00
Canada	1483	8.6	17 211	73.0	79.8	0.79	0.84
Sweden	1233	9.0	13 771	74.2	80.2	0.61	0.71
France	1105	8.6	12 803	72.0	80.3	0.76	1.12
Germany	1093	8.2	13 323	71.8	78.4	0.83	0.73
Holland	1041	8.5	12 252	73.5	80.1	0.64	0.92
Denmark	791	6.0	13 329	71.8	77.6	0.83	0.88
UK	758	6.1	12 340	71.9	77.6	0.91	0.88

Source: OECD (1990).
* All information 1987 except: Canada, life expectancy 1984, perinatal and infant mortality 1986; Germany, life expectancy 1986; Holland, infant mortality 1986; France, perinatal mortality 1984.

spent more than 2.5 times as much per capita as the UK. It is also clear that some countries at very similar levels of wealth in terms of GDP (for example Denmark and Germany) may spend quite different amounts of their wealth on health care.

A number of different explanations have been offered to account for the differences between countries in their levels of expenditure. One factor that may play a role is the level of health professionals' earnings, especially those of doctors, which are undoubtedly high in countries such as the USA. A very different explanation would point to the important role of the general practitioner in systems like the NHS in acting as a filter or gate keeper limiting access to more expensive hospital facilities. Another factor that clearly distinguishes systems like the USA and Britain is that the former is an open system in which no actor — the doctor, the patient, the hospital, the insurance company or the government — has the full capacity and incentives to control the volume of medical activities and the costs that ensue. Typically in the USA, doctors or hospitals bill patients' insurance companies who ultimately recover their costs from patients' employers, who hope in turn to pass on these costs to the general public in prices to the consumer. The health-care system in the USA has historically been a highly inflationary one because of this capacity of actors to pass on their costs, and this process stands in direct contrast to the UK where a closed financial system operates in that the total amount of finance available to the NHS is set and controlled centrally by the Treasury and, to a large extent, cannot be expanded further.

However, the most general explanation offered to explain differences in countries' levels of health-care expenditure is that the greater a country's wealth the greater will be not only the amount but also the *proportion* of the wealth devoted to health care. Support for this view comes from analyses of data (such as in Table 1) for a number of different countries which produce highly significant correlations between countries' GDP and the proportion of GDP allocated to health care (Maxwell 1981). Such analyses may also be used to predict the level of health care that might be expected for a particular country given its GDP. It has been suggested that, for example, the USA consistently spends more than expected and the UK less than might be expected from its GDP. However, others have argued that such analyses are inappropriate and use misleading exchange rates to calculate standardized expenditures (Parkin et al. 1989).

VARIATIONS IN MEDICAL CARE

It will not be surprising in view of the above differences in funding to discover that the extent of medical intervention also varies between countries. Thus the rate of surgery in the USA and Canada is at least twice that in the UK, once differences in population size and structure have been taken into consideration. A recent study of hysterectomy (McPherson 1990) showed the age-standardized rate per 100 000 women as 700 in the USA, 600 in Canada, 450 in Australia, 250 in the UK and 110 in Norway. Similar international variations could be shown for tonsillectomy, cholecystecomy and prostatectomy. These international differences are not confined to surgery. Aaron and Schwartz (1984) showed a wide range of differences between the USA and the UK. In the USA, twice as many X-ray examinations were carried out per person; there was six times greater computer tomographic scanning capacity; three times more kidney dialysis treatment was provided; and between five and ten times more hospital intensive-care beds were available.

Variations within countries

Much of the international variation in rates of medical treatments may be accounted for in terms of general differences in economic prosperity of different countries. There is also a tendency for fee-for-service systems of paying the doctor to be associated with higher use of technical procedures, such as investigations and greater resort to active treatments, such as surgery, because such forms of care tend to be more financially rewarding (Abel-Smith 1976). However, it has become increasingly apparent that there are variations in surgical and medical procedures *within* countries that are as great as those that pertain between countries. It is less easy to explain such variation in terms of gross economic incentives. Thus a six-fold variation in tonsillectomy rates and a four-fold variation in hysterectomy rates have been found for different areas within New England (Wennberg & Gittelsohn 1982). Two New England cities which were socially and demographically similar, Boston and New Haven, were examined in more detail. Whilst Boston had 2.3 times higher rates for carotid endarterectomy, the rates for cholecystectomy and hysterectomy were two-thirds, and for coronary bypass surgery only half, of those in New Haven (Wennberg et al. 1987). Similar variations have been found in different regions of the NHS. For example, rates for hysterectomy per 100 000 women have been found to vary between 181 in Mersey and 287 in North-East Thames, whilst rates for tonsillectomy varied from 144 in Trent to 251 in North-East Thames (McPherson et al. 1981).

Explanations for medical variations

Studies showing variation in the performance of treatments between areas within a country raise fundamental issues. It is extremely unlikely that variation in morbidity in the populations served could explain very much, if any, of the wide variations found in such studies. Moreover, it is unlikely that differences in consumer demand could explain large amounts of the differences in treatment rates prevailing in populations of similar social composition. One factor that is clearly implicated is supply. It can be no coincidence that the two-fold differences in surgical rates in the USA compared with the UK is mirrored by there being twice the number of surgeons per capita in the USA. However, where studies have attempted systematically to examine the effects of supply (e.g. McPherson et al. 1981) it has only been possible to explain a small amount of the variation in rates of treatment this way. It is clear that, for many procedures, the main problem is inherent uncertainty about the appropriate indications for treatment and the precise value of treatment in terms of outcomes. It is known that clinicians can vary enormously in the diagnostic and history-taking procedures used in making decisions about elective surgery (Bloor 1976). However, to produce large and consistent differences in rates between areas, such individual differences in clinical opinion and approach must also be influenced by local or regional preferences or customs, otherwise the effects upon variations in treatment rates produced by individual differences in clinical style would be cancelled out. Therefore, at the heart of any explanation of variations in treatment rates is professional uncertainty, lack of agreement about the indications for intervention and the value of intervention. Local and international variation is known to be greater for procedures such as tonsillectomy, prostatectomy and hysterectomy where professional uncertainty is greater than for procedures such as cholecystectomy where some degree of consensus has emerged (Wennberg et al. 1982).

CRITERIA FOR EVALUATING HEALTH SYSTEMS

Health-care expenditure and health status

The main reason why so much uncertainty surrounds many medical and surgical procedures is that they have not been properly evaluated. It is very difficult to distinguish specific effects of a medical therapy from other possible causes of change in the course of illness, such as placebo effects and spontaneous changes in the underlying disorder. For this reason it is often argued that only a *randomized controlled trial* (RCT), where patients are randomly allocated between the treatment group and a control group and differences in subsequent health status compared between the two groups, is adequate to distinguish real treatment effects. Very few medical interventions have been evaluated by means of such demanding methods (Cochrane 1971). Some would argue that, especially when RCTs might pose ethical problems because of the need to withhold treatment, medical treatments can still be reasonably evaluated by less exact methods such as, for example, longitudinal observational studies in which the impact of therapies on groups of patients are recorded and compared with untreated comparison groups. However, such studies are still all too rare (McPherson 1990).

Greater uncertainty surrounds the relationship between overall levels of health-care expenditure and benefits in terms of health status. In Table 1 the expenditure figures for health care in a range of western countries are compared with a number of the most recently available health-status measures. Life expectancy is a global measure that summarizes the mortality rates prevailing at all ages. It is apparent from the table that the USA, despite spending much more on health care than other countries, does not enjoy more favourable life expectancy than countries such as Denmark and the UK with quite low per capita health-care expenditure. The infant mortality rate is a quite widely used indicator not only of infant health status but also of whole populations. Again it is clear that the USA does not enjoy infant mortality rates commensurate with its high health-care expenditure. The table finally examines perinatal mortality (late fetal and neonatal deaths) on the basis that this measure may be regarded as a more sensitive measure of the quality of medical care available in a country (Waaler & Sterky 1984). Here too the USA compares quite unfavourably with the other countries.

Other analyses of the relationship between countries' levels of health-care expenditure and mortality rates have similarly failed to find evidence of the negative correlation that might reasonably be expected (Cochrane et al. 1978; Maxwell 1981). Indeed, the one variable that tends to predict mortality rates from such comparisons of national data is the gross national product (GNP), i.e. the overall level of wealth of the country (Cochrane et al. 1978). This would of course be consistent with the arguments of McKeown that social and economic factors have historically exerted far greater influence upon health than have medical measures (see Chapter 1). In view of the evidence that mortality rates are largely influenced by social, economic and environmental factors rather than medical care, it might well be argued that mortality rates are not appropriate measures of health status with which to compare countries' health-care systems. Rather, it might be argued, the main impact of health services is intended to be upon *morbidity*. In particular, the objectives of health services are to reduce the impact of illness in terms of pain, discomfort, disability and other aspects of health status. However, as indicated in Chapter 18, instruments for measuring these outcomes of health services have only recently been developed and there are numerous logistic and methodological problems that would make the comparative assessment of different health-care systems extremely difficult. At present, therefore, the only available data with which to evaluate the *effectiveness*, in terms of impact upon health, of different health-care systems is mortality.

Efficiency

It has been suggested that there are six criteria that should be used to evaluate the quality of health services: effectiveness, efficiency, accessibility, equity, social acceptability and relevance (Maxwell 1984). From what has been said above it should be clear that there are basic difficulties in examining the effectiveness of health-care systems, particularly problems of measuring outcomes. The scope for using the other five criteria are examined briefly below.

Efficiency is a term which is frequently applied to health care but seldom used with much clarity. The efficiency of an engine is the relationship between the actual and the theoretically possible amount of energy used to achieved a desired output. The closer the machine gets to the lowest level of energy use considered possible, the greater its efficiency. In human systems one normally compares the costs of two or more alternative ways of achieving the same output or result, with the less costly alternative being regarded as more efficient. The scope for increasing efficiency in health services is potentially enormous. For example, in a wide range of problems, out-patient or day-case care can be substituted for longer inpatient management; or the nurse or general practitioner may replace more costly hospital care. Efficiency is examined by health economists using techniques such as cost–benefit analysis, in which all the costs of two or more alternative therapies or ways of organizing care are compared. This requires taking into account the costs of alternative treatments, such as any additional burden imposed on the family or other carers, as well as formal health-care costs.

The British government sought to achieve numerous 'efficiency savings' from the NHS during the 1980s. However, in practice, this has often meant reducing levels of spending available, which should not be confused with real improvements in efficiency because saving money can often be associated with deteriorating efficiency. Efforts have been made to measure efficiency more directly, but the exercise has proved particularly difficult. One solution has been the development of 'performance indicators' (such as average length of hospital stay, throughput of patients per annum, and turnover interval between cases occupying a bed) that can be measured for different units, hospitals and districts. However, such measures can be quite misleading. A unit may appear to be performing more efficiently if patients' mean length of hospital stay is lower than other units. However, a full cost–benefit analysis might show that this short length of hospital stay involved transferring higher costs to the community by premature discharge together with unresolved complications of treatment that actually led to many patients being readmitted. It is also possible that varying lengths of stay in different units are due to different levels of severity of disease in the patients admitted.

It is even more difficult to compare health-care systems in terms of efficiency. In general, the length of stay in hospitals in the USA is considerably shorter than in Britain. Economic pressures have been the main factor driving down lengths of stay in the USA. Unfortunately, lengths of stay tend to be a matter of local practice and tradition and optimum length of stay has rarely been subjected to the kind of scientific examination adopted by Deyo et al. (1986), who were able to show from a randomized controlled trial that shorter lengths of bed rest were as effective in the management of backpain as longer stays.

Another aspect of efficiency would include consideration of 'bureaucracy' or administration costs of health care since such costs do not apparently make a direct contribution to patient care. The NHS fares particularly well compared with most other systems. For example, it has been estimated that the USA spends as much as 22% of its health expenditure on administration costs, compared with about 6% required by the NHS (Himmelstein & Woolhander 1986). High administration costs arise from a combination of fee-for-service and the need to itemise and bill every procedure. It is of interest that, as the NHS begins to experiment with 'internal markets', both health authorities and hospitals will require a great deal more information of this kind and administration costs will rise sharply.

Accessibility

This criterion is concerned with how readily available health services are. The health-care system with the most visible problem is the more market oriented one of the USA, in which some 15–20% of the population may have inadequate health-care insurance. No other western health-care system permits this degree of financial inaccessibility. Given that for those who are insured in the USA out-of-pocket expenses at the time of seeking care are higher than in European systems, it is remarkable that consultation rates are no different between systems. A different kind of problem of access is the necessity to wait for admission for treatment. This would appear to be very much more of a problem for the publically funded and provided services of Britain and Sweden and is one major reason why in both these countries proposals have been implemented to increase the incentives for hospitals to reduce waiting times by a more competitive structure of revenue.

Equity

Equity with regard to health involves addressing some very complex issues, especially when trying to compare the performance of different health-care systems. Thus a distinction can be made between equality of access (the extent to which different social groups have access to health services) and equality of health status (the extent to which different social groups enjoy similar levels of health). As other chapters in this book have shown, social differences in health status can be caused by a wide range of social, economic and environmental factors and the scope for intervention by health services, no matter how broadly defined, may be modest. Some would therefore argue that it is more reasonable to confine attention to comparing different health-care systems' efforts to achieve equality of access, although even with this more modest criterion there may be substantial social and cultural factors influencing use of health services. Other problems complicating quantitative comparisons of inequalities are that the social groupings (such as classes) are not consistent between countries and that social and cultural factors can influence individuals' *perceptions* of their health status (see Chapter 3).

With regard to social differences in health status, it is clear that all European and North American societies continue to experience differences in mortality between social groups, and the view that social democratic welfare states or socialist societies have eradicated such differences is misguided (Illsley 1990). Thus a comparative study of Denmark, Finland, Norway, Sweden, Hungary and England and Wales showed that in all countries mortality amongst men with the highest level of education was 40–60% lower than men of the lowest educational level (Lahelma & Valkonen 1990). In general, some of the lowest inequalities in health status appear to be found in Sweden, a country which has probably the strongest and most active commitment to welfare policies. Nevertheless, even in Sweden there are occupational and regional inequalities in mortality arising from work hazards, dietary- and alcohol-related diseases and other unexplained environmental factors (Diderichsen 1990).

All health-care systems have taken some steps to reduce or eradicate differences of access by income. At one extreme, in the USA a substantial proportion of the population do not have full access to health care because of inadequate insurance. Such individuals have to resort to a 'second-class' system of publically funded health care which has experienced particularly tight financial restrictions in the last 10 years. At the other extreme, financial barriers to access are largely removed from most European systems, and further steps have tended to be taken centrally to reduce regional inequalities of access. Particularly successful was the impact on the NHS of the Resource Allocation Working Party (RAWP), which resulted in England and Wales having the least regional inequalities in the geographical distribution of doctors when compared to France, Germany and Holland (Townsend & Davidson 1982).

Social acceptability

In those health-care systems where an attempt has been made to assess consumers' views about their health care, the majority of respondents have expressed positive satisfaction. Indeed, a standardized survey of consumers in a cross-national survey that included citizens of Canada, the USA, England, Finland and Yugoslavia found that only 5% of respondents expressed dissatisfaction with their doctor's care, and rates of dissatisfaction did not appear to differ significantly from country to country (Kohn & White 1976). The most common complaint across systems focused upon the length of time spent waiting to see the doctor. Other studies suggest that dissatisfaction with information provided by health professionals is also a universal problem. Some health-care systems generate unique complaints. It is unlikely that any other health-care system than the NHS would continue to wake patients up so early that a full 43% of patients complain about this aspect of being in hospital. Conversely, American consumers focus more critically than the consumers of other health-care systems on the high costs they face from medical care. Americans also differ fundamentally from citizens of other countries in that, while they are generally satisfied with their own care, they view the health-care system as a whole as unsatisfactory and in need of fundamental change (Blendan & Donelan 1990).

Relevance to health needs

Relevance is the last important criterion emphasized in Maxwell's list for evaluating health services. At the extreme it is possible to conceive of a health-care system that takes little or no account of the health needs of the population it served. Thus it has often been a key problem in third world countries that the health-care system has developed largely to conform to the standards of western high-technology medicine and, whilst relevant to the needs of urban social and political elites, it has failed to address the often more basic health needs of the rural majority populations. Such stark failures of relevance are less easy to identify in western health-care systems and involve major initial difficulties in defining the health needs of populations.

Nevertheless, one very promising line of research has begun to open up the more focused and manageable issue of *appropriateness*. To what extent are the treatments provided in a health-care system appropriate to the patients who receive them? The methodology for addressing this question is complex and may take different forms, but one approach essentially involves asking representative samples of relevant clinicians to rate the appropriate indications for a particular medical or surgical intervention (for example, which test results, past medical history and other patient characteristics would be appropriate indications for someone to undergo coronary artery bypass graft (CABG)). These agreed indications are then used to analyse the characteristics of samples of patients who have actually undergone the particular procedure. This methodology has been largely used in the USA and has produced quite startling results. Retrospective analyses of case records showed that for patients who received carotid endarterectomy, about one-third were rated as appropriate, one-third equivocal and one-third inappropriate. Similarly, one-quarter of coronary angiographies and one-quarter of endoscopies were rated as equivocal or inappropriate (Brook 1990). These studies give support to the view that a substantial proportion of the treatment provided in the USA may be of questionable value in terms of outcomes and may occur as much out of a more general optimistic bias and faith in technology in US culture or, more cynically, because of strong financial rewards built into fee-for-service medicine.

This methodology has now been applied cross-nationally. Two panels of physicians and surgeons, one from the USA and one from the UK, were asked to rate a large number of indications in the form of elements of case histories, in terms of appropriateness for coronary angiography and also for CABG (Brook et al. 1988). The US panel of doctors rated a much larger number of case-history indications as being appropriate for either procedure. The two panels' agreed sets of indications were then applied to real case histories. Firstly, they were applied to two samples of US patients who had undergone coronary angiography. The US panel's ratings resulted in 17% and 27% being rated as inappropriate, whereas the UK panel's ratings identified 42% and 60% as inappropriate. The ratings of indications were then applied to another sample, US patients who had undergone CABG. By the US criteria 13% and by the UK criteria 35% of operations were inappropriate. There are, therefore, quite powerful differences of views about the scope for benefit from medical treatment in medicine, despite the fact that medical science and medical training are very similar in the two countries.

MARKETS VERSUS REGULATION IN HEALTH CARE

In many respects the many complex difficulties faced by health-care systems can be subsumed into two broad types of problem. Firstly, health-care systems need to obtain adequate funds to pay for the health-care needs of the populations they serve and mechanisms are required to ensure that such funds do not outstrip the capacity of the funder to pay. Secondly, mechanisms are required to improve the effectiveness and efficiency of health services, particularly in the light of evidence of ineffectiveness and inefficiency of the kind briefly reviewed in this chapter. No health-care system appears to have addressed either problem satisfactorily and there is a constant and increasingly international search for solutions to both problems. Again in order to simplify the discussion, it is possible to detect two alternative strategies that have been pursued by governments, sick funds, health providers and other agencies concerned with the provision of health care in attempts to address the twin problems just identified. One strategy has focused on competition. It has sought to intensify the scope of market forces in the field of health care. The hope has been that competition between providers of health care would force them to reduce their costs as well as maximize their efficiency and effectiveness in accordance with the logic of market competition in other spheres of commerce. The second and contrasting strategy has been to introduce regulation into the operations of the health-care system. Faced with evidence of inefficiencies such as wide and unaccountable variations in clinical practice and use of resources, this solution has attempted to use methods of centralized planning and managerial control of health budgets. The competitive strategy is best characterized by the US system and the regulation/planning strategy is more typical of European systems.

The competitive strategy was pursued in the USA throughout the 1980s. Government finance for planning of health services was withdrawn and instead support was given to encourage competition, especially to promote the development of Health Maintenance Organizations (HMOs). HMOs were established in which a group of health providers offered a complete package of health-care services to consumers at an annually agreed price. It was hoped that HMOs would compete with each other in terms of the attractiveness of the package of services offered and their price. Finally, competition was encouraged by increasing the proportion of health bills paid out of pocket by the patient in the hope that this would increase consumer sensitivity to costs. To date there has been little evidence that pro-competitive strategies have succeeded in the main objective of driving down the highly inflationary costs of US health care.

The planning and regulatory strategies of European health services are too diverse to encompass in a brief chapter. To varying degrees in each country regulation has included efforts to set overall limits to expenditure on health care, particularly in the hospital sector; setting doctors' fees, regulating the introduction of high-technology medicine. This strategy has been largely successful in containing costs, but analysts are less happy with the evidence of continued inefficiencies and unexplained variations in most European systems, and countries such as Sweden and Britain continue to be concerned with their health-care systems' unresponsiveness to the consumer and the persistence of waiting lists as unresolved problems.

Convergence of health-care systems?

Some observers (Enthoven 1990; Ham et al. 1990) have argued that pure strategies of either market competition or central planning and regulation have failed to address the key problems of health services and have suggested that there is now evidence in many health-care systems of a convergence towards a mixed approach combining elements of both strategies. Again it is impossible to encompass all the varieties of strategy emerging in each country, but some commonly occurring themes can be detected. One theme is that of 'peer review', in which particularly clinical decisions that may result in large use of resources such as admission to hospital and decisions about surgery are subject to external review by colleagues. This has gone much further in the USA where peer review is current and intended directly to influence use of resources, whereas in Europe it has to date largely been retrospective and used more for educational purposes as in medical audit.

The second theme is the development of information systems to monitor and measure the activities and outcomes of health care. The intention is to use increasingly sophisticated information technology to inform all the parties to health care — the doctor, the patient and the purchaser in particular — about the efficiency and effectiveness of health-care activities (Ellwood 1988).

A third common theme emerging in health-care systems to varying degrees is the desire to separate out the purchaser of health care (such as the health authority or sick fund) from the provider (such as hospitals) and to increase the degree of choice that the purchaser has between different providers. In systems such as those in Britain, Holland and Sweden the intention is to induce competition within a publicly funded system. The hope is that a system which incorporates all three elements (peer review, increased attention to audit of outcomes and scope for funders to choose between providers who compete in terms of quality and price) will produce a solution to the many dilemmas of modern medical care.

REFERENCES

Aaron, H. & Schwartz, W. (1984) *The Painful Prescription*. Washington, DC: The Brookings Institution.
Abel-Smith, B. (1976) *Value for Money in Health Services*. London: Heinemann.
Blendon, R. & Donelan, K. (1990) The public and the emerging debate over national health insurance. *New Engl. J. Med,* **323,** 208–212.

Bloor, M. (1976) Bishop Berkeley and the adenotonsillectomy enigma. *Sociology,* **10,** 44–61.

Brook, R. (1990) Relationship between appropriateness and outcome. In: A. Hopkins and D. Costain (eds) *Measuring The Outcomes of Medical Care.* London: Royal College of Physicians.

Brook, R., Park, R., Winslow, C. et al (1988) Diagnosis and treatment of coronary disease: comparison of doctors' attitudes in the USA and the UK. *Lancet,* **i,** 750–753.

Cochrane, A. (1971) *Effectiveness and Efficiency.* London: Nuffield Provincial Hospitals Trust.

Cochrane, A., St. Leger, A. & Moore, F. (1978) Health service input and mortality output in developed countries. *J. Epidem. Commun. Hlth,* **32,** 200–205.

Deyo, R., Diehl, A. & Rosenthal, M. (1986) How many days of bed-rest for acute low back pain? A randomised clinical trial. *New Engl. J. Med.,* **315,** 1064–1070.

Diderichsen, F. (1990) Health and social inequalities in Sweden. *Soc. Sci. Med.,* **31,** 359–367.

Ellwood, P. (1988) Outcomes management: a technology of patient experience. *New Engl. J. Med.,* **318,** 1549–1556.

Enthoven, A. (1990) What can Europeans learn from Americans? In: *Health Care Systems in Transition.* Paris: OECD.

Field, M. (1973) The concept of the 'Health System' at the macrosociological level. *Soc. Sci. Med.,* **7,** 763–785.

Ham, C., Robinson, R. & Benzeval, M. (1990) *Health Check: Health Care Reforms in an International Context.* London: Kings Fund Institute.

Himmelstein, D. & Woolhandler, S. (1986) Cost without benefit: administrative waste in US health care. *New Engl. J. Med.,* **314,** 441–445.

Illsley, R. (1990) Comparative review of sources, methodology and knowledge. *Soc. Sci. Med.,* **31,** 229–236.

Kohn, P. & White, K. (1976) *An International Study.* Oxford: Oxford University Press.

Lahelma, E. & Valkonen, T. (1990) Health and social inequalities in Finland and elsewhere. *Soc. Sci. Med.,* **31,** 257–266.

Maxwell, R. (1981) *Health and Wealth.* Lexington, MA: Lexington Books.

Maxwell, R. (1984) Quality assessment in health. *Br. med. J.,* **288,** 1470–1472.

McPherson, K. (1990) International differences in medical care practices. In: *Health Care Systems in Transition.* Paris: OECD.

McPherson, K., Strong, P., Epstein, A. & Jones, L. (1981) Regional variations in the use of common surgical procedures. *Soc. Sci. Med.,* **15A,** 273–288.

Organisation for Economic Cooperation and Development (1990) *Health Care Systems in Transition.* Paris: OECD.

Parkin, D., McGuire, A. & Yule, B. (1989) What do international comparisons of health care expenditures really show? *Commun. Med.,* **11,** 116–123.

Townsend, P. & Davidson, N. (1982) *Inequalities in Health: The Black Report.* Harmondsworth: Penguin.

Waaler, H. & Sterky, G. (1984) What is the best indicator of health care? *Wld Hlth Forum,* **5,** 276–279.

Wennberg, J. & Gittelsohn, A. (1982) Variations in medical care among small areas. *Sci. Am.,* **246,** 120–134.

Wennberg, J., Barnes, B. & Zubkoff, M. (1982) Professional uncertainty and the problem of supplier-induced demand. *Soc. Sci. Med.,* **16,** 811–824.

Wennberg, J., Freeman, J. & Culp, W. (1987) Are hospital services rationed in New Haven or over-utilised in Boston? *Lancet,* **i,** 118.

Index